# Believing in Preaching

[8]A valuable guide to help preachers connect biblical passages with their own life experience is Robert C. Dykstra, *Discovering a Sermon: Personal Pastoral Preaching* (St. Louis: Chalice Press, 2001). For helpful sermons preached in the midst of personal and congregational conflict, see H. Beecher Hicks, Jr., *Preaching through a Storm* (Grand Rapids: Zondervan, 1987).

## Chapter 7: How Preaching Shapes the Faith Community

[1]Louis Thomas, *The Lives of a Cell: Notes of a Biology Watcher* (New York: Viking Press, 1974).

[2]Dietrich Bonhoeffer, *The Communion of Saints: A Dogmatic Inquiry into the Sociology of the Church* (New York: Harper and Row; and London: William Collins Sons, 1963, o.p. 1927).

[3]Ibid., 117–44.

[4]On the existential power of perceiving one's identity in communal terms, see Teresa L. Fry Brown, *God Don't Like Ugly: African American Women Handing on Spiritual Values* (Nashville: Abingdon Press, 2000).

[5]Alexis de Tocqueville, *Democracy In America* (New York: Vintage Books, 1956, o.p., 1848)

[6]Robert Bellah et al., *Habits of the Heart: Individualism and Commitment to American Life* (Berkeley: University of California, 1985).

[7]One of the authors has written on this topic. See Mary Alice Mulligan and Rufus Burrow Jr., *Daring to Speak in God's Name: Ethical Prophecy in Ministry* (Cleveland: Pilgrim Press, 2002), especially chapter 1. Other resources for considering communal shaping of preaching: Rufus Burrow Jr., "Personal Communitarianism and the Beloved Community," *Encounter* 61 (2000): 23–43.

[8]Miroslav Volf, *After Our Likeness: The Church in the Image of the Trinity* (Cambridge, UK, and Grand Rapids: Eerdmans, 1998), 11.

[9]David G. Buttrick, *Preaching Jesus Christ: An Exercise in Homiletic Theology* (Philadelphia: Fortress Press, 1988), 69.

[10]L. Susan Bond, *Trouble with Jesus: Women, Christology, and Preaching* (St. Louis: Chalice Press, 1999), 16.

## Chapter 8: What about God?

[1]This topic is discussed in depth in chapter 4.

[2]For a study of six leading models of preaching in the African American community, see L. Susan Bond, *Contemporary African American Preaching: Diversity in Theory and Style* (St. Louis: Chalice Press, 2003).

[3]For one of the few recent full-scale theological interpretations of God's presence and activity in all phases of preaching, see Marjorie Suchocki, *The Whispered Word: A Theology of Preaching* (St. Louis: Chalice Press, 1999).

[4]One way of doing so can be found in Teresa L. Fry Brown, *Weary Throats and New Songs: Black Women Proclaiming God's Word* (Nashville: Abingdon Press, 2003).

## Chapter 9: Listeners Respond to Preaching in Diverse Ways

[1]The interviewee statements in this cluster of "deepening faith and commitment" often contain elements that are reminiscent of themes that appear in the clusters of thinking, feeling, and acting. Nevertheless, we identify "deepening faith and commitment" as a distinct cluster because interviewees who speak of their response to the sermon in this way often describe responses that indicate that thinking, feeling, and actions affect one another in helping deepen people in faith.

[2]Some of the material in this section is reminiscent of the discussion of the roles of feeling in the sermon in chapter 6. The present material focuses particularly on how people reported they respond to sermons through feeling at the time of preaching as well as afterward, whereas chapter 6 reports more generally on how listeners perceive the roles of emotion while hearing the sermon itself.

[3]Samuel D. Proctor sets out an approach to sermons that are particularly designed to deepen people's spirituality in *How Shall They Preach? Effective Preaching for Vital Faith* (Valley Forge: Judson Press, 1992).

⁴We sketch qualities of preaching that listeners say engage them in Mary Alice Mulligan and Ronald J. Allen, *Make the Word Come Alive: Lessons from Laity* (St. Louis: Chalice Press, forthcoming).

⁵See Ronald J. Allen, *Hearing the Sermon: Relationship, Content, and Feeling* (St. Louis: Chalice Press, 2004).

⁶Because different preachers, like listening communities, are diverse in personality, habits, and theology, it follows that each preacher needs to discover his or her optimum approaches to preparing sermons and to arrange his or her schedule accordingly. Church boards and lay leaders need to be informed of the need for the minister to devote significant time each week to sermon preparation.

⁷Henry M. Mitchell often urges preachers to set a behavioral objective for each sermon. In his *Celebration and Experience in Preaching* (Nashville: Abingdon Press, 1990), Mitchell details a holistic approach to preaching that involves mind, heart, and will.

## Chapter 10: Preaching and Pluralism in the Congregation

¹Other discussions of dealing with diversity in the congregation, and that approach the subject from different points of view, include Joseph R. Jeter Jr. and Ronald J. Allen, *One Gospel, Many Ears: Preaching and Different Listeners in the Congregation* (St. Louis: Chalice Press, 2002), who ponder differences in processing the sermon related to age, types of mental operation, gender, social place in the congregation, multiculturalism in the congregation, and theological orientation; and James R. Nieman and Thomas G. Rogers, *Preaching to Every Pew: Cross Cultural Strategies* (Minneapolis: Fortress Press, 2001), who help preachers respond to congregations through the different cultures that are present in almost every congregation.

²E.g., Emmanuel Levinas, *Totality and Infinity*, tr. A. Lingis (Pittsburgh: Duquesne University Press, 1969, o.p. 1961), 114–118; idem., *Otherwise than Being or Beyond Essence,* tr. A. Lingis (The Hague: Martinus Nijhoff, 1981, o.p. 1974), 49–189. For an approach to preaching deriving, in part, from Levinas, see John S. McClure, *Otherwise Preaching: A Postmodern Ethic for Homiletics* (St. Louis: Chalice Press, 2001). For an introduction to Levinas, see Ronald J. Allen, "Preaching and the Other," *Worship* 76 (2002): 211–24.

³For works that help the preacher move toward a thick description of the local congregation as a culture, see C. Eric Lincoln and Lawrence Mamiya, *The Black Church in the African American Experience* (Durham, N.C., and London: Duke University Press, 1990); Thomas Edward Frank, *The Soul of the Congregation: An Invitation to Congregational Reflection* (Nashville: Abingdon Press, 2000); Nancy T. Ammerman, Jackson W. Carroll, Carl S. Dudley, and William McKinney, eds., *Studying Congregations: A New Handbook* (Nashville: Abingdon Press, 1998).

⁴A preacher could carry a notebook in which to record insights that emerge from such encounters, as well as from comments heard in meetings, pastoral calls, and other life settings.

⁵For more detailed considerations regarding interviewing in the congregation, see John S. McClure et al., *Listening to Listeners: Homiletical Case Studies* (St. Louis: Chalice Press, 2004), chapter 9, "Approaches to Interviewing in the Congregation," 149–64.

⁶A specific process could be agreed on by the church board, for instance an occasional group could be chosen (for a set period of time) to offer feedback to the preacher; or a team could be prepared with specific questions for interviewing representatives from groups within the congregation.

⁷Our interviews began with questions that are not directly related to preaching but that often help the interviewer get a sense of the congregation as a listening context. The responses to these questions can also be clustered, and can help preachers and other leaders get a sense of how the congregation is attractive to people, and a sense of which values, activities, and feelings are most important to the congregation. These questions are: Tell me about how you became a part of this congregation? What are the most important things that happen in this congregation? Describe a typical Sunday morning in this congregation.

⁸For other studies, see footnote 1 of this chapter.

⁹For an overview of thirty-four different styles of preaching, see Ronald J. Allen, *Patterns of Preaching: A Sermon Sampler* (St. Louis: Chalice Press, 1998).

¹⁰Of course, preachers should never violate their theological integrity in order to shape sermons in ways that have a good opportunity to engage listeners.

# Believing in Preaching
## What Listeners Hear in Sermons

Mary Alice Mulligan

Diane Turner-Sharazz

Dawn Ottoni Wilhelm

Ronald J. Allen

CHALICE
PRESS

ST. LOUIS, MISSOURI

Cover art· (c) Getty Images
Cover and interior design; Elizabeth Wright

This book is printed on acid-free, recycled paper.

Visit Chalice Press on the World Wide Web at
www.chalicepress.com

10  9  8  7  6  5  4  3  2  1          05   06   07   08   09

**Library of Congress Cataloging–in–Publication Data**

Believing in preaching : what listeners hear in sermons / Mary Alice Mulligan ... [et al.].
    p. cm.
  ISBN 13: 978-0-827205-02-3 (pbk. : alk. paper)
  ISBN 10: 0-827205-02-3
  1. Preaching.  I. Mulligan, Mary Alice, 1952-
  BV4211.3.B45 2005
  251–dc22

2004014953

Printed in the United States of America

# Contents

# Preface

When pastors are asked how they learn to improve their preaching, chances are they mention the books they have read that are written by other ministers or by preaching professors. They may also speak about conferences they have attended or conversations they have had with other preachers in which they discussed what does and does not seem to work in the pulpit. Most ministers count on these resources to guide and revise their habits of sermon preparation and delivery. However, an often untapped resource for ministers is the local congregation, made up of people who listen week after week to the minister's preaching. People in the pews are easily overlooked as resources to help identify what makes for better preaching.[1]

Believing that people who regularly listen to sermons can help preachers improve their preaching, a research team began a four-year project, sponsored by the Lilly Endowment and administered by Christian Theological Seminary, Indianapolis, in which we asked 263 laity from twenty-eight congregations to report on what helps, and what hinders, effective preaching communication from the pulpit.[2] In individual and small group interviews, the research team (composed of active church people familiar with the skills of interviewing, both lay and ordained, from various denominations) asked a series of questions to help uncover what assists people in engaging with the sermon and what leaves them cold.

When we on the team of interviewers began working, we imagined we would write one book on the results. We planned to share what laity reported helps them enter into the meaning of a sermon and what keeps them from hearing what the preacher is saying. The book was envisioned as containing our findings related to three traditional categories: those who engage more easily with emotions, those who listen more carefully when a logical argument is given, and those who connect with the sermon because of a connection with the preacher (what we might call "heart," "mind," and "relationship"). However, we were not eager to publish a simple "how-to" book for increasing worship attendance. Such psychological and sociological manuals are already available from church growth authorities and others. Instead, we wanted a book that would assist ministers and priests in their reflections about their preaching, specifically a book that would facilitate theological growth and congregational maturation. We also hoped that the book would be accessible to laity who were interested in what other pew-sitters had to say about sermons.

The material that these listeners to sermons shared with us is so rich and thought-provoking that we are publishing not one but four books on the findings. The first book, *Listening to Listeners*, presents six slightly abbreviated interviews as case studies from actual transcripts, with brief commentary, to show the reader the seriousness with which laity listen to sermons and the meaningful results they report from good preaching.[3] The second book, *Hearing the Sermon,* lays out the major categories on which the project originally based its investigation: *pathos* (emotions), *logos* (intellect), *ethos* (character and relationship), and embodiment (delivery).[4] This volume, *Believing in Preaching,* presents the diversity of answers found in the interviews by clustering material around ten individual chapter topics, and reveals the range of ideas active within many congregations. The fourth book, *Make the Word Come Alive,* presents specific advice and suggestions for preachers gleaned from the interviews.[5] Each of the books may be read independently, for each addresses a different topic and has a specific purpose in mind. The books may also be read together, giving the reader four separate ways of mining the rich information gathered from this extensive project. Care has been taken that the books do not repeat findings. Nine separate authors, with quite individual perspectives and intentions, participated in the writing of the books in the series. In addition, the authors have tried to minimize the use of the same material from a transcript in more than one book, except in cases where excerpts are used to illustrate quite different ideas.

The Lilly Endowment, represented by Chris Coble, and Christian Theological Seminary, Indianapolis, under the presidency of Edward Wheeler, have been generous in their material support and sincere in their encouragement, especially as the project developed and evolved. Nancy Eiesland, professor of the sociology of religion at Candler School of Theology, Emory University, advised the project. For all these gifts, we truly thank them.

The authors of this book also wish to extend their gratitude to Melissa Green, whose indefatigable hours of transcription work and meticulous proofreading of transcripts made our research analysis far easier than we could have asked or imagined. Also, Owen Cayton and Kara Brinkerhoff, project assistants, worked many hours setting up interviews and working with the individual transcripts, coding interviews for anonymity, and converting them to CDs. We thank them for their professionalism and willing spirits.

Our greatest appreciation goes to the congregations and their members, who opened the doors of their faith and invited the researchers in. Without their wisdom, candor, and testimony, we would have nothing to report.

# Authors

**Mary Alice Mulligan** is director of the chapel and teaches preaching and Christian ethics at Christian Theological Seminary, Indianapolis. She is ordained in the Christian Church (Disciples of Christ) and has served churches in Illinois, Indiana, and Tennessee. She coauthored with her husband, Rufus Burrow Jr., her most recent book, *Standing in the Margin: How Your Congregation Can Minister with the Poor (and perhaps recover its soul in the process)* (Pilgrim Press, 2004)

**Diane Turner-Sharazz** is instructor in homiletics on the Homer J. Elford Chair of Homiletics at the Methodist Theological School of Ohio. Ordained in the United Methodist Church, she has served as a minister in local congregations in Ohio. Some of her recent works include contributions to *Patterns of Preaching: A Sermon Sampler* (Chalice Press, 1998); *Preaching: Word and Witness;* "The Role of Music and Prayer in African American Spirituality" in *Pace;* and chapters in *Abingdon Women's Preaching Annual* (Abingdon Press, 1998).

**Dawn Ottoni Wilhelm** is assistant professor of preaching and worship at Bethany Theological Seminary in Richmond, Indiana, and is ordained in the Church of the Brethren. After several years of pastoral ministry, she recently completed her doctoral work at Princeton Theological Seminary. Dawn contributed a chapter to *Anabaptist Preaching: A Conversation Between Pulpit, Pew and Bible,* ed. David Greiser (Cascadia Publishing House, 2003).

**Ronald J. Allen** is Nettie Sweeney and Hugh Th. Miller Professor of Preaching and New Testament, Christian Theological Seminary. He was cominister, with his spouse, of a congregation of the Christian Church (Disciples of Christ) in Nebraska, authored the textbook *Interpreting the Gospel: An Introduction to Preaching* (Chalice Press, 1998), and edited a companion that illustrates thirty-four ways to construct sermons: *Patterns of Preaching: A Sermon Sampler* (Chalice Press, 1998).

# Introduction

One hundred and twenty-eight typical churchgoers were individually interviewed regarding how they listen to sermons. They came from twenty-eight congregations, which varied by denomination, size, setting, worship style, and ethnic make up. Each person was asked to fill out a paper questionnaire, and then engaged in a conversational interview that lasted about an hour.[1] The interview covered various areas of the preaching experience. Questions ranged from "What do you think God is doing during preaching?" to "How does preaching shape your community?" to "Tell us about a sermon that caused you to think or act differently." The interview questions were set up to investigate four general areas of the preaching event—the listener's perception of (a) the relationship with the preacher, (b) the content of the sermon, (c) the feelings stirred by the sermon, and (d) the preacher's embodiment of the sermon.[2] However, we quickly discovered a wider range of ideas than we expected. *Believing in Preaching* presents selections from the diverse answers given in the individual interview conversations with church members and regular attendants. The reader will see some strands of a categorical arrangement at times, but the primary layout of material here is of a different warp and woof. We have gathered answers within topical clusters. The range of answers is quite surprising in some areas. In other areas, significant agreement and important trends surface. Occasionally, the authors here summarize what listeners said, but

1

much of each chapter is composed of direct quotations extracted from the interviews, reproduced to show the variety of answers. This approach allows the laity's own words to say what needs to be said about what helps or hinders the communication process between pulpit and pew, and retains the nuances of the responses. By and large we have not edited the listeners' styles of speaking; many of the comments have the flavor of oral speech. Our task is to present the material in thematic clusters and add our analysis and interpretive comments.

One of the most important findings of our study is the remarkable diversity with respect to how people listen to sermons in the typical congregation. As an interviewee stated, "obviously different people are going to give different answers." Indeed, the authors of this book no longer speak of *the* way people listen to sermons, as if all of us hear sermons in the same way. We speak instead of the different clusters or patterns of listening that are present even in the same congregation, and certainly in different congregations.

We suspect that the range of perspectives on preaching voiced by laity in this project are typical of ones found in other congregations across the Midwest and South, and perhaps throughout much of North America.[3] However, the interviews in this project reinforce the fact that each congregation is distinct. Preachers should not assume that the perspectives on preaching printed in these pages are the same ones that pertain to their local congregations. As we discuss in more detail in the final chapter, preachers need to listen to the particularity of the individual congregations they are called to serve.[4]

In this book, specific topics are covered chapter by chapter. The interview material is clustered around ten specific topics, each of which is reported and explored in its own chapter. Although this book is a joint effort by the four authors, because of the extensive amount of material, each author chose specific topics on which to focus her or his reading and research. Thus, we list here the chapter topics and the person who authored the first draft of that specific chapter—chapter 1: "How Do These Listeners Understand the Purposes of Preaching?" Ronald Allen; chapter 2: "The Role and Authority of Scripture in Preaching," Dawn Ottoni Wilhelm; chapter 3: "Embodiment of the Sermon," Diane Turner-Sharazz; chapter 4: "Listener's Relationship with the Preacher," Mary Alice Mulligan; chapter 5: "Controversy and Challenge in the Preaching Moment," Dawn Ottoni Wilhelm; chapter 6: "Roles of Feeling in Preaching,"

Ronald Allen; chapter 7: "How Preaching Shapes the Faith Community," Mary Alice Mulligan; chapter 8: "What about God?" Mary Alice Mulligan; chapter 9: "Listeners Respond to Preaching in Diverse Ways," Ronald Allen; chapter 10: "Preaching and Pluralism in the Congregation," Ronald Allen and Mary Alice Mulligan.

There are occasions when chapter materials touch one another, as when a respondent explains the importance of the preacher's physical presence in the pulpit (embodiment, chapter 3) in discussing controversial subjects (chapter 5). We have usually limited inclusion of the material to a single chapter, yet recognize that calling attention to such connections is not repetitious, but important in understanding the intricacies of the preaching event.

The authors do not simply lay out a spectrum of listener responses (e.g., from "hot" to "cold") but group the responses according to clusters. In fact, we sometimes refer to this work as "the cluster book." An effort to construct a spectrum from "hot" to "cold" would be artificial. To be more accurate and helpful, the authors offer selections from the interviews that demonstrate the rich variety we discovered in the pews. Rather than polarizing the responses, we attempted to choose answers that reveal the significant diversity of those interviewed and the depth and seriousness with which people listen to sermons while recognizing that answers can be grouped together around traits that they have in common (clusters). Thus, the reader is given access to a sampling of the complexity and interconnection of answers. The intention is to allow those laypersons who were interviewed to speak for themselves.

The respondents were guaranteed anonymity; that is, as far as is reasonable, the readers of any publication coming from the study would not be able to identify the interviewees, their preachers, or their congregations. However, when it is helpful for the reader to understand a particular interviewee's remark, notes concerning gender, age, ethnicity, size of congregation, geographical setting, or denominational affiliation are supplied. Because context is often an important factor in attempting to understand why a particular technique or type of preaching succeeds or fails, there are also occasions when brief explanatory comments are appropriate, such as noting that the congregation has had eight pastors in twelve years, or that an interview took place just a few days after September 11, 2001, or that the interviewee has been a member of the congregation for forty-five years. There are also occasional quotations from the interviews with the preachers themselves, reflecting the preachers' sense of how particular efforts may or may not have engaged their listeners.

Because we assured anonymity to the persons interviewed for the study, we have made slight and occasional emendations in language in the quoted material to remove indications of the personal identities of the respondents, but only in ways that do not affect meaning. For instance, we substitute the terms *pastor, priest,* and *minister* interchangeably, recognizing that the type of congregation could be identified by the clerical reference. After some discussion, we also intentionally deleted gender reference in the pronouns used to discuss the clergy. The reader will notice that most qualifiers have been eliminated in introducing a person's idras. In most instances, it is not integral to the chapter to identify whether the speaker was a man or a woman, younger or older, from a small town or large city, African American or Anglo, from a small congregation or megachurch. However, when helpful, we used identifying labels if they seem important to interpreting the comments of the interviewees. We note, for instance, when persons in small congregations share ideas with those in large churches, or when persons in similar situations reveal divergent thoughts about what helps them connect with the sermon.

Each topical chapter was written with the following flow as a guide: The chapter begins with an introduction of the topic, including how we are using key terms. We also identify some of the specific questions asked from which we gathered material for the chapter. This is followed by the largest section of each chapter, which contains direct quotes from the interviews. There are also accompanying summary statements indicating a degree of agreement within answers and similar matters. The quoted material is usually presented according to a pattern (or schema) of clusters and sub-clusters of similar ideas, which the authors set out. The **cluster headings** are indicated by **bold type** and the *sub-clusters* by *italics*. Brief commentary may assist quotations in this section. The third section reflects on what we are learning about preaching from the presented material. Are there convergences? We include theological reflection on the stated topic that investigates how the listeners' understanding of preaching fits with and even shapes their understanding and living out of the Christian faith. The authors hope that as lay readers discover their own thoughts echoed in the ideas of those who were interviewed, they will also recognize and take advantage of this opportunity to reflect on the ideas of others in the light of our shared faith and beliefs about the church. Each chapter ends with a brief fourth section containing a word to preachers about the material presented, paying special attention to how sermons can be used to reinforce listener preferences that are appropriate to the theological heart and purpose of the faith, and what to do when it may be important to attempt to educate the congregation's listening preferences. This fourth section includes a few questions to guide further considerations about preaching. We invite ministers to consider forming a clergy group to study and work together on strengthening their preaching in light of these words to preachers. Of course, the reflections and questions may be used individually as well.

Our research has continued to support the belief that preaching is important in the lives of believers and congregations. Those who sit in the pews week after week show they are eager for a significant and timely word to feed their faith and witness. They are continuing to come to worship because they are "believing in preaching." We offer this book as an encouragement and sign of hope for the church.

# How Do These Listeners Understand the Purposes of Preaching?

The central concern of this first chapter is signaled by a question we asked people interviewed for the study. "When the preacher stands up to preach, what do you hope will happen to you as a result of listening to the sermon?" The goal of this question was to find out how our interviewees think of the purpose(s) of preaching. What do they say they want from a sermon? Other questions called forth responses around this concern. "What do you think your pastor is doing when she or he preaches?" "Tell me what preaching does in this congregation that other things do not do?" "What would be missing if there were no sermon?" Listener responses to still other queries contribute to this exploration. For example, when asked "What do you think God is doing in the sermon?" some people replied, "Speaking to the minister, who then speaks to the congregation."

## What These Listeners Say about the Purposes of Preaching

Listener statements about the purpose of preaching are quite diverse; indeed, we identify eleven clusters of perspectives. While we separate these gathering points for purposes of discussion, they are interrelated, and a single listener often voices ideas from more than one cluster. In particular, the first (the sermon teaches) is frequently given content by the second and third (the sermon explains the Bible and/or the word of God) and given practical implication by the fourth (the sermon applies the Bible/word of God to life). Differences among the various viewpoints are often matters of degree and emphasis. Many listeners, in fact, describe the sermon as having multiple purposes.

First, nearly two-thirds of the respondents say that a major purpose of preaching is to **teach or instruct** the congregation and the individuals within it. The listeners sometimes identify the content of the instruction (e.g., the Bible, Christian doctrine) but sometimes do not specify what the sermon should teach. One listener both summarizes this motif in the material and illustrates how themes intertwine.

> I think the preacher is trying to do a couple of things. I think one would be to give instructions to the members, I think, to reinforce our faith by giving us more instruction about the Bible or about faith-related principles. I think to give a better understanding of just what Christian faith does to help us through problems in our lives. I also think the minister is trying to motivate the membership. If by chance those things can make you feel better about the challenges that you're going to be facing in the coming days, then that's an additional benefit.

Another interviewee sounds a similar note that is found in several interviews.

> I think the sermon is an opportunity to teach, because I think the huge majority of those who call ourselves Christians are relatively illiterate as far as the whole Bible is concerned and the history. I think a lot is taught in seminary that we should probably know and don't. I also think our pastor really strives to connect with what's going on in the world.

Again, we see the intertwining of themes: teaching in such a way as to connect with today's world.

A number of persons interviewed speak of the sermon in a related second way as **explaining the Bible**. As we see in chapter 2, the attitudes toward the Bible voiced by the study population are quite diverse. Nevertheless, most listeners think that one aspect of the preacher's work is to explain it, as we hear in the following remark:

> I think the sermon is primarily to teach you more about the Bible. I think it teaches you about the principles of what the Bible is trying to emit and how it might apply to your life. I don't think that the Bible is read verbatim. I think as you try to take the context and then you try to apply it to situations that you might find yourself in today, or, in some cases, a situation that the world is in today.

For most of these listeners, teaching is more than repeating the content of the Bible, as someone else says:

> The sermon is not a history lesson. I think so often that many ministers preaching straight from the scripture turn it into history lessons, but then they never make the connection. You have to connect it. You have to give something. Say, "Why is the life of Daniel important to me?"

The sermon honors the social contexts of the Bible while making it contemporary. For some interviewees, however, teaching is mainly repeating the content of the Bible and applying it directly to our time.

More than simply as explanation of the Bible, many people, regard the sermon as **the word of God**, or **as interpreting the word of God.**[1] These categories are sometimes difficult to separate in the responses because some congregants equate or nearly equate the Bible with the word of God, and some see the sermon in the same way (either as almost a direct quote from God or as containing or witnessing to the word of God). Other interviewees include the Bible in the word of God while recognizing other ways that God speaks.[2] Some listeners think of the preacher not so much directly speaking the word of God but more **interpreting** it. Some listeners do not use the category "word of God" in relationship to the sermon.

For instance, one African American listener says vividly, "What the sermon does particularly–I like it in the African American context–is to charge the air with words from God." The preacher's words are not automatically the word of God for this community member, but when the preacher responds to the movement of the Spirit, the preaching becomes "an instrument used by God."

A hearer in another congregation emphasizes that the sermon "lifts up God's word and the interpretation of it with commonness" that all can understand.

I certainly feel that God speaks to us through prayer and through listening to scripture. But when whoever is preaching gets up, that person is also speaking God's word to us. If that person is prepared, and opened him or herself to believing in the Lord's Spirit, which I thoroughly believe all our ministers do here, then God is going to be speaking through that person who is standing in front of us and has a message for us if we have the open heart and ears to hear it.

However, the claim that the sermon can speak God's word does not mean that everything in the sermon is automatically clear and self-interpreting. This congregant continues,

We know the phrase "active listener," and it is a two-way thing with the sermon with questions sometimes. I've told [name of senior minister] a number of times I wanted to raise my hand and say, "Hey, preacher, what do you mean by that?" or "Hey, preacher, I don't agree with that," but so far I've managed to control myself.

While this listener accords a high authority to the sermon, the person also recognizes that interpretation is involved and believes that the community can help.

Most persons who participated in the interviews would concur with the following response: "I think preachers are sharing their interpretation of God's word and God's desire or wish for humanity on this earth."

Fourth, many people speak of the aim of the sermon as **applying teachings of the Bible or Christian faith to life**. They want to know how to make theological sense out of circumstances in which they find themselves, ranging from international and national situations to home life. After explaining, "I don't think a sermon should be sugar-coated," a parishioner says forcefully, using the Old Testament as an example, "Show me what it says in the Old Testament and how I can apply it to my life." This respondent wants to know, in very practical terms, what a biblical text calls the congregation to do.

Still another interviewee provides a summary of the ways many people experience the relationship of these first themes.

I'm listening for a sermon that is based, that they cite their scriptural foundation for whatever they are teaching for the day. I like to know where we're going, what the beginning and end of the sermon is, and what the point of the sermon is, what the three or four or five key areas that they're going to talk about. I like for it to be something that can be applied to one's daily life, and as you leave you feel like it's something that you can truly use.

The emphasis on preaching providing "something you can use" permeates the survey. Many people who make comments similar to this one often want to know what the sermon calls them to believe and do in their every day life settings. They are eager for the preacher to help them name the implications of the sermon that are specific to their own households, congregation, and city. The listener quoted above gave an example. A sermon on the importance of practicing forgiveness in the Christian community helped this person recognize the need to seek forgiveness from another person. The listener felt much better after doing so.

As a fifth cluster, some people seek for the sermon to help them **deepen their relationships with God or Christ**. "I would hope that the sermon would cause people to grow closer to the Lord and enhance their walk with God, that they would better love and serve God because of the preaching that they hear, that it would inspire them on their own to grow in Christ." We hear a similar note in another response: "The sermon would be something that would somehow connect me with God." Taking up the language of feeling, another says, "I hope to feel closer to God at that point during the sermon...I want to be drawn as much as possible." This parishioner wants to feel like "you're getting deeper." In many of the interviews, we hear a deep sense of yearning to experience an increasingly significant relationship with God.

A sixth cluster of responses gathers around the motifs of **inspiration, lifting up, empowerment, and motivation**. While we could certainly find differences among these different qualities, they share the idea that a goal of preaching is to awaken individuals and the community to greater awareness of the divine presence and to more faithful living. For some listeners these purposes work together. "No doubt education, to educate, to motivate, and I'm going to throw in this phrase, 'uplift.' I think if you can educate and motivate people, the uplifting happens." Another congregant desires for the sermon to "lift me emotionally to a place I'm not at that time. Sometimes that's a big lift." Most of the persons who speak in this vein see the uplifting as an empowerment for faithful witness. In this trajectory, one remark speaks for many: "I hope the preacher is going to say something that will make me be inspired to go out and do more than I am presently doing."

Inspiration and uplift sometimes result from sermons that cause the members of the community to examine themselves, as another person says, "Preaching for the congregation should at times make you feel a little uncomfortable, which it does in this church. I used to think that was a bad thing. It's not a bad thing. It helps you to see where your faults are, your flaws are, and to acknowledge them and try to want to better them."

In chapter 7, we discuss whether and how the sermon helps shape the congregation as community. For now, as a seventh cluster, we report that a noticeable number of hearers identify a purpose of preaching as **unifying the congregation**. While it is not always clear whether these listeners think of the congregation as a true community or as an aggregate of individuals, they believe that the sermon plays a significant role in helping the congregation develop the capacity to work together. For instance, one person sees the sermon as "rallying the troops." A more expansive comment is, "I think that ideally the preacher is standing up to call together the people of God and to continue to form the community…and to join people together as one in that act." The aim of bonding as a community in the gospel is to provide support for people within the church as well as for the church as a body to witness in the world.

Eighth, while again not a majority perspective in the sample, a goodly number of hearers say explicitly that they would like for the sermon to **cause them to think about the Bible or issues in life** in ways that push them beyond the edges of their current perspectives. A person interviewed puts it this way when asked to say what the preacher is trying to do when preaching: "I think it really depends on the pastor. Some pastors, I think, have their own opinions about things, and they try to carry those opinions to you. Other pastors, I think, try to stimulate you to thinking and not really try to force an opinion on you." This listener continues approvingly, "I think our pastor is stimulating our thinking. To some degree the preacher is saying, 'Here's what I think,' but at the same time I think the preacher is challenging you." Similarly, another listener opines that a sermon should "make you sit back and think and listen and reflect and learn." Another listener says, "I hope that I will be challenged to think about things or see things in a different way…I guess what I hope at my best is to be intellectually challenged." At the risk of imposing too great a burden on preachers, we report other words along this line: "I hope that I will have at least one little 'Aha' in every sermon, that I will be changed in some way, that I will have my eyes opened or my ears opened." Even when that does not happen, "I'm still content to sit through an entire sermon."

Some listeners say they appreciate mind-stretching sermons even when they do not agree with the preacher. A congregant deplores "robot-type congregations" that ministers have "trained" to think in certain ways. This congregant likes it when the sermon contains something that "really stands out or I question" and people respond after the service, by talking energetically with the preacher and among themselves about the points of difference. This hearer believes that such differences, when handled respectfully, can become points of clarification and "growth." Another interviewee remembers a sermon with disturbing ideas: "It stirred up emotions of hurt and anger." However, "Over time you begin to realize there was something being said there that you needed to listen to."

Several respondents emphasize that they do not expect preachers to have all the answers about God and life. But they do want sermons to help them.

> I really love the sermons that are about things that we're uncomfortable about, and the times when preachers say, "You know, I just really don't understand this, but here's what I've been thinking about." I love it when people get up and say, "I'm struggling with you on this."

For such folk, it is less important that the sermon hands them an answer than that the sermon provides a space within which preacher and congregation can struggle and stretch.

A few listeners who make up a ninth cluster say that the intention of the sermon is to help them **sort out what they believe**. Several persons interviewed, represented by this comment, overtly state a primary purpose of preaching in such terms, such as the following: "I want to know what God has to say about a subject. What did God say? A human being can say anything, but we need to know what God said and what God would do." Using a story of Jesus teaching a crowd and vocation of the preacher, one person says succinctly, "Here's somebody who knows and who explains to those people in the crowd what the truth really was. That's what *we* want." Many listeners hope the sermon will help them learn Christian doctrine and apply it to life. "I would think the preachers are trying to lead us to a better understanding of who God is, trying to help us see more clearly what our role is here on Earth, what it is that God would have us do." This person yearns for sermons to help answer theological questions, "Like, for example, 'Why do we suffer?'" This viewpoint resonates with that of another hearer who hopes the sermon will result in "the ability to make some sense out of those things going on in life." Several listeners want the preacher "to give me the basis for why the pastor is believing" the ideas in the sermon.

> Our pastor explains. Our pastor doesn't just come out, "This is wrong because I say it's wrong," but looks for scriptural backing of what the sermon is saying, and reminds us, "What do you think Jesus Christ would say about this if Jesus were here today? What would Jesus' stand be?" Our pastor is effective in giving reasons for the stand that the sermon takes. The pastor doesn't just say, "Believe this because I'm your pastor and I tell you this is what you ought to believe," but will say, "This is why. This is my stand on this issue." The pastor gives a logical defense or apologetics of why that's the stand.

Such listeners want the sermon to help them discover what they can believe, and why.

Few people in our survey speak explicitly of the sermon's role as **converting people**, a tenth cluster. However, this concern does appear from time to time.

> I'm proud that our preacher every Sunday issues somewhere in that sermon a gospel call. One of the things that depress me is when I go to churches and I don't hear that. It's not just a Billy Graham Crusade message, but it will just be woven in to make sure you assess yourself.

For such respondents, a primary purpose of the sermon is to convert.

For the final (eleventh) cluster, several members in diverse settings insist that the sermon should bring **a message that is distinctively Christian and that will help the congregation manifest distinctively Christian identity and vocation**. One member says, "The sermon is not just to make you feel good, which you can get at the Rotary Club or the Kiwanis Club or somewhere else." A sermon similar to what you hear at a service club or get from self-help resources is "pretty much just what a psychologist says about this and what some philosophers have said. They quote a bunch of people…and it's basically just 'Gird up your loins' and 'Go for it' and 'Find the strength within you' and 'Tell yourself you can do it.'" Such talks are "fine for Kiwanis," but, the same interviewee continues, a sermon should "lead you to the truth and to the Lord." Sermons should point to "a higher level of spirituality," a "calling to service," and even "a holy lifestyle."

Another interviewee says the sermon is to "call us together to be a people unique,"; that is, "a people with peculiar practices and things that set them apart from the rest of the world. Not in a bad way, not to be separatist or anything, but to shape us and help us engage the world in a different way." These listeners speak for many people in our study who want the sermon to help them understand life from a Christian perspective and to guide and empower them in living faithfully:

> If a church is absent of the story and meaning of Christ, to me it's just another building, brick and mortar, wood and stone, where people gather, shake hands, smile at each other, feel good about themselves, and go home and don't really get anything. It would be to me like going to a restaurant, waiting in line, getting to the table, candlelight and nice atmosphere. "There's not any food tonight, but we're glad you came." We did feel welcome. On your way out, "Thanks for coming." But when you got out, why would I come back? I went to eat. Everything else was an enhancement, but I went there to eat. If I didn't get anything to eat, then I wasted my time.

For many of these listeners, preaching is not only the main course of the service of worship, but a main course of life. Like the main course, preaching provides the substance—the vision and energy—out of which they live.

### Reflections and Insights on How These Listeners Understand Preaching

One of the most persistent themes in the interviews is the high degree of importance that most of these listeners place on the sermon. When asked what would be missing if there were no sermon, one listener voiced a thought shared by many, "I wouldn't want to come." This person relies upon the sermon to bring "a word from God." On the one hand, this attitude among laity should reinforce the preacher's confidence in preaching, and should encourage pastors to continue working hard at preaching. On the other hand, it suggests that many people in contemporary congregations need a more adequate theological grasp of the nature and function of the service of worship as a whole.[3] Scholarship in worship over the last forty years has increasingly emphasized that the service of worship should be not just a collection of liturgical knick-knacks (e.g., hymns, prayers, passing the peace, the Lord's supper) to set up the sermon, but should embody a coherent theological vision in its movement and practices, of which the sermon is a piece. Through its liturgical structure, actions, and content, the service as a whole should represent a Christian vision of God and the world.[4] Preachers need to help many congregations develop an overarching understanding of the service of worship, and the role of the sermon as contributing to the flow of the service.

Many of the listeners in our study generally echo the Reformation emphasis on the sermon as an event of teaching. This perspective is not surprising since the majority of the interviewees come from congregations descended from the Reformation or the Radical Reformation. The idea of the sermon as teaching also made its way into churches that see themselves related to the Counter Reformation. These folk generally hold that the sermon is to help them develop theological perspectives on life. Many folk understand teaching to be the *raison d'etre* of preaching.

We note considerable pluralism in the ways in which the sample population regards both the content and methods of the teaching. With respect to content, a handful of listeners seem to conceive of the sermon, almost by definition, as *the* word of God. Most think that preaching offers an *interpretation* of the word of God. Listeners differ as to the relationship of the Bible, the word of God, and the theology voiced in the sermon. In the midst of the pluralism, however, we detect a theological problem that is shared by many people in their differing viewpoints. Few of the listeners articulate criteria by which to gauge the degree to which the teaching in a sermon is theologically adequate. When listeners hear a sermon, how do they tell the degree to which it is a faithful interpretation of God's purposes for the world?

Two criteria crop up often in the interviews. A very common criterion is *fidelity to the Bible*: a sermon is trustworthy when it is true to scripture.[5] This viewpoint raises the question, of course, of what it means to be true to the Bible. As we discover in chapter 2, opinions vary as to the nature of the Bible and its authority, but most of the congregations in the study are in denominations or movements that are coming to recognize that the Bible itself contains a diversity of theological viewpoints, some of which are in tension with one another. To be sure, congregations do not always follow (or accept) developments in theological conversations in the denomination, the seminary, and broader Christian movements. Nevertheless, listeners may need assistance from the pulpit when voices in the Bible conflict with one another, when the Bible is silent on (and does not contain a useful analogy for) an issue, or when the Bible voices a viewpoint that goes against the grain of the congregation's deepest convictions about God. We suggest that a preacher or congregation cannot appeal singularly to "the Bible" as criterion for determining the authenticity of a sermon since the Bible itself is not a singular voice.

This issue is part of a larger canvass. Most of our listeners tie the purpose of preaching directly to explaining the Bible, as if the Bible were the only source of the knowledge of God and as if the sermon must be an exposition of a biblical text to be fully Christian. While some theological families concur with this judgment, others in the Christian household think of the Bible as a primary but not exclusive guide to the divine presence, and see the purpose of preaching, in a broader theological frame, as interpreting the presence and purposes of God. For such preachers and communities, the Bible is typically a significant, even primary, part of the sermon, but for them the presence or absence of the Bible does not, in and of itself, define the purpose of the sermon.[6]

As we note more fully in chapter 6, "Roles of Feeling in Preaching," a smaller number of listeners believe that certain *feelings* reveal that a sermon is trustworthy. For example, one listener recognizes God's word is being spoken because "It touches you in some deep way." Some people indicate that the Holy Spirit is the source of such transverbal awareness. To be sure, feeling plays an important role in the ways in which human beings "know."[7] However, we want to remember that the simple presence of an emotion is not inherently a guarantee that the emotion is born of the Spirit. A feeling may—or may not—arise in response to the Spirit. A congregation needs norms by which to evaluate the degree to which feelings are reliable indicators of faithful guidance. The sermon may be an arena in which to explore these things. Of course, members of the congregation need to be involved in other forms of Christian education.

The laity's desire for the sermon to teach is welcome. Many parishioners are aware that they need to know more about the Bible, doctrine, making ethical decisions, and other matters in order to function as deeply as possible as Christians. Many laity (and preachers) recognize that sermons, at twenty to forty minutes a week, cannot assume the whole teaching responsibility for a congregation. The preacher can certainly use the sermon to reinforce the importance of congregants taking part in other educational opportunities in the congregation (such as Bible school and other study groups) and can help the congregation recognize the learning that takes place in events such as mission trips and in broader congregational practices.[9]

## A Word to Preachers

We now turn to some possibilities for ways a minister might respond to the preceding theological reflections on how persons in our interviews understand the purposes of preaching. When preachers have a sense of what people in the congregation expect when hearing a sermon, they can engage in critical theological reflection on how to relate to listener expectations. Can the preacher wholeheartedly embrace the laity's attitudes towards the sermon? That is, can the preacher try to develop sermons that give them what they want? Or, should preachers theologically affirm some aspects of the congregation's hopes for the sermon while urging the people to modify others? Or, will the preacher need to help the congregation significantly rethink what they anticipate from a sermon? If the latter, the preacher needs to consider how to urge the congregation to shift their expectations in a way that the congregation will consider inviting.

We have highlighted several avenues of shared understanding of the purposes of preaching while also calling attention to exceptions to these trends. Because preaching is always contextual, local pastors should not respond only to the perspectives that surfaced in our study, but to the ones that are alive in the communities in which they preach.

Since the historic claims of the church and the words of the listeners underscore the importance of preaching, it makes sense for ministers to preach, from time to time, on *the purposes of preaching.* Such sermons would help the congregation enter more fully into the world of the sermon.

If a congregation does not have a theologically adequate under-standing of the service of worship, a preacher and other leaders of the congregation are called to help the community enhance their perceptions. An enlarged understanding of the service of worship will not only enhance participation and increase what the congregation receives, it will also more fully honor God.

We further noted that listeners need to possess adequate criteria by which to evaluate the relative faithfulness of a sermon. As L. Susan Bond, a noted authority in the field of preaching, says in her significant book *Trouble with Jesus* that one of the most important purposes of preaching is to help congregations develop a critical awareness of how we come to interpret certain ideas, feelings, actions, and circumstances as consistent or inconsistent with the divine aims for the world. The preacher can use the sermon to model for the congregation how to engage in theological reflection.[9] A minister can help congregants discern norms that emanate from a responsible vision of God.[10] A part of this task, of course, is to help the congregation articulate a clear and coherent perception of how the Bible, feelings, and other resources can contribute to the congregation's under-standing of God's presence and purposes for the world.

Several appropriate perspectives on the purpose of preaching generated by the interviewees suggest things a preacher might do when developing a sermon.[11]

- One of the most pervasive understandings of the purpose of preaching is for the sermon to instruct the congregations. The preacher can seek for each sermon to help the community make theological sense out of its world.[12]

- Many listeners underscore the importance of the sermon explaining the Bible. While the sermon needs to be more than a history lesson, the preacher needs to be sure that the sermon typically helps the congregation honor the meaning(s) of the text in its historical, literary, and theological contexts.[13]

- However, many listeners emphasize further that the sermon needs to move beyond being a history lesson to helping the congregation make sense of the Bible and other Christian perspectives for today. Preachers can construct a sermon with a view towards how the message can help the church name implications of the message that are specific to the contemporary congregation and the world.

Such exercises can be extended to other aspects of the purposes of preaching. How will a message help a community deepen its relationship with God? In what ways might a homily lift up, motivate, and empower the hearing community? How might a message help a congregation come together as community? In what fashion could a sermon cause the congregation to stretch its thinking, acting, or feeling?

The remarks of our listeners challenge two assumptions commonplace in some contemporary preaching circles. For one, some preachers are reluctant to critique congregations for fear of alienating the listeners. In contrast, several laity recognize that, at times, the sermon cannot be "sugar coated," and that, indeed, one function of preaching is to bring them to confront aspects of themselves and the world that may need to be rethought or reshaped. A number of listeners recognize that such confrontation is necessary to help them mature in faith and to bring about a congregation or world that more fully manifests the purposes of God. We hope that these listeners' remarks will encourage preachers to speak, when necessary, a discomforting word to help congregations turn away from complicity with evil and to turn towards the gospel.[14]

The other assumption relates to the form and function of the sermon. Since the 1970s, many preachers and writers in the field have recommended inductive and indirect approaches—often relying heavily on image, experience, and narrative—that leave listeners in the position of coming to their own conclusions regarding the meaning of the sermon. Advocates of these innovative approaches often dismiss more deductive and directive styles. However, many of the persons in our interview sample state a preference for sermons that communicate straightforwardly the possibilities for belief and witness. As one of the listeners cited above said, "I like to know where we're going, what the beginning and end of the sermon is, what the point of the sermon is." Indeed, one of our respondents expresses an even more straightforward preference. This respondent likes for the preacher to indicate, "three points and I [the preacher] am through." Because most congregations likely contain listeners in both of these clusters (and others), ministers should probably include both kinds of sermons (as well as some that are amalgams of the two) over a season of preaching.[15]

As readers leave this chapter, it could be constructive (as intimated earlier) to consider the questions, How do the listeners in my congregation understand the purpose(s) of preaching? What do the members of this congregation think the pastor is doing when she or he stands up to preach? Readers could consider how the clusters of understanding in the congregation compare and contrast with one another, and with the preacher's notion of the aims of the sermon. The preacher could bring these different perspectives into conversation with one another. In a similar way, readers could ask how preaching actually functions in their congregations, and could identify things that preaching does that other things do not do. A preacher, then, could help the congregation name and reinforce qualities associated with preaching that help the congregation become a community of the gospel and remedy those qualities that frustrate that goal.

# CHAPTER 2

# The Role and Authority of Scripture in Preaching

According to the listener responses in our survey, one of the most passionate and persistent interests of those who listen to sermons is the role and authority of scripture in preaching. Across denominational affiliations, through the comments of young and old, male and female, persons of various ethnic identities and from a variety of congregational settings and sizes, listeners who participated in this study recognize a vital and essential relationship between the written word in scripture and the spoken word in preaching and worship. Whether the Bible relates what is strange or familiar, challenging or comforting, the vast majority of listeners interviewed believe that scripture is something more than print on a page. It is alive with meaning and relevant for today.

In particular, the vast majority of interviewees speak of the Bible as central to preaching. Referred to as "scripture," "the Bible," "the Book," "the word of God" or simply "the Word," many people attribute the authority of preaching to the preacher's use of scripture. In response to the written questionnaire that asked listeners to prioritize thirteen elements that may help the hearer engage the sermon (including such items as touching the emotions, telling hearers how to behave, the use of memorable stories), 60 percent of people who completed the questionnaire cite "make the Bible come alive" as one of their top four priorities, with only 9 percent of respondents listing it as eleventh or lower on their priority lists. One writes, "If the Bible is a dead book, why is it so important? A 'live' commentary can change lives today."

However, amid the deep commitment and widespread longing to engage with scripture in the worship of God we also hear a variety of approaches to the interpretation of scripture, its role, and how it functions authoritatively in the sermon. In the oral interviews, listeners describe the role of scripture in preaching through a number of different functions or metaphors as the "foundation," "road map," "study guide," "compass," "tool," "backbone," or "basis" for the life of faith. Although some insist that the "whole objective of the sermon is the Bible teaching of the Bible, explaining the Bible, and interpreting it," others assert, "I want the sermon to be based in the scripture text, but it does not have to be." Although some interviewees express appreciation for "straight Bible teaching" in sermons, many others are "willing to accept the fact that there are various ways of interpreting what's written down."

### What These Listeners Say about the Role of Scripture in Preaching

Because the Bible is mentioned by so many listeners, and their comments reveal an array of perspectives and understandings regarding the interpretation and authority of scripture in preaching, it is important to consider at least five clusters of comments related to the Bible in preaching among those who were interviewed. These include comments related to **teaching about the content of scripture in the sermon, the importance of interpreting scripture in its historical and literary contexts, the authority attributed to scripture** by the listener, **the broader range of resources that are authoritative and meaningful in preaching**, and the importance of **the relevance of the Bible for today** in and beyond the preaching moment. Although these overlap considerably in the comments of listeners, each of these categories will be explored after first considering listeners' overarching interest in being taught the content of the Bible through preaching.

In describing the role of the Bible in preaching, listeners frequently refer to the importance of **teaching about the content of scripture in the sermon**. As one of the primary purposes of preaching described in chapter 1, teaching about scripture in the sermon emerges as a vital interest among people in the pews. In commenting on the role of the Bible in preaching, one person is adamant that "the whole role of preaching" is to teach listeners about scripture. Another listener asserts that the role is "to show people the teachings of Jesus or God. That's the kind of role preaching has to me. It teaches you." One listener's comment is representative of the thoughts of many: "I can read the Bible as well as the next person, but I may not understand what it means. So if you can know what the Bible says and explain what it means, then certainly that has a very significant role, a very significant role in the effectiveness of the sermon."

This comment not only reveals the importance of communicating the Bible's meaning but it also suggests for this listener that scripture's meaningfulness is intimately related to *perceived notions of the authority of scripture* and the listener's perception of the "effectiveness" of the sermon. According to the comments of many listeners, preaching that engages others with scripture involves an awareness of the ways in which biblical interpretation, authority, and relevance interact in the preaching moment. Further complicating the interplay of these ingredients (each of which is addressed more fully below) is the fact that not only is the preacher's approach to scripture of consequence, but the approaches of the listeners must also be heard and considered as vital to the preaching event.

Of course, it is a considerable responsibility to teach others about scripture and perhaps a daunting prospect for preachers who cannot assume their hearers share a common level of familiarity with biblical texts. However, it may be comforting and encouraging for preachers to realize the enthusiasm with which many listeners speak of their desire and receptivity to a message that enlightens their understanding or offers a moment of insight into the deeper meaning or relevance of scripture. Several interviewees view the sermon as a vital opportunity to gain knowledge and insight related to scripture texts. They value preaching that provides spiritual education and edification. One comment reflects the thoughts of others: "I read the Bible every day, but half the time it's difficult to understand reading it by myself. There's nobody there to help you. I would have spent a lifetime studying if I could have afforded it. I like some of that from the sermon."

Whether a text is familiar or not, listeners express appreciation for hearing sermons that offer a fresh glimpse or *new insights into the Bible:*

Sometimes I've heard a sermon on a scripture that I've heard all the time, and a minister can preach on it, and it just sheds a different light. Like Revelation has never bothered me that much, but a couple of years ago my pastor preached on Revelation and what it meant and it took the scariness out of it. It never did scare me, but I was too lazy to delve into it to see what all these things meant. My pastor brought it up to the surface because I know people that really fear Revelation.

Those who feel less informed about the Bible (or admit feeling discomfort around others who are more biblically literate) voice deep appreciation for preachers who read scripture, interpret it, and share life experiences that relate to the text. In addition to these listeners, those who are more familiar with the Bible also express deep longing to learn more about a scripture passage. Categories of biblical interpretation, authority, and relevance converge in the comments of many listeners, including that of one person who speaks of the pastor's ability to share Bible stories in ways that are relevant, accessible, and meaningful:

> To me it's like the preacher telling me a story that I haven't read and making it personal by reading the gospel, interpreting it, and giving a life experience when telling the congregation about that. My kids, when they were little, you can read them stories, and they can hear the same ones over and over. That's kind of how I am whenever I hear any Bible teachings, because I didn't have that experience as a kid. Today I feel uncomfortable if I'm in a group of people that's very knowledgeable about the Bible because I am not. I'm learning by hearing and reading. That helps me.

Many others hope that preaching may teach them about the *Bible as a resource for right living and God's values or intentions.* At this point, categories of biblical teaching, authority, and relevance intersect once again as many listeners are interested in hearing sermons that draw on scripture as a teaching tool in learning how God's purposes are revealed in scripture and how the Bible relates to daily living and current concerns. In the words of one listener:

> I think the role of the Bible in preaching is to teach us what God wants us to do and the lessons. All the stories are told for a reason, kind of like lessons. It's kind of like a history

book. It tells you what happened and what the outcome was from the circumstances of what they did, from the action—kind of giving us a warning like as we do as parents.

Another reason for valuing scripture also reveals a pragmatic interest on the part of listeners. For some, the purpose of biblical preaching is not primarily related to the personal lessons to be learned, but to the *social benefits to be gained from the regular exploration of scripture* in worship. One listener values biblical preaching that provides children with a "moral structure" that is of social and cultural significance, and comments on the role of the Bible in preaching as well as in Sunday school classes:

> It seems to me that, in modern life, parents who are themselves not related to the church and really agnostic would be better off if they said, "Look, my kids are going to go to church. They're going to go to Sunday school and church to learn this stuff partly because it's our culture. Now you can throw it over when you get to be an adult if you want but at least you have something to shoot against. You ought to know those things just as a matter of cultural conditioning if nothing else."

This listener and several others appreciate the value of learning more about scripture as it relates not only to our individual lives but to our relationships with others and the larger society to which we relate.

Fortunately, most listeners understand that numerous challenges are involved in the task of preparing biblically oriented preaching and one person speaks for those who hope their pastor will take up this challenge:

> I feel strongly that preaching should come from the Bible. It should be biblically based. It's a complex compilation of books that I think obviously has been studied and analyzed, and there are multitudes of perspectives, but if you don't start there, I'm not sure what you'd be preaching about.

A few listeners express their appreciation for biblically based sermons when they speak positively about the lectionary. People belonging to very different communities of faith also appreciate scripture reading before the sermon that is "well done."

More often people comment about numerous occasions when preachers referenced several different scripture texts in the same sermon. Whereas some listeners express a desire for "periodic and perpetual references to scripture" and affirm the preacher's ability to name texts that support and relate to a particular biblical theme, others "do not see the need to quote the scripture here and the scripture there within the sermon."[1] For many, learning about the Bible through sermons and worship is a high priority but *biblical preaching is not a matter of using frequent Bible quotations. For these listeners, preaching is biblical when the Bible is the leading force or direction of the sermon so that the preacher does not need to quote different texts as* much as to center the sermon on one biblical text or theme.[2] In fact, some assume that the Bible "is always there. It doesn't have to be overtly there, but it's there. It doesn't have to be pointed to or waved or slapped, but it's there." This listener and others appreciate scripture's presence in worship but do not need or want to hear numerous citations or references to different texts. One listener voices considerable frustration in trying to follow a preacher who moves between several texts in the same sermon:

> The preacher is flipping back and forth so fast. By the time I get to the next one that's already read, the preacher is on to the next one. After a while, I'll sit back, okay. I don't like the flipping back and forth. A few, that's fine, but when you're reading ten, fifteen, twenty verses just back and forth, just flipping back and forth. You can look around and most everybody is trying to flip back and forth in their Bibles.

Among those who voice interest in sermons that address multiple scripture texts in the same message there is a clear and *strong desire for the preacher to focus on one biblical teaching, idea, or image.* In the words of one listener who appreciates the preacher's ability to reference the larger framework of the biblical witness yet also remain well focused:

> There are a lot of preachers that I have heard who, it really is, almost like a fountain of cool water the way that they open the scriptures and explain them and use other scriptures to tie together so that the Bible becomes really a unified whole. That is my ideal with a good sermon. I think I started by saying, even without stories I enjoy someone teaching a Bible study, but a good preacher who holds our attention is one who really does turn on the light on scripture in such a

way that it does become a unified whole, and it explains itself, and it interprets itself. That's what I like, and I look for in a good sermon.

Most of the listeners interviewed in this study are emphatic that the Bible needs to be a central part of the sermon. Aware of the challenges this presents to preachers, many people are persistent in voicing their need to be more fully informed about the Bible and its relevance for their lives. For reasons of spiritual edification and enlightenment, personal guidance and social benefit, an overwhelming number of interviewees accord the teaching of scripture a high priority in the preaching of the church.

As these comments regarding the teaching of the Bible reflect, preaching that relates to biblical texts (and biblical preaching in general) necessarily involves preachers and listeners in a second major cluster (and one that is closely related to the first for many listeners), **interpreting scripture from the standpoint of its historical and literary settings**. Many listeners in our study reveal an appreciation for biblical interpretation that involves both a *reverence for scripture and an awareness of the complexities of the task*. In the words of one listener, "There are inconsistencies. You can't take it all equally seriously. You have to take it seriously but not literally." Another listener recognizes that the four gospels cover many of the same stories "but you get different versions. Which is right and which is wrong?" Without referencing specific hermeneutical methods (such as historical critical methods or literary approaches to the biblical writings), many interviewees offer insightful and even sophisticated descriptions of various aspects of biblical interpretation. Commenting on the interplay of text, context, pretext, as well as spiritual discernment in the process of biblical interpretation, one listener offers an assessment of what is involved in biblical exegesis for preaching:[3] "I'm not talking about just stringing texts along to bring your viewpoint, but looking at the context, looking at the culture, looking at everything that's there. I believe that it is read intentional with revelation, with the hope of revelation." Another congregant articulates both a deep devotion to scripture and the importance of giving consideration to the context within which biblical texts were written and transmitted. Exploring the dynamic relationship of social, cultural, and literary elements moving through the Bible, this member voices confidence in God's word as it holds meaning for our world today:

We have the Bible, and God's word to us is found in the Bible, but we have to understand that it was written by people living in a time different from ours and people who were from a culture that is very different from ours and saw life through a different set of filters from what we do, and we cannot understand scripture accurately unless we are willing to learn about those people and their ideas and their living conditions and their beliefs as formed in conjunction with the neighbors with whom they lived if we're looking back in the Old Testament times, as well as in Jesus' day and the contact with Greeks and Romans.

Several listeners comment on the need for faithful and studious care on the part of preachers who examine the text in search of its meaning for today. Their words not only reflect considerable awareness of what is at stake in the interpretive process, but also reveal appreciation for the fact that the study of scripture may yield new and challenging insights. Glad for the preacher to share his or her interpretation of a text, one listener speaks of the ways preaching provides an opportunity for the congregation to consider various perspectives that may encourage their own deeper reflection on the Bible:

> The Bible is so unexplained at times itself, we would really love the pastors' explanation, their understanding of it. And I think that our ministers have been pretty good about it. "Hey, you know? This is my belief. This may not necessarily fit in line totally with yours, but this is how I see this passage," and they relate it. I think their whole point is that as much as they're studying, as much as our pastor reads and as much as the pastor equates things to the world, we're still learning new things. I think that's one of the things that has connected with this particular congregation.

Related to this appreciation for new learning, some listeners express respect for the variety of interpretations that may arise from studying any one text, and one person even names God's intention of having diverse interpretations of scripture: "I'm willing to accept the fact that there are various ways of interpreting what's written down. The longer I guess about my own personal Christian growth, the more I realize that it may actually be that way by divine intent."

For others, what is of concern is not so much the variety of interpretations that may challenge or excite the listener but the fact that some texts seem especially difficult to understand. In particular, several listeners mention struggling with the meaning of Old Testament texts and appreciate that the study of the canon can greatly enhance understanding as the preacher prepares sermons: "If you're going to study the Old Testament, you need some education in order to come to correct conclusions about a great deal of what the Old Testament says." For one listener, some passages in the book of Psalms are particularly disturbing because of their violent images or content and this person is glad for the pastor to help set these texts alongside other texts: "The preacher will pick a psalm and then go back to some other scripture that led up to that, why that person said that. It makes me feel a little better." One person asks for help in approaching texts that are difficult: "We don't always understand everything the Bible is trying to say and why it went on the way it went on, especially the Old Testament. It's very hard to understand. So maybe make a connection between all that and how that can be seen today."

Another listener sounds a very different note and expresses excitement in gaining greater familiarity with Old Testament texts: "When you read about the creation of humankind in maybe the first ten pages of Genesis, that's a heck of a movie right there. The way it starts out, it's enough just to get people to keep reading the book of Genesis." This listener, like many others, appreciates hearing strange and challenging biblical stories and longs for preaching that addresses a variety of texts. Whether texts are challenging, intriguing, or frustrating, many listeners long for sermons that offer interpretive help and engage them in considering scripture texts anew.

Among the few who voice *a measure of suspicion regarding the role of biblical interpretation in preaching* and who see it as exerting an unnecessary or even harmful influence over the literal meaning of texts, one listener attributes the congregation's growth to preaching that communicates biblical truths in immediate and relevant ways: "First of all, from the pulpit a doctrinal fidelity is maintained. Biblical truths are not twisted. They're not interpreted. Scripture is brought forth in a current way that's applicable to today and to living today."

However, most listeners speak positively of the need for interpretation, and some not only speak of the pastor's role in studying the Bible in preparation for preaching but also note the need for listeners to engage in biblical interpretation as well. The comments of at least a few listeners reflect their active engagement in the process of interpretation before, during, and after the preaching moment. These listeners are very clear about their role in the process of biblical interpretation, and one person expresses not only willingness but a sense of active responsibility for grappling with the meaning of texts and participating in biblical interpretation. According to one congregant, "Whether they ever happened just like that, like it says in the Bible, is not important to me. I like to know that's the basis. So you want to read the scripture for yourself and see what I think my own interpretation is before. I hear it from somebody else. But I like to hear other people's interpretations as well." Another listener claims personal responsibility for the interpretation of the Bible, and holds a more cautious view about the preacher's use and interpretation of scripture. In response to the question, "What makes a sermon true?" this person states:

> As long as it comes out of the Bible. As long as it's not just taking one verse here and one verse there. I like to read the verses before and the verses after to make sure about what they're saying. There are even times I've gone home and I'll read it after, because my pastor skips around a lot. I'll go home, and I'll look at a verse and read the verses before and the verse after to make sure. Not that I don't believe, but I want to read it myself and make sure that the preacher's telling me the truth. I don't want to be blindly led.

Finally, another member speaks with appreciation and respect not so much for the respondent's part in the interpretation of scripture, but for the interpretive work of church leaders through the years whose insights may help enliven biblical preaching for the church today: "I do like the idea that the centuries of church leaders studying the Bible have some collected knowledge." All of these listeners, representing a range of denominational affiliations and church traditions, name the listener's role as crucial to the interpretation of the sacred texts.

Whether focusing on the preacher's role or the listener's role in interpreting scripture, many listeners view the *role of the Holy Spirit as integral and vital to the preaching moment* and believe that the Spirit is a close companion of the Bible, so that "both scripture and the Spirit have to be present." Although God's participation in preaching will be addressed in chapter 8 ("What about God?"), it is important to consider the comments of listeners who view the role of the Spirit as essential to the interpretation of scripture. One person strongly believes that the sermon will "be built on research and Spirit indwelling thoughts" of the minister, and another asserts, "I think all of preaching should be based upon the Bible, which can be interpreted different ways depending on how a particular pastor feels she or he is being led by the Lord." When asked what the pastor is doing when standing up to preach, one person explains, "Expounding the word of God. They've studied. They've researched, hopefully led by the Holy Spirit. They deliver the sermon, and then the sermons that they deliver are the word of God."

In describing the sermon as "the word of God," this listener introduces a phrase that many others draw on but use in a number of different ways. Although, as we noted in chapter 1 (on the purposes of preaching), it is impossible to assess the precise meaning of the term "word of God" for each listener, it is certain that many interviewees refer to God's word with very different meanings or reference points in mind. To some, "The Bible is God's word" and scripture is nearly equated with the word of God. For these listeners, one knows or encounters God primarily through the Bible, which stands as the centerpiece of the proclaimed word: "If you believe that the Bible is the word of God, then that's where you get to know God. So that's why I think it's best. God is the most important thing, but getting to know God is through the Bible."

For others, the Bible reveals God's word but there are *complications in the transmission and communication of scripture* that need to be recognized. Commenting on the role of the Bible in preaching, one listener states, "I believe it is the revealed word of God, but I also believe that it's not clear in my mind that the translators are following the original script that may have been revealed." Another listener speaks respectfully and frankly about wrestling with the relationship between the written words of scripture and what the listener believes may be the word of God: "You know there are people that believe that everything in the Bible is automatically the word of God, but I just wonder sometimes if it is, if everything in the Bible is the word of God, some things that I don't believe that are in the Bible."

Yet another comment reflects the priority given to the word of God in preaching while indicating a fluid movement or shared sense of meaning attributed to bible text, sermon, and the word of God:

"When the pastor gets up there and delivers the sermon, the only thing that I'm spiritually interested in is the word. If the pastor is delivering the word out of that Bible, God allows that word to come."

Finally, there are those who refer to the *word of God in more dynamic terms*, as something that thrives through written and spoken discourse, so that the sermon requires a measure of artfulness and skill on the part of the preacher. The comment of one listener reflects this living and active sense of the word of God, revealing the convergence of biblical authority, interpretation, and relevance in preaching:

> God's word is the primary authority. Yes, I like sermons that are connected to that. There's reference made to actual biblical text. It's related to biblical text and connecting, taking that and connecting it to what's happening in our lives today. So there's a skill there. There's an art form there in being able to do that. Some pastors do it better than others. To make it come alive. God's word is not dead. It's very dynamic and alive today. It's reflected in people's lives, and it's obviously reflected because people's lives do change. And they do change as a result of hearing the truth and God's word. Lives changing is probably the greatest proof that God's word is alive, and it's not dead. The Living Word– that's why it has been referred to as the Living Word.

The vitality with which this listener describes the relationship between the written words of scripture and the spoken words of the sermon reflect a confidence in the eventfulness of preaching as it may provide an occasion for transformation in the lives of those who hear God's living word. For this person, preaching involves the listeners in an engagement with the Bible and with God's word moving through scripture in such a way that the preacher is instrumental to the task of biblical interpretation.

Perhaps most interesting of all for the task of biblical interpretation in preaching is the fact that the listeners in our study describe the role or function of scripture in very different ways. People listen to sermons hoping to hear the written word interpreted or drawn upon for very different purposes, and their sense of the third cluster, **the confidence that scripture is authoritative in preaching**, is closely related to the ways in which the preacher appeals to scripture in the sermon. Listeners name at least three ways that the Bible functions authoritatively in the preaching moment: when the preacher communicates something about the *content of scripture* (its specific concerns or general principles), focuses on the *God who is revealed in scripture,* or makes *faithful use of biblical imagination in preaching.*[4]

For example, many listeners long for preaching that focuses on *the content of scripture,* and describe the Bible as functioning authoritatively because of its thematic content, principles, or concepts that guide the life of faith. Some insist that the words and content of the Bible are to be reported in as straightforward a manner as possible: "If you add to the word or take away from the word, I've got real problems with you, and that's when I want to walk out." Others insist that "the sermon needs to be based on biblical principles" and refer to the Bible as a "map," "guide," or "directory." These listeners speak of the sermon as it conveys a biblical idea or theme, relating the content of faith through biblical principles: "I think it's important to be able to take that quote from the Bible or that concept or context of the Bible and to expand on it. It isn't so much the Bible itself I guess as the concepts that it conveys or tries to convey itself. It's the concepts then whether you're pulling it from the *New International* or whatever version." Among the many listeners who view the authority of the biblical text through the communication of biblical principles or ideas in preaching, one person noted the pastor's ability to weave several stories and biblical characters into a single biblical theme. In describing a meaningful Father's Day sermon, this listener reports:

> The pastor gave us four or five examples. The whole sermon wasn't spent on Job's life or Abraham's struggle. The preacher mentioned those, briefly brought us back to what that Bible story was about, where they came from, what they encountered in the middle, and where they ended up. Five or eight minutes on each one, and before you knew it, the sermon was over, but it was enjoyable. You were almost bombarded with the same theme in four different individuals.

Although few listeners give specific examples of sermons that help develop their knowledge of or relationship with God, a second function of scripture in preaching that underlies the comments of several listeners is to render *biblical stories or messages about God that deepen the hearer's encounter with the Divine.* One interviewee speaks of the authority of scripture and the sermon in worship and anticipates hearing a divine word in the preacher's message: "I know that my God is going to speak to me." Although few people in our study describe preaching or sermons that have helped them to know more about God and God's nature, several people make comments that reflect a strong desire to know God through listening to stories of the Divine recounted in the Old and New Testaments. When asked about the authority of scripture in preaching, one listener draws from a particular biblical passage as it recounts something of God's relationship with humanity: "Back to Jonah when God told him to go to Nineveh and he didn't and what happened. I think using those kind of experiences from the Bible when God's people did not do what they were told to do and the consequences of those actions gives you more authority than stories just of everyday life without any kind of vision or thought about God."

Besides the content of scripture and the hope of knowing more about God through biblical stories explored in the sermon, a third function of scripture in preaching that relates to the interpretive work and authority of the sermon is named by other interviewees. Many people speak with great appreciation for preachers who can engage the hearer through the *faithful use of biblical imagination* in preaching. According to several interviewees, the preacher's creative use of biblical images or expansive portrayals of biblical characters provide a welcome opportunity for listeners to encounter the God of the Bible in new and enlivening ways. One listener expresses appreciation for numerous sermons when the preacher spoke and "I personally visualized something that has been conjured by the spoken word." For another person, the reenactment or dramatization of a biblical text proves meaningful:

> We had never been to the church before. They did a reenactment. Although the congregation had kids, they did a reenactment of the death on the cross and the resurrection. I can't even think what the name of the song was, but there was a guy that sang this long song about it while they were doing it. I don't think there was a dry eye in the congregation when it was over. It was one of those that just really moved you.

For another listener, a stirring account of Jesus' temptations brought the text to life as the preacher recounted the events of scripture in creative, evocative, and faithful ways. In remarkable detail, this listener remembers a particular sermon:

One that was important to me was when Jesus came down from the temptations. The preacher imagined what Jesus would have gone through after forty days. He would have been hungry. He would have looked for something to eat. He would have been perplexed because of the questions the devil asked. He would have been very tired, because it would have been an exhausting experience. He would have wondered about the choices he made. The pastor just went through that in terms of everyday experiences for the people. Yet, it wasn't a scripture text he followed except that when Jesus came down, Jesus was human and so Jesus experienced the same things we did.

As this and other comments suggest, the way that the Bible functions in preaching (or the appeals that the preacher makes to scripture when preaching) reveals something of the listener's perception of the authority of the biblical canon and strongly influences the sermon's claims on the lives of the listeners.

However, in the fourth cluster, the listeners in our study also include many people who appreciate **a range of resources that are authoritative and meaningful in preaching, including some that go beyond the Bible**. Whether interviewees consider the Bible, personal experience, church tradition, human reasoning, or other resources to be authoritative for the life of faith and for the sermons they hear, listener comments tend to cluster around three views of the relationship of scripture to other authoritative resources in preaching.

For some of these listeners, the *Bible is the exclusive or nearly exclusive source of authority in preaching.* One person refers to scripture as "the sole base of authority when it comes to ministry" and another interviewee voices concern over cultural influences on biblical interpretation: "We try to make the Bible conform to our culture, rather than making our culture conform to our Bible. I think it should be the very basis of everything we do in the church."

However, for many other interviewees, even if the Bible is the leading or dominant source of divine authority in the sermon, *scripture is not the sole authority for pastors to draw on in preaching.* These listeners reveal an appreciation for the ways in which biblical texts interact with other resources for the life of faith. For example, one listener views scripture as "one of the guides" for Christian faith and another asserts that the Bible may "lend some credibility to what's being said" in the sermon but it does not function as the sole authority for preaching. Frequent mention is also made of personal experience or current events as these may be related to scripture. Without devaluing the role of scripture in preaching, one listener comments, "I think there should be part of the Bible in your sermon, yes, but the rest of it could be personal witness." Another person expands notions of personal experience to include the experiences of the cloud of witnesses throughout the centuries: "Sometimes experience in what the congregation may need or the church may need at that time. Sometimes it could be a word from the saints. I would say the Bible is very important, but there are also a lot of other resources that can be called upon to bring the church to where it needs to be, in order to work in the world."

A few listeners refer to *other materials as authoritative for preaching and note that the sermon may or may not make reference to scripture at all.* These alternative resources include classic literature, current newspapers, and "a lot of different readings" that may not necessarily be placed in conversation with the Bible in preaching. Interviewees who mention other sources of authority for sermons tend to value the immediacy or relevance that these bring to the sermon without necessarily diminishing the role and authority of scripture in preaching. For example, when one listener was asked about the Bible's role in preaching and what would happen if the preacher presented a sermon "out of a magazine" instead of the Bible, this listener's response neither dismisses the role and authority of scripture in preaching nor demands that a biblical passage be the leading resource for the sermon:

> Everything that we go through in life that has a lesson, it's probably all in the Bible, but a preacher might go to a magazine. I think that's helpful, because the scripture is nice and it tells us they went through the same thing. But then when the preacher brings it back to, for example, if a certain member of our conregation did this—or something we communicate more about—then we'll get the feeling of what the sermon's saying. I think it's okay, because the preacher's trying to connect it with us.

This listener's comments and those of many others reflect a final category of interest related to the Bible's role in preaching, its interpretation, and authority in preaching; namely, the importance of the **relevance of the Bible for today**. Even more than biblical interpretation, authority, and other resources for preaching, listeners speak with great passion and urgency about the need for scripture to connect with their lives, and the vast majority of persons interviewed insist that it is essential for the preacher to render the Bible in ways that are relevant and meaningful for the life of faith. Some cite their concern for "applying scripture to everyday life" so that its meaning is not only accessible or understandable but "can be related in some way to me." These listeners are explicit in naming their confidence in the Bible's relevance and in its applicability to current events and life situations. According to one listener, "I feel that anything that's going on in the world, whether it's terrorism, racism, homosexuality, whatever it is, it should be discussed in the pulpit, because everything that's going on is biblical. Everything is in the Bible and everything that's in the Bible applies to our lives today." For this person and several others, the Bible can relate to any number of contexts and it holds meaning for individuals and communities across time and geographic locations. Echoing this, another listener speaks with conviction about the Bible's relevance for today and laments the fact that others relegate scripture to a thing of the past: "They think it's something that doesn't apply to this age and why would you waste your time either reading it or memorizing it, and if you do that, you might as well forget it as far as I'm concerned."

With high regard for the authority of the Bible and its ability to provide guidance for present day hearers through the words of the preacher, one listener summarizes the thoughts of many: "I think the Bible has to be our guide to living our life, and therefore the Bible should speak to what's going on today. So a pastor or a preacher ought to be able to make the Bible reference come alive for today."

For the most part, however, listeners tend to describe biblical relevance as it relates to one of three arenas of life, and their comments cluster around these specific areas of applicability: *relevance to personal life, relevance to community and/or congregational life*, and *relevance to the world*. Although there is certainly overlap between these and many listeners recount the need for scripture to address multiple arenas of life, most center their comments on one of these three arenas.

Those who focus on *the relevance of the Bible for today as it pertains to personal life* comment on the need for scripture to relate to individual needs and struggles. Referring to the Bible as "the book of love," one listener asserts that the Bible offers priorities or direction as to what is worthy of attention and what may be put aside in one's life: "It tells you what to do, what not to do; what to be bothered with, what not to be bothered with." At least one listener was openly appreciative of the preacher's ability to offer practical examples of daily conduct by using "illustrations of people like I am, like contemporary people," and another speaks eagerly of a pastor who preaches in ways that allow "preaching and the word in the Bible to be exemplified in day to day living."

At a very personal level, another person listens to the Bible in preaching as it addresses specific needs and gives immediate care and help when addressing life's problems: "I think scripture aids people in their life, their understanding of life and their problems, how to go about solving them, and where to look for help."[5] The intimacy and familiarity with which this person speaks of the Bible's role in faith and preaching may inspire pastors to consider how some listeners consult the Bible in their daily questions and struggles. However, at least one listener warns of preaching that reduces scripture to simplistic answers and insists that God in scripture is not simply concerned with providing moral lessons:[6] "God didn't do that and say, 'These are the rules and that's it,' and leave it that way. God gives us stories and lessons and says, 'This is why I'm saying this. This is why you should do this, because if you don't do this, this is what can happen.'"

A second arena of life that is of interest to many listeners is that of the *relevance of the Bible as it pertains to community and congregational life.*[7] More than one listener voices a longing for sermons that relate scripture to relationships with others and the larger contexts of life in church and society. One listener describes a sermon that was particularly engaging and commends the preacher for bringing scripture to bear on one's relationship with other family members:

> The pastor started out with a biblical perspective and then slowly, almost if you think of a coiled spring, brought it around and around, and it kept getting closer and closer to you as an individual and what you could do. The concept, everybody can grasp the concept and nod their head and say, "Yes, that's right. You're right on with that." Then as it gets closer and closer to home, and how you have people looking to you, and how your actions speak louder than your

words, and how you react, respond, and engage your family really defines you.

At least one listener voices respect for a pastor who addresses needs within the congregation and commends the preacher for relating biblical texts to the financial needs of the church. Noting that the pastor did not care to preach about church finance and was aware of those who might accuse the preacher of being self-serving, the congregant asserts, "Are people losing their focus about giving back to God? That is part of the instruction of the Bible. The pastor did a series, saying, 'We need that right now.'" For this listener, even a topic that is unpopular among church members takes on greater meaning and possibility as the pastor relates it to scripture.[8] For the preacher who hopes to build up the body of Christ and strengthen the worship life of the local church, it is important to relate scripture to matters of congregational interest and concern.[9]

Beyond family and congregational life, others indicate that *biblical relevance to the world* is of great importance to preaching and several listeners appreciate sermons that link scripture to the church's role in larger circles of life and the concerns of the world.[10] For one interviewee, the congregation's relationship to the wider world arises out of scripture's mandate and the Bible's relevance to neighbors near and far. This listener not only assumes that scripture is authoritative in offering guidance for the church's mission to the world but asks the preacher for help in relating the Bible to wider spheres of interest:

> It's important to me that it not just be talking in thin air. It has to have some relevance to what's happening for me that I can see parallels and understand why whatever story we're talking about from the Bible or whatever point is being discussed, why that matters in 2001. What's happening in our city or in the world at large? I need to see that connection. Sometimes I'll get there on my own, but maybe not. I like to see that as part of what's talked about.

To facilitate connections with the wider world (and to personal and corporate concerns as well), many listeners in our study appreciate the preacher's use of illustrations or examples drawn from various settings and current resources: "A really intelligent, well read minister has the ability to pull this illustration from a novel, from a movie, from a play, from the newspaper and pull these things in."

However, at least a few listeners caution against becoming "too focused on worldly things" and one raises concerns over sermons that "talked about social issues but they were from the standpoint of sociology, not from the Bible." Once again, issues of scriptural authority (or the priority of scripture over other authoritative resources) come into play as listeners grapple with what it means to relate the Bible to their larger life and world. Still, most listeners not only assume that themes from the Bible are relevant to society and the world at large but also expect that the words of scripture offer meaningful insights for Christian faith and practice that lives and thrives in the world. One listener reflects this passionate commitment to making connections between scripture and the needs of the world:

> I think that I can hear the story of the Good Samaritan or I can hear another biblical passage, and that means one thing. I can hear the tale of starving children in Somalia, and that means something else. But undoubtedly what I hear in the preaching at this church is the link that says, "Okay, here's a biblical basis for why you should model this kind of behavior. Here's a present worldly condition." What comes from the pulpit to me is the link that says, "And here's how your actions can or cannot influence the welfare of someone else."

The larger impact of scripture in the church's witness to the world is also heard in the words of another listener who hopes to serve others in ways that are faithful to the Bible: "We base our sermons on biblical and everything, but I think it is much more meaningful when we can relate that today—what we can do with it: 'Hey, that's what happened. That's what it meant in those times. What can we learn from that to make an impact on life today in this world—maybe not for me, but for someone somewhere?'"

Just as these comments reveal a keen sense of scripture's authority and its meaningfulness, so do we hear listeners speak to the vitality of the biblical witness in the world. There is little doubt that the preacher's ability to relate scripture to various arenas of personal, corporate, and global concern is a high priority for many listeners of sermons.

### Reflections and Insights on How These Listeners Understand Scripture

The listeners in our study express strong affirmation of the Bible's role in preaching, as well as a longing to learn more about the words of scripture through the words of the preacher. As a shared resource for the life of faith, most listeners view the biblical text as central to the sermon and hope their pastors will help explain its meaning and relevance for their lives. Sometimes exciting, sometimes challenging and often enigmatic, listeners agree that the Bible is a worthy, even essential, conversation partner and vital to Christian worship, faith, and practice.

But what exactly is the nature of biblical preaching? And what does it mean to preach sermons that are based on or related to scripture? If, as most of the comments indicate, biblical preaching means more than referencing as many passages from the Bible as possible in a given sermon, then a deeper analysis of scripture's role in preaching is called for if we are to explore what is possible in terms of teaching others about the Bible in preaching.[11] Underlying a passion for preaching that explains or teaches listeners about scripture, it is important to identify the different ways people speak of the biblical canon functioning in sermons. The listeners in our study reflect myriad ways of approaching the Bible and describing its potential meaning and relevance for our lives. In particular, we identify five categories related to scripture that listeners name and are important for preachers to consider when preparing and presenting sermons.

First, the vast majority of listeners voice a keen desire to learn more about scripture and scripture's meaning for their lives. The search for meaningfulness in the Bible also includes interests in gaining greater familiarity with the contents of scripture, in understanding what the Bible reveals about God, and in wrestling with texts that are particularly troublesome or difficult to understand. The listeners in our study, those who speak of their familiarity with scripture as well as those who speak of their lack of familiarity, articulate a sense of interest and responsibility for understanding the Bible and view the sermon as a crucial opportunity to learn more about scripture.

Related to this is a second category, that many listeners in our study also reflect a measure of appreciation for the complexities of the interpretive task. Several people reveal an awareness of differences or potential differences in interpretation and look to their pastors for help in guiding them through different understandings of a text. However, it is important for preachers to note that very few listeners are able to describe the process of interpretation itself, and listeners do not mention theological criteria that may help or hinder the faithful interpretation of scripture. This means that even if they have an intuitive sense of what is helpful or disturbing, there is little awareness on the part of listeners as to how they may theologically assess the sermons they hear. The preacher, then, has both a tremendous opportunity and a great responsibility in the preaching moment: He or she may not only present an understanding of scripture's meaning, but also invite listeners into the process of biblical interpretation so that listeners may discover the Bible's meaning and learn how to interpret texts for themselves.[12] Through modeling different approaches to biblical hermeneutics (e.g., historical-critical, literary) and/or presenting sermons that invite listeners into the interpretive process itself (i.e., inductive modes of preaching), preachers may teach listeners about theological criteria for biblical interpretation even as they engage listeners in an encounter with the text.

The third category that arises in the comments of listeners is the authority of scripture in preaching. Without naming scriptural authority *per se*, many listeners reflect diverse understandings of the Bible's authority for preaching and reveal appreciation or frustration for the ways in which the preacher appeals to the Bible as an authoritative resource for the life of faith. Many persons appreciate when the preacher appeals to the content of scripture, its concepts and lessons, through biblical stories, themes, or principles that arise out of specific texts, as these are authoritative for Christian faith. For others, the Bible functions authoritatively in preaching when the sermon communicates stories or messages about God that deepen the hearer's encounter with the Divine. The comments of a few listeners indicate that scripture is authoritative in preaching when the preacher draws on its images and symbols to express something of the original revelation of God. For these persons, biblical texts may occasion a current revelatory moment or experience through the faithful use of biblical imagination in preaching. It is important for preachers to realize that scripture functions authoritatively for different people in different ways and that even among members of the same congregation, listeners appeal to scripture's authority in preaching in very different ways.

In addition to biblical interpretation and authority in preaching, a fourth category of interest among the listeners in our study includes references to many other sources of authority that may interact with or even supersede the authority of the biblical materials. These include personal experience, church tradition, other written materials, and works of art. The seemingly endless combination of authoritative resources may be perceived as bane or blessing to the preacher, but it is wise for pastors to be aware that the appeals one makes to scripture and other authoritative resources may help establish or diminish the claims of the sermon for the listeners.

Finally, a fifth category of interest among the listeners who were interviewed for our study is the importance of biblical relevance. With passion and a sense of urgency, nearly all listeners want to hear the ways that scripture connects with one's personal needs and struggles as well as with the needs of the congregation and local community. Moreover, biblical relevance to the world is of great importance to several listeners who voice their confidence in the Bible's connection to global concerns. Remarkably, most listeners tend to gravitate toward only one of these arenas and do not mention the others as important to their sense of scripture's relevance for their lives. However, there is considerable danger in neglecting any one realm of biblical relevance because in doing so, preachers risk reducing scripture to specific agendas of concern. For example, if only personal relevance is considered, preachers risk committing "the age-old homiletical sin of moralizing" so that the Bible may be presented as rules or suggestions for better living rather than proclaiming God's way in the world.[13] Or, if the only realm considered is the arena of biblical relevance in the larger world, we risk reducing scripture to political agendas or revolutionary mandates that may or may not be grounded in the particularity of human experience. Because nearly all listeners assume scripture's relevance across time and geographic locations, it is surely important for preachers to remind listeners that the Bible also addresses various arenas or realms of concern, including personal, social, and global questions related to faith and practice.

## A Word to Preachers

Listener comments regarding the role of scripture in preaching not only reveal a strong sense of the vitality of scripture for the life of faith, but also raise several questions that may help guide the preacher to a deeper encounter with listeners in preaching.

First, given the strong desire among listeners to learn more about the Bible, what does it mean to teach listeners about the Bible in preaching? As our research shows, most congregants seek and expect the preacher's help in approaching scripture in their search for the Bible's meaning and relevance to life. In light of other purposes of preaching outlined in chapter 1, it is important for preachers to determine the scope and specific goals they may establish in relation to teaching listeners about scripture and encouraging communities of faith and individual members to continue the work of exploring scripture and its potential meaning, authority, and relevance for their lives. Working in concert with Christian educators and Bible study leaders in the local congregation, pastors are wise to consider how various ministries of the church may help address this need to understand not only the content of scripture but different ways of interpreting and engaging scripture as it relates to the life of faith and the world around them.

Second, what does the preacher need to be aware of in terms of his or her own inclinations and perspectives regarding biblical interpretation, authority, and relevance in preaching? Given that these three categories overlap significantly in listener comments, it may be helpful for preachers to reflect carefully and critically about a number of different aspects related to each of these. For example, look back over six to eight of your best sermons from the past year and take note of what you observe: What methods of biblical interpretation do you tend to draw on when preparing sermons? In what ways is scripture authoritative for you (through its content, its revealing something about God, as a source of imaginative encounter)? Whether you preach on texts designated in the lectionary or choose texts weekly, do you notice that you are repeatedly drawn to certain genres of scripture or parts of the Bible in preaching? Also, as you relate scripture to the questions and concerns of the people, do you notice yourself tending toward any one sphere of life–personal, communal, or global? If so, it is wise to consider how you will redirect or expand the range of references made to different arenas of life. A careful assessment of your own orientations and inclinations may uncover tendencies that you are not fully aware of, or it may simply encourage greater awareness of areas that are not adequately addressed.

Third, and as a close accompaniment to the above considerations, the preacher needs to consider the listeners' involvement in biblical interpretation, authority, and relevance before, during, and after the preaching moment. The listener's role (and the role of the congregation as a listening community) is not always taken into account by preachers who readily assume sole responsibility for interpreting biblical texts on the congregation's behalf. However, the comments of listeners in our study reveal that people in the pews consider themselves to be integral to discerning scripture's claims and those of the sermon on their lives. In addition to educating listeners about the Bible, it is important to consider how you will involve listeners in the process of biblical interpretation before, during, and after the preaching moment: perhaps through small group discussions, Bible studies led by other members of the congregation who lead sessions related to the scripture text for upcoming worship services, and so on. In listening to the listener, you may hear about the particular texts and questions that the congregation brings to the preaching moment.[14] Finally, consider the wide array of preaching forms you may employ in order to creatively engage listeners with scripture in the preaching moment. Inductive modes of preaching, problem solutions approaches, expository, lectio continua, dramatic enactments, and other modes of sermon design may help a variety of listeners to encounter scripture anew. Through these and other approaches to scripture in preaching, you may provide occasions for listeners to engage the Bible as they encounter God in worship.

# CHAPTER 3

# Embodiment of the Sermon

What brings the sermon to life? How does it move from the word on the page to the ear of the listener? As the sermon comes through the preacher, what happens to make the preached word effective? What is it about the preacher's presence that invites listeners into the sermon? These are important questions that are often dealt with in a chapter near the end of preaching textbooks. Categorized under "delivery," it is, by implication of its position in the book, the last thing that needs to be considered before one stands up to preach, though not necessarily of lesser importance than other aspects of the preaching process.

As listeners discuss the ways that sermons engage them through the preacher's physical presence and delivery, we hear how important this is to their experience of the sermon. While a few persons discount the "how" of the sermon presentation, and state that content is the only important aspect of the sermon, most listeners identify the way the sermon is presented as an important aspect of engagement for them as listeners.

In our study, we ask interviewees such questions as: "Would you describe for me a preacher's presence in the pulpit that was really good–whose delivery was really engaging? What are some things a preacher does physically (while delivering a sermon) that help you want to pay attention? How do the physical conditions of being able to hear and see the preacher affect the way you pay attention to a sermon?" In responding to these questions, the interviewees indicate that they are affected by more than demonstrated technical delivery skills or physical movement. While these aspects are important and respondents often refer to issues of technical delivery, they also take on the question of presence, which is more complex in nature. They give consideration to the preacher's preparation, the interiority of the message being preached, sincerity and authenticity, the preacher's confidence, passion and authority, and the place of the Spirit as evidenced in the preacher and the sermon. Many of these things incorporate the person and way of being of the preacher, which precede one's actual standing up to preach. In listening to the various responses, the coauthors feel that the subject matter in our study deserves early consideration in the book.

Additionally, the authors–in company with many others in the preaching community–think that the term *delivery* is inadequate to describe and image our understandings. The term *embodiment* more accurately and appropriately characterizes the substance of that which brings the sermon to life and affects and engages listeners in sermons. So what exactly is embodiment? Embodiment, in terms of preaching, is the incarnation of the proclaimed word, the enfleshed word given life at a particular point in time, making the proclaimed word *present* to a particular people through the preacher.[1]

### What These Listeners Say about Embodiment

In general, listeners describe embodiment as vital to their engagement with the sermon. They look for and expect the preacher not only to have appropriate content in the message but also an ability to relate to the congregation in such a way that the message has life and engages them experientially at the time the sermon is preached. As such, most persons are able to name and describe embodiment qualities that are important and meaningful for engaging them in the sermon.

Throughout the study, we find that specific responses to questions regarding embodiment cluster around several qualities–**eye contact, voice** (and its various components)**, gestures and movement, attire, language and grammar, perceived preacher preparation, and presence**. In some instances, there are sub-clusters within the general clusters.

**Eye contact** is mentioned by a majority of respondents as a quality that is vital for their engagement in the sermon. They speak of this importance in a variety of ways–sometimes naming eye contact directly, and, at other times, identifying particular hindrances that interfere with eye contact.

One person, when asked what helps to engage the listener in the sermon, gives this immediate response, "Well, eye contact first of all." Another states:

> When they look around a full congregation, they engage you. They kind of seek different people out and actually catch their eye. I think that brings it closer. It's like they're actually talking to you. They turn around and talk to the choir, the associate pastor behind them. I think that's very engaging to let everyone know that they're speaking to everyone, not over everyone, but to them. That, to me, catches my attention.

One listener points out the connection that occurs as the result of eye contact: "There's an immediacy and an awareness of what's going on, rather than they're just standing here and talking to this room and hoping that able-bodied people will pick up the message. There's actually a connection to this group." Another person describes the way the pastor tends to avoid contact by looking off in a corner. "Our pastor is not looking at us. Sometimes for effect, yes, but most often the preacher is looking off into the chapel or looking at the corner up here. This is a little disconcerting."

Many interviewees name the reading of sermons as a major hindrance to eye contact. This person reflects the sentiment of many others:

> I think it's vitally important that preachers don't word-for-word read a message. If you want to know what really turns me off is when somebody's got to have their head down reading for twenty or thirty minutes to me.

One interviewee is upset with the pastor whose eyes seem to be closed during preaching. The listener is unsure as to whether the eyes are actually closed, or if they just appear closed because of the physical construction of the eyes. In either event, the result is that this listener feels some disconnection from the preacher and the message. The listener implies here that eye contact is more than a physical act of the preacher looking at the "audience." It is a point of connection. This listener feels as though people are not being addressed in the sermon because they are not being seen. The eye contact is significant because of the connection and the immediate "relationship" that occurs in the seeing and being seen. This is an important point for the listeners.

Another important and engaging quality is **the voice**. This includes such sub-clusters as *tone, pitch, volume, inflection,* and *modulation.* A few respondents provide general comments regarding a particular quality of voice, such as a preference for deeper voices. However, most persons do not express a particular preference. Neither do the majority of listeners identify a preference to listening to one gender over another.

A considerable number of listeners comment on various qualities of *tone.* Most listeners speak in terms of the degree of voice inflection, finding themselves engaged by preachers who are expressive in their speech, using appropriate voice inflections. On the other hand, a large number of listeners identify a monotone voice as a real problem. One listener describes some monotone preachers who were brought to the church as guest pastors. "They are absolutely, completely lost up in the pulpit. They're monotone. They're deadpan in the delivery of their message, and so the message is lost." A person in a different congregation makes the point that, "Even if it's the world's greatest message, it will still put you to sleep."

While speaking in monotone is the most agreed upon tonal issue for listeners, one listener takes issue with a different aspect of tone. This listener approaches tone from the perspective of how some preachers use an unnatural voice or way of speaking. They use a "preaching tone." The listener says,

> The adoption of a particular tone in delivery to me is like throwing a wet blanket over the congregation. It's a serious, somber delivery which, to me, tries to create a mood that indicates this is a serious sermon you're about to hear. It's like if you heard a train whistle, you would know that train is going by. To me, if a preacher has to adopt a somber, funeralistic tone (and not only the tone but the way that the words are spaced out and accented in order to create the mood of a sermon), there must not be very much in the sermon itself. I just hate that. I can't tell you how much I hate that, and I probably shouldn't say this either, but…it just seems to me that every other church you go to, you hear this minister's tone and delivery that drives me batty.

For this listener, the use of a preaching tone is an emotional issue. The same listener goes on to give preachers advice on this matter.

To the extent that the pastor can be conversational, but not too conversational, deliver it in a normal way. You do want a professional job. You appreciate someone who can deliver a sermon professionally with charm and charisma and good word choice, but also do it in a way that you're not thinking the fact that this is not the way this guy talks normally; he's adopted some kind of false façade in his communication which really just sort of throws you off.

For this listener, the somber tone and style of delivery is superficial and inauthentic. It interferes with the listener's perception that the preached word is sincere and/or of worthy content.

A different aspect of voice is *volume*. While some respondents name a preference for softness or loudness, others prefer variation in volume. One listener expresses this preference: "It doesn't have to be shouting. A little bit of that goes a long way. Loud is not necessarily good. Once in a while, a little loud wakes people up." For this listener, volume is related not just to the effectiveness of the message, but serves another function—to foster attentiveness to the sermon. Regarding variation in volume, one listener speaks of the pastor who will raise and lower the voice, based on whatever is being talked about. Another listener gives an even more vivid response to this issue:

Oh, I want you to make noise. I want you to be loud. I want you to talk. If we're in the same room I want you to even talk where you have to whisper. Then I want you to get loud again. I don't want you to just "Dadadadada." I want some fire. I didn't come to just sit and listen to a story. If you're going to tell me a story, make it good. I'm an animated person. I want to feel your story. If you want to tell me about your trip to Cleveland, make it interesting. That's the way I look at pastors. They have to be animated. They have to entertain us. I don't know if that's the right word to use, but you almost have to be entertaining. The preachers with engaging delivery have range in their voice. In other words, sometimes they'll take the volume down really low, and then sometimes they'll bring the volume up."

For this listener, the use of volume and voice is closely connected to the liveliness of the delivery.

Another aspect of voice is proper *enunciation and clarity of speech.* Several people bring this out as important for them as they listen. Other listeners pick up on the quality of clarity as they encounter problems in understanding the preacher's words. For one listener, a different issue is implied. "If you put your hand across your mouth, that's saying you're unsure of what you're saying or something. There's some insecurity there." The listener goes on to say that when one is preaching to people, one has be sure that the message is clearly projected.

**Body movement** and **gestures** comprise another cluster of responses. Included in this are physical movement in and around the pulpit, as well as aspects of *energy* and *enthusiasm.* Listeners generally have clear opinions about their preferences and understandings of how body movements are able to engage or hinder engagement with the sermon.

Most listeners feel that some movement of hands, eyes, and body is important in engaging listeners in the message. "Hand movements are actually what keep the eyes focused. Your movements keep people focused on you," says one person. Another says, "I feel with my heart first of all, but I am also moved by expression of a pastor in delivering the word. The hand gestures bring the word." This person speaks of the way that gestures that could be seen make the proclaimed word more intensely felt by the listener. One interviewee prefers that preachers temper the use of gestures because of the association with a particular kind of preaching: "I don't like a lot of gestures. You can tell that I don't like hellfire and damnation. No pounding, no waving of the arms, getting out from behind the pulpit and coming down. I think you can get your point across without that."

One person describes the pastor's use of gestures in this way:

> Our pastor doesn't have wide Bible-thumping gestures. This person has a much more, if you will, sort of presidential tone to the delivery when doing a traditional sermon from the pulpit. The preacher doesn't wander far from the pulpit. When really wanting you to get something, the pastor will lean forward with the forearms on the pulpit. This preacher's gestures are really not a far-reaching sort of thing that I notice. There are pastors who get all over the place, and I just get disoriented. So I prefer they stay where they are.

There is agreement among a number of listeners that movement, affect, and content need to be congruent. One person puts it this way:

> I think infrequent large movements, like talking with your hands, but not all the time and not in a jittery way, are okay. I think movement, facial expression, and tone of voice should all be reflecting the content. They certainly shouldn't be counteracting what you're talking about. Facial expressions— I think when they're natural, they really help a lot. But when they seem put on or somehow at odds with what's being said—Have you ever had someone talk to you about something really painful and smile the whole time because they're uncomfortable?—then it's distracting.

Another listener comments on the difficulty of using gestures too frequently: "There are some gestures that you get to see the same one again, and again, and again. It isn't a turnoff by any stretch of the imagination, but it becomes redundant. If you emphasize everything, suddenly nothing is being emphasized, if you know what I mean."

When considering gestures and movement, a number of listeners speak about *movement of the preacher within the pulpit area*. Listeners present diverse views on this matter. One persons says, "I think a little movement is okay. Too many pastors don't have movement. Get out from behind the pulpit. It's okay by me. Take a little stroll or something for emphasis. I don't see a problem with that." On the other hand, another listener says, "Now I've seen on television some of these televangelists roam all over the chancel, up and down the aisles while they're talking. That drives me absolutely wild."

A third listener makes an important point about movement:

> It depends on where they're going to do this and what their audience is composed of. Here in this church, we are more traditional in that you stand up at the pulpit and give your sermon and sit down. You don't have to go into a three-ring circus act, because as you well know, we think very strongly of the word. The word is the important thing.

A number of persons describe the *energy and enthusiasm* of the preacher as having an impact upon the listener's engagement with the sermon. For one listener, preaching energy and enthusiasm mean that the preacher is "going to be able to reach people." For another, this indicates that the preachers "have conviction. That makes me want to believe that they believe in what they are saying."

One listener describes an enthusiastic preacher as one who "wasn't rigid, engaged appropriate gestures, engaged appropriate voice inflections. The delivery of the message and animation, conveyed the enthusiasm on the message. There are pastors I've listened to on the radio–radio messages–that you can tell they are enthused about the delivery of their message." One interviewee describes the preacher's interaction with the congregation as engaging. "If the congregation is responding with praise and thanksgiving, the minister responds as well, using a lot of hand motions. You can sense the energy." The preacher's enthusiasm energizes the congregation.

While persons are able to affirm the need for energy and enthusiasm on the part of the preacher, they are also able to identify problems that could interfere with the listener's engagement in the sermon. One problem mentioned by several listeners is over-animation of the sermon on the part of the preacher.

> I think sometimes people get overly animated. They become very theatrical, boisterous, loud, even physically doing some stuff that I think doesn't seem to be scripturally sound, and tends to draw so much attention to themselves and their style of preaching. Maybe it's part of their need to be charismatic. I think some people think they're charismatic when they're not.

An entirely different issue is that of **attire**. A modest percentage of hearers indicate this as an important factor in the embodiment of the sermon. Other hearers are not overly concerned with how the pastor dresses, unless it becomes a hindrance to the listener's engagement with the sermon. For this first listener, the preacher's appearance affects the motivation to listen to that person. "Well, the preacher comes in well dressed, cleaned up, sharp, and usually you think, 'I want to listen to this person.' The appearance makes you want to listen, makes you want to sit in your seat and listen." Another listener suggests that preachers dress in ways appropriate to the context in which they are preaching. For instance,

> Our congregation tends to be on the older side. Basically the average age is sixty or sixty-five. So some of those folks prefer that the pastor be up there in a robe and a suit and tie.

I think it probably means more to them than it does to me. I didn't grow up in the church. So I don't have some of these notions of what a pastor is supposed to be like.

Several persons indicate a preference for the preachers' wearing of a robe or vestments. For one person, the robe "identifies them as a member of the leadership." For another, "There's something about a robe, and I think it's that I get the picture of Christ. Like when ministers raise their hands like that [gesturing upraised hands], that will get my attention." For other listeners, the matter of dress is related to the appropriateness for the message and venue. One listener summarizes this view:

> I wouldn't want man or woman to be before me with too much on that would distract me from what they're saying to what they're wearing. I love robes. But to preach, the attention really needs to be on God.

One area that we did not initially consider in the area of embodiment, but which was brought up by several listeners, is the issue of the *preacher's preparation*—how well the preacher seems to be prepared to preach. When we speak of the preacher's preparation, we are generally speaking of how well preachers are prepared to move from what they have already written on the page to the actual proclaiming from the pulpit. However, in a few instances, the comments refer to general preparation of the whole sermon. The listeners' perception of the preparation affects their engagement with and their determination of the effectiveness of the sermon. Sometimes it is the preacher's familiarity with the message that is key. One listener says,

> It goes without saying that if a preacher can deliver a sermon without having to read every word, it's more effective. We have a pulpit where the preacher can step to the left and away from the podium. You're still with the confines of the pulpit, but you're not standing behind the podium. All of the good preachers that we have had have stepped over to the left and basically leaned over toward the congregation and communicated, and then stepped back to the podium to read something that needs to be read or to find out where they are on their outline. That's always helpful. I'm not sure every preacher can do that. I don't hold it against a preacher who isn't able to get away from the written text.

Another listener has a slightly different perception about use of notes. "I've listened to sermons where the pastor is constantly going back to notes. To me, that would indicate that one's not as familiar with the material or the delivery or the presentation as one really should be for the benefit of the listener." The minority voice on use of notes and reading the manuscript comes from this listener who speaks of one pastor who reads the sermons:

> Now, by all accounts this is the absolute worst thing in the world to do. Frankly, I found these sermons to be very dense in content. It is clear that the preacher put a lot of time into thinking it through and structuring it, and in a short period of time, the minister could communicate an enormous amount of content. For me, that reached out to me, because I was prepared to invest in that. I think other people were turned off by it.

For another listener, preparation or lack of preparation can be noted in the sermon's organization or lack thereof.

> I find it offensive when it doesn't appear that somebody has spent very much time thinking through the organization of a sermon. If it seems to be just meandering around, and I can't quite follow where we're going and where we've been, I get irritated, because I would never have a lecture like that. I feel like I ought to be able to insist on a similar amount of preparation from somebody who's doing this. This is a vocation.

Another listener states,

> I've been very impressed by pastors who will not lose their train of thought, will deliver a sermon, and it almost seems impromptu. They're very much in tune with what they have to share that day. They are very familiar with what they're going to say and how they're going to say it. They are in control of the situation as far as delivering the message. So I'm impressed when they deliver that message without a lot of notes.

Other indicators perceived as lack of preparation are delineated in the following statements. "I don't want a bunch of fumbling with papers and notes and things. That's their job, and that sermon should be rehearsed and polished. If they want to try it out, try it out on their spouse or their kids or somebody else. Don't try it out on me on Sunday morning." Or, "We had one pastor who would even get up sometimes on Sunday morning and say, 'Let's have another song, because I'm not real sure what I'm going to preach about.'"

For the following person, preparation serves as incentive for the listener:

> I think if I see that they're interested, that they've done their homework. I think you can tell early on whether they put some effort in developing their sermon. Once I sense that they have worked to give this to me, that makes me want to listen. Sometimes I have heard a sermon that I felt was scripted. They just got up and read it. It was like, "I've got to do this. That's what I'm paid to do." I think the congregation can sense that.

In the book of Ezekiel, chapter thirty-seven, there is an image that seems appropriate as we move into the area of **presence**. Ezekiel speaks of being taken to a valley filled with dry bones. After some discussion with the LORD about whether the dry bones could live again, Ezekiel eventually proclaims the God-given word to the bones, and the bones come together in an appropriate and organized fashion, even acquiring some flesh and muscle upon them. Yet, with all of the bones, muscles and flesh coming together in an appropriate manner, there is still something missing. It is the breath, that which will give them life. The image of the enfleshed bones without breath parallels the way these interviewees consider rhetorical skills and techniques without presence. It is presence that gives life to skills and techniques such that the message and the techniques come together.

This whole area of presence is nebulous and hard to grasp. As listeners describe presence, they identify a number of qualities that contribute to it. However, many listeners' descriptions lapse into nebulous phrases such as, "There's just something…," or "the preacher just…," because they can't quite put their finger on the definitive answer to the question of presence. In the study, the qualities described tend to cluster around the following areas–the perception of *the connection of the preacher with God, the demeanor of the preacher* (includes the preacher's comfort with him/herself, knowledge of self, the preacher's carriage, etc.), and *the perception that the preacher has confidence and authority.*

A number of persons who respond to the question of presence refer to *the preacher's connection with God* and the way that this affects the reception of or engagement of the listener with the sermon. One listener puts it this way:

> I think one of the things I've felt very definitely with this preacher is the demeanor, the whole approach, physical manner in which the preacher gets into the pulpit, saying, "Come Holy Spirit," etc. I have a feeling that it's not just a job. The preacher is not just performing a duty, because the person decided to be a preacher. This is a very meaningful thing. There is a spiritual dimension there that immediately makes me feel it's important. It's important for the preacher, therefore, it's important for me. I felt with another minister it's business, and it doesn't pay well. It doesn't pay well enough. I just didn't feel there was much of a spiritual dimension.

One interviewee tunes into what the Spirit seems to be doing with the preacher. This person is also listening for heartfelt delivery.

> It was just like someone who had already been with the Lord and wanted to tell you about it. This preacher could just... You were on the edge of your seat all the time. There was more of a lecture, teaching kind of thing. It was not the emotional, jumping up and down kind of thing, but yet, there was something about the person's aura, the way the person would bring it forth.

These listeners are hoping to perceive that the preacher has been with God or that the preacher is being led by God in the preaching moment. This connection with God is an important quality for these hearers.

Another aspect of presence is *the preacher's demeanor*. This is sometimes thought of in terms of the perceived comfort of the preacher. Is the preacher comfortable with herself, comfortable in his own skin? in the role as preacher? Comfortable with the word being preached? One listener tackles this aspect of demeanor and the effect upon the congregation.

> I can tell you elements of what I think. Basically, it's got to be somebody that feels comfortable with being there. You've got to have maybe all the elements of being able to get up

and do public speaking. That has, I guess, a lot to do with what I'm saying about feeling comfortable. I have seen people..., 'Am I saying the right things?' That conveys out to the audience, to the congregation, the people. You have to have that comfort feeling, because a lot of people may not really feel comfortable in church. You don't want this uptightness of somebody who's not sure what they're thinking about up there.

One listener describes another preacher, saying,

This is a short person, but when preaching, this preacher has a big presence at the church. The preacher is comfortable— comfortable in the pulpit, comfortable around people. You can tell this person is not afraid of personalities. I get a sense that this preacher would preach the same way if the church had only twenty-two members. Plus, this person is a good communicator.

Another respondent suggests that a preacher's comfort can be detected as that preacher allows her or his personality to become a vehicle for the preached word:

I feel like it's good for preachers to allow their personality to show through in their sermon, but sometimes I feel like they're so self-conscious, it's almost like they're fighting against their personality or who they are. Sometimes I feel like the sermon is more about them than it is about God or trying to be a conduit of God. Usually, that doesn't work very well.

The more comfortable the preacher is, the more possible it is for the preacher to bring his or her whole self, personality and all, into the preaching moment. As the previous listener tells us, the discomfort and self-consciousness that can overshadow the preacher's personality can sometimes shift the focus upon the preacher and away from God.

Demeanor is also perceived in the way that preachers carry themselves. This can be experienced in various ways. It can be physical presence or in terms of *a quality of confidence and a sense of authority*. For instance, one listener describes one preacher as being tall and standing tall. Another says, "The body language kind of tells you something about the spirit of the person, the sincerity, the real emphasis." Another states,

> I think for me, as I think about this person, what impressed me or what spoke to me from this minister's manner in the pulpit was the minister's commonness. This person spoke like one of us instead of like an authority. The preacher spoke as though the preacher was living it.

This listener has a perception of what it means for a preacher to speak "like an authority." It appears that this listener is engaged by this particular preacher's presentation of the message. So, whereas the listener may be turned off by one who speaks "like an authority," it seems that the preacher is given authority by this listener because of the "commonness" of the preacher's demeanor.

Another listener describes a combination of qualities that comprise an appealing and engaging demeanor of preachers. "Then there are those ministers like Howard Thurman who just speak–the preacher's presence, feelings. The tone in which they speak, almost with an air of authority that is uncommon, but yet a humbling of the spirit all alone, trying to resonate a point."

For another interviewee, an engaging demeanor is evidenced in a bolder confidence and authority. This type of presence is tied into the preacher's confidence in God and the assurance that the preached word is word of God for "this people in the this place at this time." The interviewee notes such presence can be heard in the preacher's words:

> "Look, I'm here to preach the word of God. I want to preach the word of God. Regardless of what you say or do, this is what God wants you to know, and when it's all said and done, we're going to be convicted by the word of God." The pastor's presence, it doesn't say, "Here I am," but it's "Here's God. This is it." And it's a good thing, and I like that. The delivery is always excellent.

Listeners speak of presence as that quality or combination of qualities that exudes from the particular persona of the preacher and that gives evidence of the preacher's connection with God, her- or himself, and the sermon being preached. This presence is also evidenced in preachers' willingness to give themselves fully to the preaching moment and the endeavor, to God, and to the congregation, so that the preached word can become a living word through that preacher.

### Reflections and Insights on Embodiment

For the majority of people in our study, the way the preacher embodies the proclaimed word is a major factor in engaging the listener in the sermon. The "how" of the sermon has the potential to enhance or hinder the receiving of the message, to engage or turn off the listener.

We anticipated that listeners would confirm our understandings about embodiment skills and that they would tell us about the particular qualities that were most engaging. And they have. We had also hoped that those interviewed would be able to tell us what behaviors or lack of skills most negatively affect the listeners' engagement with the sermon. Listeners are helpful in articulating hindering behaviors. Listeners are also helpful in painting a rich picture of sermon embodiment through their descriptions and experiences of engaging sermons and preachers.

As we reflect upon the material received, we realize that a key word that seems to describe engaging embodiment is "connection." The listeners are engaged when they perceive various connections occurring with the sermon and/or the preacher within the preaching moment.[2] First, when listeners perceive a connection with the pastor, that is, the pastor is intentionally connecting with them through the delivery of the sermon, the sermon is more engaging. The listeners experience in this a willingness of the preacher to connect with them. This happens through eye contact, appropriate volume, language usage that is appropriate for the context, and presentation that seeks to hold the listeners' interest, such as voice inflection, variation in pace, etc. Listeners want to know that they are being addressed through the way the sermon is embodied as well as through sermon content.

The connection between preacher and listener takes on much more importance or urgency as one considers the understanding of the role of the preacher. If the preacher is understood to be liaison between God and the congregation, or is standing as representative of God to the people, then the preacher's willingness or unwillingness to connect with the listeners may infer something to the listeners about God. Questions arise. Does God seek to—and is the word intended to—connect with us through the proclaimed word? Is God willing to look at/see us, and willing to ensure that the word reaches our ears? Preachers are the vessels through which this connection is to be facilitated. On the other hand, even if the preacher's role is not perceived as liaison or representative, the preacher is still in the position of being the called proclaimer of the word to the people, the one whose responsibility it is to make sure that the word is not only spoken but given the opportunity to be received. People are investing themselves in the listening (thankfully, someone is listening!), but finding it frustrating when the hearing of the proclaimed word is hindered. The preacher is to be intentional about connecting with the listeners. It is the preacher's responsibility to make sure that all is done to facilitate the connection of the word and the listener through the preacher's embodiment of the sermon.

Secondly, the listeners are engaged when they perceive that the preacher has connected with the sermon that is being preached. When listeners sense that preachers tarry in the sermon process, seeking a word of truth for this community, and that the sermons even impact the preacher, several things occur. The result is that the listener perceives the preacher not only as preacher but also co-listener to the word that is being proclaimed. The word is not only a word for the congregation; it is also a word that is meant for the preacher. If the scripture being dealt with envelops, covers, even scratches at the core of the preachers, confronting and convicting them, then the listeners perceive the impact on the preachers that has come through the encounter. If the preachers connect with the sermon, then the message proclaimed is experienced as authentic.

When preachers internally experience the word, they bring a depth to the message that is missing when they have only experienced a superficial encounter with the sermon. The proclaimed word is to be delivered as a word that the preacher knows, that the preacher believes. In turn, the word becomes more believable to the listeners. Some of the respondents in the interview describe this as the preacher "preaching from the heart." There is a passion that results when the sermon is internalized and has been filtered through the preacher's own joys and sorrows, the preacher's own faith journey and life experiences. The preacher speaks that of which the preacher knows–preaching a true word, a word that rings true in the preacher's own heart and understanding, and then testifies to its truth. Listeners are engaged when they believe that the preacher is telling the truth.

Third, listeners engage when they perceive that the preacher is connecting with God. This is, in some ways, related to the listeners' perception of the preacher's faith. Fred Craddock puts it this way:

"The preacher is expected to be a person of faith, passion, authority and grace. Faith makes one believable, and if the messenger is not believable, neither is the message. The absence of faith is almost impossible to disguise for any period of time."[3]

Additionally, listeners may perceive the preacher's connection with and dependence on God through their experience of the proclaimed word as ringing true with sound scriptural understandings and as ringing true within their own spirits. This connection may be perceived as a spiritual presence when the preacher is speaking. The reality is that when the preacher does have a connection with God, it can may often be sensed within and by the congregation during the preaching moment (as well as outside of the pulpit). Generally, congregations expect their pastors to be persons who pray, and pray consistently. They expect that the preacher seeks to connect with God. Unfortunately, this is not always the case. We hope, however, that preachers will intentionally open themselves to God throughout the sermonic development and the actual proclamation of the message—inviting the Holy Spirit throughout the entire process. When listeners perceive that connection with God, they are more engaged in the sermon.

Each of these three areas of connection—the preacher's connection with the listeners, with the sermon, and with God—contributes to the listeners' engagement with the sermon. For the preacher to deemphasize either connection is to risk the most fruitful connection of the message with the listening community.

Although many interviewees confirm the authors' understandings about effective and engaging delivery techniques, there is one thing that we did not anticipate. That is the depth of feeling that is sometimes associated with a listener's response to particular qualities of embodiment. This is especially noted around behaviors that listeners experiences as negative, such as the verbatim reading of manuscripts, or preachers who do not speak loudly enough to the heard. For instance, listeners sometimes feel disturbed or insulted by the preacher's verbatim reading of a manuscript and used words like "hate" to describe their feelings. Or they want to shout at the preacher to talk louder or look at them. For most of the listeners that we interviewed, the preached and embodied word carries significant worth and value for the listener. It may be the very word of life that they most need to hear on that day. When the connection is disrupted and the communication of the proclamation is hindered, it very often evokes an emotional response.

We learn in this study that most listeners care how the sermon is presented, and that they desire for preachers to be intentional in their efforts to get the message across in an engaging manner. This is true across the demographic board: across age, gender, ethnic, and denominational lines. We are impressed by the diversity of responses. While there are some denomination, cultural, and local parish preferences, listeners are just as likely to differ within the same congregation as with those outside of their particular environments. Additionally, the authors are aware that stereotypical ideas exist regarding the way that certain cultural or ethnic groups respond. For instance, some believe that African Americans would be most attracted to preachers that are emotional and very animated, and that Anglos would not. While some African Americans in our study express attraction to this type of preacher, not all find this type to be most appealing. On the other hand, there are some Anglos who express attraction to emotional, animated preachers.[4] Responses differ both within and among diverse groups, but also give evidence of similarities across denominational, cultural, ethnic, and gender lines. In general, we learned that listeners of all "stripes" desire effective communication of the proclaimed word, and want it presented in an engaging manner within their context.

### A Word to Preachers

Listeners care how you preach. The way you deliver and embody the sermon says more to them than that this person has skills and techniques to get a message across, to deliver a sermon. Ultimately for listeners, the whole of embodiment of the sermon is more than the sum of its parts (skill, techniques, etc.). The way you embody the sermon gives to the listener some indication of your desire and intention to engage the congregation in the sermon.

Our research shows that we as preachers need to begin to think about embodiment at the beginning of our preparation, not just the moments before we enter the pulpit. Charles Bartow suggests that embodiment begins much before the sermon is actually preached. In fact, the embodiment of the sermon commences at the beginning of the sermon preparation process. It begins with the initial encounter with the scripture. In the *Concise Encyclopedia of Preaching*, Bartow makes the point that

> the delivery of sermons begins with the speaking of the texts upon which those sermons are based. This is so because the

texts of scripture themselves, for the most part, are texts of oral discourse. They are meant to be heard, felt, and acted upon. However, to know texts in terms of what they can do to those who read them, the texts have to be said. They require a human voice and body. If sermons seem to be lifeless when they are spoken from the pulpit or if what liveliness they have appears to be artificial and forced, the cause very possibly may be the preacher's lifeless reading of the text.[5]

Delivery begins with the preacher's engagement with the scripture, continues through the sermon development, and, finally, moves through the preacher to the listening ear.

The encouragement is for us, the preachers, to enter into the encounter with the topic or the biblical text experientially. We can read the scriptures aloud, with expression. Hear the words. We can enter the scripture and allow ourselves to experience the dynamics of the actions, images, phrases, scents, and textures. Entering into dialogue with the text, allowing it to speak to us and ask questions of it, adds depth to our understanding. We have the opportunity to spend time in prayerful meditation and thoughtful exegesis as we consider how the texts speak to us and our particular contexts. When we develop the sermon, it matters that we always keep our listeners in mind, considering how this message speaks, and how we can best communicate this word, to them.

As a result of our analysis of the interviews, we have several suggestions to make. When we get up to preach, it is important to establish engagement with the listeners through intentionally allowing ourselves to connect with them—allowing ourselves to see the listeners, as well as making sure to project our voices out far enough to reach them, and to preach interestingly enough to keep them awake. We can use our hands and bodies in such ways as to invite listeners into the meaning and nuances of the message. We also need to speak in ways and words that allow the listeners to catch and grasp meaning.

The one aspect of sermon delivery that causes the most frequent discussion and difficulty with listeners is the act of reading, as opposed to orally telling or proclaiming, the sermon. This perceived disconnection between the sermon and the listener encompasses at least two of the areas that are needed to engage the listener in the sermon. In the area of perception, it affects the connection with the congregation because the preacher does not have eye contact with the congregation. It may also seem to be more of a dispassionate lecture than a sermon. Additionally, the need to read the sermon is sometimes perceived by the listener as the preacher not having the sermon internalized. It may appear that the sermon is not from the heart because the preacher is not familiar with the sermon–the preacher does not seem to know the message.

Listeners are very clear that word-for-word reading of a sermon manuscript greatly interferes with the listener's engagement with the sermon. The manuscript, in itself, is not necessarily the problem. It is the preacher's use of it. The use of a manuscript becomes problematic when the preacher's eyes are continually focused on the paper, thereby interrupting eye contact with the congregation. It is problematic when the reading of the manuscript sounds like the presentation of an academic paper or a lecture. It is especially problematic when the language used in the manuscript is abstract and/or written as a literary piece, as opposed to an oral script.

The above begs the question as to what the preacher should do if he or she prefers to use a manuscript. Many preachers find it especially helpful to write out a full manuscript as a means of organizing their thoughts and incorporating the message within, even if they do not use the manuscript in the pulpit. Whether you take it to the pulpit or not, it is helpful for the preacher to become as familiar with the manuscript or the content of the sermon as possible. Repeated reading of the sermon out loud facilitates this. It not only familiarizes and helps the preacher to further internalize the message; it allows the preacher to discern its oral nature. This can be facilitated in several ways: by using a large enough computer font that allows you to glance down rather than bury your head in the paper; by strategically placing the paper on the pulpit so that eye contact is maintained; by constructing the manuscript creatively so that it serves the purpose of the message (e.g., emboldening words to be emphasized, adding extra spacing between ideas so that you know when to pause, highlighting areas that need to be presented exactly). However, familiarity with the sermon is still key.

Some persons choose to memorize the entire sermon verbatim. If persons can do this well, that's fine. However, this type of memorization may not be the best solution for many, as one can become as tied to the exact wording of the memorized script as one can be to the written manuscript. A better tactic is being familiar enough with the sermon that you do not have to read every word.

Joseph Webb, a prolific contemporary writer in the field of preaching, in his book *Preaching Without Notes* encourages preachers to develop a sermon outline, determining what content supports and brings this to life, and then memorizing the outline through repetitive rehearsal.[6] The result is that the preacher knows the key ideas and related content, yet is not tied to every word within the sermon; has the opportunity to connect more fully with the congregation through eye contact and rapport with the congregation; and can be more spontaneous, opening herself to insights that may come during the preaching moment. If the preacher has been carefully and thoroughly preparing through the week, if he has opened himself to the movement and work of the Holy Spirit throughout the sermon's development, then there may be those times that an inspired word comes that focuses the message and speaks to that moment in the life of the congregation. Caution! A preacher shall share the insight only if it comes out of the preparation. Know that not everything that comes to mind is inspired and in line with the focus and purpose of the message, nor is it necessarily theologically sound.

It is important that we respect the congregation and God enough to be prepared to preach. We can prayerfully enter the preaching moment with the assurance that we have sought the word to be preached to this congregation in this place at this time. If we are familiar enough with the sermon we can present it without stumbling. In humble confidence in the God who has called and sent us to proclaim the word, we will be able to stand tall as preachers whose strength, authority, and confidence come from the Lord.

In closing, we encourage preachers to think about how you are displaying that preaching is a priority in your ministry. How are you intentionally making time to pray, study, and meditate upon the scriptures? Are you cultivating your relationship with God? Each of us needs to pay attention to how we are allowing the Holy Spirit to be a part of our sermon development from the beginning. Do you allow the biblical texts to encounter you before you preach from them? Do you believe your own sermons?

You might ask yourself to identify particular delivery skills that help you connect with listeners. Are there some areas that are growing edges for you? How can we best embody the sermon such that it brings forth a living word that engages our listeners?

# CHAPTER 4

# Listener's Relationship with the Preacher

One of the basic questions for our research concerns whether congregants' relationships with the preacher are factors in their ability to engage with the sermon. Many of those interviewed speak easily and in some detail about their minister or priest. We were interested to know whether the closeness (or lack) of relationship congregants feel toward the preacher would affect their ability to hear the sermon. Interviewers asked about a respondent's experiences with various preachers through the years in order to determine how the parishioner perceived those relationships. An additional question in this area was: "Can you tell me about a pastor who was also a good preacher?" This was often followed by asking: "What is it about the preacher that you like as a person?" Then, a final question in this section asked if the respondent believes liking the preacher (or having a relationship with the preacher) affects listening. We believed recalling details of the various persons they had listened to preach over the years would assist in clarifying whether relationship actually had an impact on whether or how they could hear the sermon.

In our interviews, a significant number of sermon listeners reported that how close they feel to the preacher makes a difference in their ability to engage with the sermon. This was revealed not only in answers to the previously mentioned types of questions about the preacher's character or the listener's personal connection to the minister, but also in other places. Sometimes questions about delivery, for instance, resulted in responses about how consistent the preacher's life was to the sermon content or how eye contact helped make the pastor seem more real.

### What These Listeners Say about Relationship with the Preacher

As the interviewed persons articulated aspects of their relationships with preachers, they seemed to focus either on a positive bond arising from their experience of the pastor in worship (perhaps indicating that was the extent of the relationship or at least that was the important part of their relationship) or they focused on the relationship that has developed beyond worship (frequently a friendship). From these tendencies, we divide listeners into five main clusters. Of those whose relationship seems limited to the experience shared in worship, we find they cluster around the idea of a **personal connection from the pulpit** (e.g., the preachers' personal stories reveal they are "one of us"). Those who report a relationship that developed beyond worship, we divide into three additional clusters: those whose comments indicated the relationship comes from **experiences within the walls of the church building** (e.g., from committee meetings or painting the youth room together), those who talk about sharing **church events with the preacher beyond the walls of the building** (e.g., missions trips), and finally those who share **nonchurch events with the preacher beyond the walls of the church building** (e.g., local ball games, casual meals, neighborhood barbecues). There is a fifth cluster of listeners who express that the **relationship with the pastor does not affect their ability to listen to the sermon**, although they often feel quite connected to the pastor both through worship and experiences beyond Sunday morning.

We look first at the cluster of answers about relationships that seem limited to or focused on what happens in worship itself. It is composed of answers that indicate a relationship develops from **a personal connection from the pulpit.** That is, the congregant feels a personal relationship because of the content of the sermon, or something in the delivery, which establishes some familiarity or sense of connection. Two quite different persons (different gender, different ethnicity) from two quite different congregations (different cities, different denominations, different settings) say very similar things about their relationship with the preacher. When asked about a relationship with the pastor and preaching, one says: "In terms of their preaching, I think that's what many people relate with their pastors on, because if you don't have a 'going out for coffee after church' relationship with your pastor, many times that sermon is the way that they speak to you. Even though it's in a crowd, they're speaking to you individually." The other answers roughly the same question: "Some experiences stick out in my mind because they tell something personal, and that connects you a little bit more. That makes you remember a little more." A member of what we refer to as a megachurch echoes this same idea, yet gives even more flesh to it discussing how this person's ministers brought children and adults to the edge of their seats with preaching:

> They make themselves a little bit vulnerable, too. They're not holier than thou, and they tell things on themselves or their family that makes you realize that none of us are perfect, and all of us struggle with many of the same things. We all strive toward a common goal, which is to try to ever increase our ability to walk as God would want us to walk. We all struggle with that. By making themselves vulnerable and a little bit transparent.

We note that this respondent feels a closeness that comes from the material of the sermon causing an identity with the preacher. Rather than personal time spent one-on-one with the minister, or even time spent in a group at church events outside worship, the relationship comes from the preacher showing that ministers struggle with the same life situations as the person in the pew. In effect, the sermon demonstrates that clergy people are as human as everyone else. The discussion goes on to reveal an especially warm appreciation for the senior pastor, whose foibles have been revealed in many personal sermon illustrations, e.g., misunderstanding a spouse's needs, getting a speeding ticket. The interviewee continues:

> Our senior minister will spend thirty to thirty-five hours a week in sermon preparation, and you can't do that in small churches because you have so many other demands on your time. It took a lot to educate our membership that, if the minister didn't show up for every funeral and every time every member went in the hospital, that was okay. They were probably going to be better served if someone else did some of that. Taking enough time to prepare the sermon

well is, theoretically, your most fruitful place in the church where others have come to hear, rather than the one on one. If that's your primary role, then you should be allowed to do it.

We might readily imagine that people in these large congregations of course have to make their major connection with the preacher during the sermon, for that is really the only time they are in direct communication together. Other meetings with the pastor may be quite fleeting (a handshake at the sanctuary door), merely business (as in an occasional committee meeting), and rare (the senior pastor does not attend all church gatherings). So, it is easy to understand in that a "relationship" with the preacher may have to come from personal connection through the sermon in large churches. However, members of small congregations report this phenomenon as well. In fact, an equivalent number of persons are sharing this type of connection with the pastor in the smaller congregations. For instance, this reply comes from one of the smallest congregations where interviews took place. Located in a small town where the minister lives in a nearby parsonage, the major relationship for this listener still seems to develop by connecting with the preacher in the sermon. Here is part of the answer from the question asked about a pastor who is also a good preacher. This is specifically addressing use of stories.

> You expect a certain amount of authority in the pastor as the one who studies the scripture. We all should, but the pastor's the one who's probably spending more time, who probably has more training. We do expect that, but I think it's also wonderful when the pastor comes across as a person with normal struggles like everybody else. We tend to put pastors on a pedestal, God bless them. We don't want to know what kind of struggles they have, and yet, we should because their struggles are our struggles. Being able to speak personally about that is one thing that great pastors can do.

Interestingly, these people who restrict their comments to the connection that develops from their experience of the minister in the preaching event still often speak in terms of having a "good relationship" with the pastor. A person from another small congregation of a different ethnicity mentions the current pastor: "Basically, it's a pretty good relationship. I feel open enough. I can approach my minister about anything." Yet there is no indication that there ever has been such a conversation.

In a number of the interviews, there is an indication that the person has contact with the preacher outside of worship, but the conversation focuses on the connection made from worship, as if that were the "real" relationship and the behaviors outside worship are just church business, a less authentic relationship. In those cases, we cluster the responses as considering worship the primary place and way of relating. For instance, one person speaks in quite friendly terms about various priests, but each time the relationship coming from the sermon seems primary.

But the current priest demonstrates what I consider Christians should be like, somebody who accepts people without being extremely judgmental. Who also is, I guess, scholarly in as much as their approach toward their sermons and being able to evoke thought-provoking type sermons that get you to thinking, not the hell and brimstone type person who is always saying, "This is the way you have to behave." That turns me off. I like somebody who can evoke thoughtful responses in you and gets your mind thinking about Christ and religion in general and being able to keep you throughout the week thinking about what they said.

Another person goes so far as to separate the relationship that exists with the minister during the week from the relationship in worship. In describing the presence of the minister during worship, the respondent explains:

Of course, I'm here a lot through the week, and I talk to Pastor, and things are very friendly. But when we're in church, you just feel that—I don't know—the pastor's holy. I don't know how to say that, but the pastor is, of course, such a religious person. What our minister says is really so. The pastor seems really godly-like almost in the sanctuary in the sermons. Sometimes I would think that's very important when you have a feeling what that person is saying is really so, and with our preacher, you do.

The interviewer then asks if how pastors appear in worship makes a difference in being able to receive them. In other words, does that sense that the preacher is really "holy" or "godly-like" make a difference in being able to hear the sermon?

Oh, yes. I think so. I don't know. I think appearance and how they present themselves leads to you more believing what they're saying, sometimes; not all the time. Some of the speakers maybe aren't that educated that you've had, but they're very likeable. When they're likeable, you're more believing in what they're telling you.

Another experience comes from a person with a tendency to drop in and out of church attendance, until the arrival of the current pastor. The relationship does not come from recognizing the pastor is like the congregants, rather something else. "The minister was here as an interim, and the pastoral style was so totally different from the previous minister. It was more of a motherly, caring feeling coming from the pulpit then. That was the turning point." Another respondent expresses appreciation for the pastor's being a woman, explaining the earliest church experiences were with a denomination that did not welcome women into ordained ministry. In answer to a question about good sermon qualities, this respondent expresses amusement at being among those interviewed, since it is known that sermons are not a favorite part of this person's church experience.

Outside of sermons I usually like the pastors pretty well. They are a part of the church. The first time I went to a church in this denomination, I was in graduate school. I found a church that had a woman pastor, and that made all the difference in the world. I did a lot better with connecting to that church. I don't know if it's just tone of voice or having a woman pastor for the first time in my life. That's not something that you see in the churches of my childhood.

Although these respondents receive something quite different from the previous respondents who felt an identity with the preachers' humanity, all have connection with the preachers from experiencing something from them in the pulpit. For one of them the bond from the pulpit even makes it easier to connect with others in the congregation.

The personal connections persons feel from the preaching event vary significantly from setting to setting and from person to person. In another large congregation of a different ethnicity and denomination, an interviewee reveals an appreciation for receiving an intimate moment with a former preacher in worship some years before. In answer to the question of what is liked about a minister who is also a good preacher: "I liked the peace, the sense of peace the preacher had and the calm setting. We were in a small congregation, and during the pastoral prayer the preacher would circle the sanctuary and sometimes lay hands on members while praying."

Another congregant from a different denomination is less detailed when asked what is liked about the person of the preacher: "They make contact with you." Some of the answers about what people receive from the minister during preaching are quite surprising. Asked what is liked about the person of the preacher, one person admits: "It's not a good example. It's just one of the things about preachers in our denomination, that southern drawl that makes you feel warm and friendly. I wouldn't say it was something necessarily that came out of the message other than the delivery." Yet, when invited to share ideas beyond the worship setting, a similar feeling is communicated: "The warmness exchange, taking an interest in you, being there when you needed the person, whether it was for counseling or an illness."

We close this cluster with a quote that mentions connections made outside of worship. However, we leave the example within this cluster because the speaker seems most focused on the sermon. The outside relationship develops because of a desire to understand what the preacher says in the sermon that might mean something particular for the hearer. Again, the interviewer is asking what is liked about the preacher as a person.

> I've been fortunate to have the opportunity to hear a lot of good preachers, but the one that I've heard the most for the last fourteen years is our senior pastor, whose strengths are not only being biblically based; our minister is very talented in the ability to illustrate with words, putting a lot of information and emotion and strength into a message.

The speaker continues with a discussion of two other preachers from teenage years who had allowed the asking of questions about sermons and about the faith. This openness meant a great deal to the teen and to continuing church connection through the later years. "At that point I was in high school and there was a caring and an understanding from the pulpit that I could just grasp every word. So I had some wonderful memories of both of those people." The interviewer then asks if these relationships enhanced the ability to listen to what is being said in the sermon.

> I think probably the relationship that evolved, because of their openness to questions about the sermons. Especially the first one when I was at a younger age, if I'd been dismissed or given an answer that was above my head, I probably would have turned it off and gone on about my way, but because there was an open channel there, the relationship evolved and allowed me to go further in listening.

The discussion is about making questions beyond worship, but it seems to us that the focus of the relationship is on the sermon and the faith. The interviewee reveals that the genuine relationship with the preacher comes from these experiences of connecting about the sermon and worship.

Although quite a few persons limit their conversation about the minister or priest to the relationship created within worship, an even larger number of the respondents report a relationship with the pastor that extends beyond the worship service experience. These responses fall roughly into three additional clusters: **within the walls, church events beyond the walls,** and **nonchurch events beyond the walls.** We look at each in turn.

**A relationship developing within the walls of the church buildings** is the second cluster to investigate. These relationships with preachers are reported as stemming from church work such as committee meetings, cleaning the church kitchen, or painting the youth room. Predictably, the responses often reveal a sense of connection resulting from shared commitments, as this person who reports having seven different functions and responsibilities during one period. "My relationship with preachers has been good, because I've been involved in so many things. As I said I was in seven things in the church here for a while and of course a lot of them, you need to talk to preachers." But for some people it is not just proximity or access to the preacher outside worship; there is also an important sense of being able to trust the pastor, which comes from interactions within the building. In responding to a question about what is liked about a preacher as a person, a member of a more liturgical church says:

> I have to say that would be our current priest. Our priest is human. It's kind of hard to explain. I know what the title is,

but I don't feel that I have to behave differently because this person is my priest. I don't feel that. The priest doesn't turn a nose down if I say something maybe I shouldn't say or behave in a manner that I shouldn't behave.

A similar trust is expressed by someone in a different setting: "The first pastor that we had when we moved here I really considered a mentor to me, and the current pastor I consider a friend as well as a pastor, someone that I'm comfortable enough with that I can complain and disagree with and be honest with."

The language of these typical members indicates a fondness, a bond, with the person they hear preach most often. They report a willingness on the part of the minister to interact with them beyond worship, yet often the interactions that they report are limited to events within the church building. Here are two typical examples. These actually come from the same congregation. We note them because of their differences. Each discusses how they have interacted with the preacher, and then answers the questions about relationship affecting listening. The first person has just been asked if having a personal relationship matters in hearing the sermon.

> Yes, it does, of course. It does, if you know a person and know how that person acts when not in the pulpit, acts in his or her life. If you think a person is hypocritical because of something you know about him or her, then that does affect negatively your receipt of the message. The opposite would be true as well. If you have come to know someone as courageous and having strong character, that gives more weight to what they have to say. There's no secret there. [*The interviewer directly asks, "Do you know the current minister?"*] Yes, I do. I do. We've never played golf before. I don't know that I've ever done anything socially with the minister, but I was the lay leader here for two years and I've served on staff parish. So I know the minister pretty well through committee leadership and things like that.

This member answers that the pastor is known even though there has been no interaction that one would call merely social at all, and no experience with the minister beyond the walls of the church building. The minister is known "pretty well" because of committee interactions. Yet this relationship, the respondent clarifies, does affect the hearing of sermons.

Here is the second example of a listener in the same congregation who feels a close relationship with the pastor, which has developed only within the walls of the church, who also answers the question about affecting the hearing of the sermon. This is confirming the question of having a personal relationship with the pastor: "Yes, I do. When I first got into church, the senior minister was very encouraging. I think with all the new members, the minister tries to take a hand in making them feel comfortable." Note, the "personal" relationship develops from what is reported as standard contact with a new member. The interviewer follows this by asking if the personal relationship impacts hearing the sermon. The answer is quite different from the fellow member above:

I don't think so. I don't think so because what I realized was when I came to the church that, as much as our minister's willing to be close to everybody, you couldn't be. I know ministers needed to be treated as a person. There's a limit. From my personal standpoint, our relationship is friends. The way it is, I pray with the pastor. Before the sermon we have a group that prays with the pastor on Sunday mornings. I'm one of the ones. It's a volunteer thing. I have numerous occasions been on committees. I'm affectionate about our minister. I don't have to be with you everyday or call you up everyday. We have the relationship is there because it started out right, and there's been nothing to change things. I have no criticism at all. Since praying with the pastor before worship I really like to know what the topic is so I can explore it myself. But I'm just as close to the pastor as I ever could be or want to be. That's still my preacher.

The response seems to recognize the limits of a "pastoral" relationship. It is almost as if the respondent is admitting that even though there is *not* a closer relationship, it does not affect the desire or the ability to listen. The eagerness to listen seems to come more from praying beforehand and knowing what the day's topic is.

As was obvious in some of the material above, it is not always easy to get the persons to discuss whether the relationship actually assist listening to the sermon. Occasionally someone begins addressing the need for relationship in order to hear the sermon, but then wanders away from the sermon piece. This one, for instance, is answering the direct question about relationship affecting listening:

Yes. Yes. That's one of the things. I think it plays a role. I think the pastor has to be open-minded, I think, and caring. It's all right for pastors to be smart and knowledgeable on the word of God and be able to be a good teacher and a good preacher, but they must–they simply must–be able to communicate and have a relationship with their people. That plays a big part in their ministry, because whatever projects they set out to introduce to their people or a vision that God gives them, the people have to see something within them– see that seriousness, that spirituality in them. I think it's important for them to have a relationship with each one of their members.

One person seems to have an opposite reaction. "For me personally, I don't have to have a one-on-one real close relationship with the person if they are an effective preacher. I like that, but I don't have to have that." Although the person admits having a personal relationship with the pastor because of serving on several committees and agreeing that it does affect listening, the bottom line seems that the sermon rises or falls on its own merits rather than the relationship with the preacher. The relationship is a nice addition to hearing the sermon, but it is not essential.

One final example: This member has an odd mix of feeling as close to the preacher as a family member, although there is little or no contact except on Sunday, and feeling the charisma of a stage presence that would draw anyone into the sermon presentation. Note the closeness.

Sure. My minister is a friend, has become a friend, but my minister is really kind of almost a father figure–the one who is the teacher, and I'm the student. I've learned a lot. This is someone who's very hardworking, who earns your respect, someone who backs up their words with actions. This is a very nice and loving person, who's really accessible and human and honest and nice. I see my minister pretty much just on Sundays. We were part of the same Bible study last series. So it kind of feels like we're family, but it's not like we talk every day or anything like that. [*Discussing the consistency between the life and words of the preacher, the interviewee continues*] That's why I pay attention to what is said, because I know how the pastor lives and works, but there is definitely a stage presence. With voice and microphone, there is definitely a stage presence.

The close feelings the congregant has for the minister apparently assist the listening, although the more polished delivery is also helpful in keeping the attention focused. Like others in this second cluster, the relationship is perceived as personal (even familial), although quite limited in actual contact (only within the church building). Perhaps this perceived closeness allows for the listener to connect with the preacher's meaning in a way that a lesser relationship would not allow.

The third cluster of responses is composed of those who talk about sharing **church events with the preacher beyond the walls of the building** (e.g., mission trips) In previous pages, we show that some parishioners seem to consider the minister a close friend when their personal contact is minimal. In this cluster, we see folks who have spent considerable time with the pastor beyond the church building, although involved in church matters, on mission trips or Sunday school events, yet some of them never deviate from seeing the pastor in the clerical role. Consider this response:

> I do have a good relationship with our pastor. We talk. From the beginning when we visited together in our house, and we spoke about things that were delicate and confidential, from that point forward there was a trust there. I think that's very important that you know you have that trust. With this pastor, we do. Honesty, trust, caring.

Another response expresses a similar appreciation, although it was made by someone from a significantly different congregation.

> We were good friends. We went calling on several occasions with our priest, where we would go out and visit folks to see if they wanted to learn more or become involved in the congregation and just to make them feel welcome. We were Sunday school teachers there, youth counselors. The priest just had a great way of making you feel as if you were a part of the bigger thing that was going on there. Our priest had a way of not involving you so much to the point that it felt tiresome or burdensome. So there was a very good balance between involvements without over-involving people. Our current priest is very busy. I just really enjoy seeing this priest

in the pulpit. There is a very kind manner about this person. We are quite happy.

For some people the closeness they feel with the minister develops from an early contact of establishing a sense of being welcome in the congregation. One member of a small town church talks about the "gentleman from the church down the street" knocking on the door when they were knee deep in boxes, still moving in. That welcome made an impression. They visited and eventually joined. Asked how important it is to relate well to the minister, the respondent chimes up, "It's important. Yes, I have to relate to them. The ones that we've had that I haven't related to really well, it hasn't kept me from coming to church, because I feel the church is the important thing, but having a minister that I feel good about is very good." The interviewer also asks if the relating makes a difference in the hearing. "I think it makes a big difference, because if you really don't like the minister, you don't come. People stop coming." A member from a more liturgical church in a larger-sized city tells a similar story:

> The reason that we joined it was because my spouse and I, at the time, we were engaged and about to become married. We belonged to different denominations, and we decided to start shopping around. The priest at the nearby church we had attended on this particular Sunday came to our home the Monday following the church service and we realized that this was actually a follow-up visit, and that was impressive. That's why we joined that church.

But it is not only the preliminary visit of welcome that makes an impression. The feeling of connection beyond the walls of the church building first came from a hospital visit for this person:

> Our pastor, I guess to me, it's almost like our pastor's become a part of our lives. My dad when he was visiting us about two years ago had broken his hip, and our pastor was there visiting him in the hospital every day, even more than I was visiting him. Our pastor really spent a lot of time, which was something I really appreciated.

There are quite a few examples of people who were involved in ministry out in the community with the pastor, or attending conferences where the relationship solidified. Yet it is difficult for people to articulate if such closeness actually facilitates listening.

> The minister did preach good sermons and was also someone you just liked, and you got a genuine feeling that you were liked, too. That is probably the first minister that I can remember who really I felt a connection to. I have been with the current minister where we've been on like youth trips where we're all sleeping on church floors or driving in vans and going places. You get a little closer when you do those things. [*Discussing qualities of a good pastor*] I do look to be challenged. I don't want somebody to tell me what I knew last week and the week before. I want them to be a step ahead of me and hopefully bring me along with them. They have to continually be growing themselves in order... Hopefully, I'm growing, too, and they'll be bringing me along.

This same respondent gets to the place of talking about the ability to listen and whether it is easier to engage with the sermon at certain times. Using unconventional terminology, the respondent praises what is referred to as the associate minister's "kick ass" sermons:

> They told us of the struggles the associate has personally with the faith, or why the denomination or certain kinds of churches sometimes are upsetting. I probably felt closer to our associate in those sermons those two or three weeks in a row than any other sermon. I think it had to do with having the freedom to be in a point in life and the point in the relationship with our church where the associate could just lay it on the line. I think there will always be value to having that personal one-on-one with somebody who helps guide your faith journey. I guess someone who understands where you are in that faith journey and can help you figure it out. Boy, there's not too much of a challenge, eh?

Perhaps the close relationship develops in this case as a result of the powerful sermon and not the other way around. That is, it is not the relationship that makes listening easier, but the solid preaching which makes the relationship easier.

The fourth cluster is composed of those who share **nonchurch events with the preacher beyond the walls of the church building** (e.g., local ball games, casual meals, and neighborhood barbecues). For these members, often the minister has become a friend. In some of the answers you can feel the reciprocal feelings between parishioner and priest. In others, there is that particular quality of an occasional contact resulting in a perceived closeness on the part of the parishioner, as if the minister had become family or close friend from infrequent, although meaningful, contact.

This response comes from someone who has crossed over to becoming quite close with the pastor:

> My spouse and I have known them personally other than just as ministers. We've had a minister drop by our house on a Saturday afternoon, because there was a problem to work out. The minister didn't know how to solve it. One minister came to our place several times and talked, needed somebody to talk to. We've been close to all of them. We've been to their house; they've been to our house.

Yet in further conversation, this same respondent makes it clear that the relationship is not all that matters in their church experience. In answer to the question of what would be missing if there were no sermon, the answer indicates an understanding of the importance of the sermon itself, although a significant focus still seems to be on the person of the preacher.

> The cohesiveness, I think, would be missing. I think the pulpit ministers are sort of the thing that holds everything together, and you rely on that person, whether it's a male or female to be that thing that holds everything together. You can go to Sunday school classes and get the same message really. A lot of times we do. If we happen to follow the lectionary in our Bible class, if it's hitting the same subject that the lectionary has, we hear it twice. I personally don't think I would go to a church if it didn't have a sermon. We rely on sermons. It punches our button for the next week.

One interesting interviewee seems to appreciate the relationship with the priest that developed over time. Although there are occasional nonchurch events, such as casually working in the priest's garden or having a meal together, the contact seems sparse although deeply meaningful to the parishioner. We insert a lengthy piece of the interview, beginning with the Christmas Eve service, which is how the interviewee first comes to be connected with the congregation.

That was the first time I came here, and I knew I was home. The priest just embraced me at that point, and we hit it off completely, and I knew I was home. I knew this was a priest that no matter what happened, what circumstances in my life or what I did, this was a person I could talk to who would not be judgmental but would point out and say, "You're messing up. You're screwing up, but I love you anyway." It was kind of reprimanding, yet full of love. Now we joke with each other and we cut up with each other. My priest is still my priest. I think the difference is this priest knows of the hurt that I've had with the church. Therefore, my priest lets some of that guard down for me. Honestly, I think that it's hard on both of us with our families far away. So, we're kind of family. I don't go to the rectory or anything like that. We meet for dinner every once in a while, probably four times since I've been here four years. On Saturday mornings, if I'm off work, if I take a Saturday off, I'll come in and trim roses or we'll work in the flower gardens together and just talk about everyday stuff. I have a wonderful priest.

The closeness begins with a feeling of acceptance from this first worship service, which was the first contact the interviewee had with the priest. From just these Sunday experiences, a number of occasions of working in the garden, and a meal once a year, the parishioner considers the priest like family. In answer to the question about their relationship assisting hearing the sermon, the respondent says:

It does completely, because I know where they're coming from. I know that the ground is level. I know that the ground is level, and I know that there's not an ounce of judgmentalism in what they're saying. I know that if they speak something, they speak it from their heart. If someone preaches or speaks against something that I don't believe in, I will not shut it out if I know that it is something that they truly believe in and that it's something that is to better me. I will never disregard it, because I know that it's done in love.

The interviewer notes that the respondent's whole body becomes animated talking about the priest. There is a leaning forward and a sitting up, as if this might be the most important part of what is going on in church for this person. The conversation comes back around to preaching again. "I think that to know the minister's life is to know where the person comes from and to truly understand their sermons." In other words, one has to know the person of the preacher in order to understand the sermon.

Another person was even more direct about how much the preacher means:

> My pastor's like a person you can go talk to. I feel very comfortable talking about anything. My pastor's just like an angel kind of. There's just something about this person, a very outgoing, very nice person. Our pastor's been down to our house for some graduation parties. Our pastor has a good connection with people.

To follow up, the interviewer asks if liking the pastor makes listening to the sermon easier. "Yes. Our pastor makes it more interesting. Like our old preacher that we had before, when preaching there would be some times when we wouldn't get a sermon basically, because that preacher wanted to talk about other things. Our current minister talks about stuff in the Bible, and we get that half-hour sermon."

There is also evidence that some people's closeness seems to come from the type of sermon preached, even though there have been various contacts beyond Sunday. Of the dual pastors in one church a respondent explains,

> I like them because they're approachable. They are down to earth. They speak clearly, to the point, but yet make it inspiring and enjoyable. I don't know how to explain it anymore than that. Just that they seem to make it more like a family situation for the whole community, the whole church. It's not them versus the congregation.

The respondent goes on to chronicle times their children had been in school together, thus the families had gone to ball games together and other things outside of church. The interviewer then goes on to ask about knowing the preacher on a personal level and whether it changes the reaction to the sermon. Although the response begins by stating "No," it seems to go on to mean that knowing the preacher makes it more meaningful. "Oh, no. Sometimes it makes it more meaningful to know that they go through the same things that we do every day. They bring it down on a level that everyone can understand."

Another person reports a close relationship with a pastor and spouse where they attended plays and went out to dinner together. When asked about their relationship assisting listening, the person replies: "Yes, I think it does on whole. I think on a week-to-week basis it probably does help if you have a good rapport with someone and someone you can trust, and especially if that person has good sermons and has a pretty good track record. It's not critical whether you like the person or not, but I think it helps.

There was a fifth cluster of listeners who express that the **relationship with the pastor does not affect their ability to listen to the sermon**, although they often express feeling quite connected to the pastor both through worship and experiences beyond Sunday morning. Content or delivery seems significantly more important in determining whether they would attend to the sermon. One person puts it bluntly, "I think that the most critical test for any preacher is if they're effective preaching to people who don't know them personally." Quite a few people, when asked if a relationship with the preacher affects their listening simply reply that it does not. A one sentence answer was: "I don't need to like somebody." Curiously, even some persons who go into colorful detail about how fond they are of the pastor could be short and firm that the relationship does not affect hearing. This person speaks in significant detail about several different pastors who had served their congregation through the years, yet when asked if the relationship affects hearing the sermon: "It doesn't. It doesn't. Now, sometimes even if you get too close or don't like a person, either way, at least with me, I am sitting there waiting for the preacher to say something that I can pounce on." Apparently, by "pounce on" this person means something one could grab hold of and mull over at length. A listener from a less liturgical traditional replies merely, "Not for me," when asked if knowing the preacher well affects the ability to listen.

Other persons express a more clearly theological reason for not being affected by relationship, as this one does.

> I think what you're talking about is an experiential thing. It changes all the time, because for me personally my ear is always turned toward lighting the light of scripture. God strike me dead if I don't divide scripture correctly. That's what I'm listening for. I really don't care who it is. I like some people, don't get me wrong. I'm not mean about it. But my thing is listening to see if they're stepping out of line.

Someone expresses a similar view, after describing in detail good relationships with certain previous pastors. A friendly, almost familial connection with the pastor outside of worship is expected within their denomination. After discussing a preacher with whom there is little relationship, the interviewer asks a second time if the relationship affects listening.

> No. I've come to believe in sanctification. There is something about the pulpit and putting yourself…It really doesn't matter. If I didn't want to be distracted, I could close my eyes and listen, but what was coming from there was not coming from the preacher really. It was coming from God. I guess I believe that, and I guess I experience that and understand that, and it doesn't…What I hear and what I get, I'm supposed to got. The vessel and the vehicle don't make that much difference.

Another answer is not unlike some of the others. Although this person gives articulate answers to many questions, asking about relationship affecting hearing caused several false starts and some stumbling:

> There are things I like about…I would…I guess what I'm looking at is when the pastor is in the role of giving the sermon, it's in a different role than I would put that particular individual and I…I just associate the two of whether I like the person on a personal level or not is relevant to the message that person is giving.

The interviewer attempts to clarify by asking directly whether a relationship is important for listening. "No. No. It's not important to me in hearing the message." Four of the above quotes in this cluster come from diverse sources: Lutheran, Anabaptist, Methodist, and Reformed traditions. These persons seem to focus on content of the sermon rather than relationship with the preacher as a key to listening.

### Reflections and Insights on Relationship with the Preacher

Everyone seems to have a relationship with the preacher. Even those who claimed they could listen to sermons irrespective of whether or not they knew the preacher relished talking about how they did know their minister or priest in various settings. We divided those settings into five clusters. Of course the divisions between the clusters are not always clear, which is one of the reasons we refer to them as "clusters" rather than a firmer term such as "category." Often persons discuss their appreciation for the minister's preaching in terms that indicate a relationship of sorts resulting from Sunday after Sunday sitting and listening to the same person preach. They might also mention a committee meeting, a conversation away from the building, or a moment in a specific sermon that created a bond with the minister. We separated the clusters to demonstrate the range of responses and the specific functions we suspect the relationships are fulfilling. Yet whether they had slept on church floors, gone calling, sat in years of committees, spent every Saturday cheering at the same ball games, or only experienced the pastor in the service of worship, almost everyone reports some feeling of connection with their preacher.

Respondents who report listening to radio preachers before going to worship often claim that knowing the person does not matter, yet their behavior indicates another ingredient. The radio preaching is not enough to feed their spiritual and religious life. They demonstrate the importance of participating in live worship services with their own community of faith. Going to worship is not just about the fellowship of a Sunday school class, not just the communal experiences of prayer and singing. It is also the preaching, being present and hearing this preacher whom they know. We consider this to be a significant finding.

We must admit we expected some patterns to surface. For instance, we expected there would be very little relationship outside the building with the pastors of the large churches, and close, family-like ties with pastors in the smaller congregations, especially those in small towns or open country settings. And certainly this was partly true. However, there were people in the large congregations who had close personal feelings for the pastor, although we suspect that some of those were grounded on quite limited interactions with the pastor. And there were people in small town congregations where the fellowship of the church body was evidently important in their answers, yet the closeness with the preacher was reported as not affecting listening to the sermon. We also wondered if there would be ethnic, gender, denominational, and age differentiations. There was some of this. For instance, we found almost twice as many males as females reporting the relationship with the preacher did not affect their listening. This is particularly significant when it is remembered that there were almost one-third more women than men in the study (seventy-five women; fifty-three men). One element we did not predict, but can easily understand, was the importance of connection with the pastor when the person had only recently come to the faith or come back to church. This tendency seemed to cross all categories. We were somewhat surprised that there was little distinction along ethnic lines. Approximately the same percentages of African Americans and Anglos appear in each cluster, except in the group that discussed their relationship with the preacher as being formed beyond the walls of the church building when they were involved in nonchurch events. Of the thirteen responses placed in this cluster, only two were African American. In the other clusters the numbers usually ran about two Anglos for each African American, which roughly equaled the percentages in the study. We found diversity of denominational groups represented within each cluster. There were as likely to be Methodists (of three traditions), Disciples, Lutherans, Baptists, Presbyterians, and Episcopalians, as there were nondenominational people and some from congregations related to the North American Christian Convention, and Anabaptists in each cluster.

One characteristic that seemed to come up again and again was an expectation that the preacher was trustworthy. Regardless of the cluster, that is, regardless of how the relationship with the pastor developed or even if the congregant said the relationship did not matter, that member wanted to be assured that the pastor would be a pastor to him or her when needed and that the sermons would be lived out in the lives of the preachers. How the listener will know whether the life was consistent with what was preached was not often clear, but we assume it came from some personal connection. However, the emphasis expressed was often on the ability to hear a trusted person. This respondent stands as a good representative, explaining what is liked about a person who was a good preacher.

> Well, I guess where I grew up, the preacher was also a spiritual person. It's not just enough to preach a good sermon, but how you respect your minister and the spirit that she or he has also has a lot to do with the person as a preacher. I think that's how our reverend was: a person who always spoke the word, but who also made you believe it. And our preacher exemplified it. It does make a difference, because if you can't respect the minister, it's hard to listen to what they have to

say. No matter how they speak it, or what terms they use, or what fancy words, if you don't see it in their living, it's very hard to accept the words they give you.

## A Word to Preachers

People are connecting with you. It is not just that they want to connect with you; they are. Yet they demand a delicate balance. On the one hand, they want someone who will be able to give them pastoral direction. They want someone theologically educated who knows the Bible. They want someone spiritual, whose prayers mean something. It is important to remember that when we preach we are not just telling the congregation about God; we are representing God. Preachers are teaching, but they are also demonstrating the faith. What we say in the pulpit and who we are on the outside are both being listened to. If congregants do not "hear" a consistency in our lives, our ability to engage the pew is lessened. And, unfortunately, our weaknesses and inconsistencies can be seen as weaknesses in the faith. We represent the faith; our foibles become the foibles of the faith. On the other hand, congregants want a human being in the pulpit. They like knowing we got a speeding ticket or we go out to eat with our spouse. It seems especially comforting when congregants hear we have struggled with issues of the faith and have survived. People want to be able to repeat what this person said: "Our current senior minister is the one I've worked with the most. Our minister is excellent in doing this job." When the interviewer asked what makes ministers excellent, the member replies, "They aren't politicians. They aren't gossipers. They do their job well. They're well spoken. Like our senior minister who is very well mannered, and I think is one of the most excellent teachers I've met since God sent me back to the church." The people who desire to have a personal relationship with the preacher cross gender, ethnic, denomination, and age differences.

We want to give a word of warning and a word of encouragement about use of personal stories from the pulpit. Many people seem to have developed a fondness for the preacher from hearing personal stories about the pastor's life from sermons. Some people enjoy that sense of hearing the pastor is "just like me" or "one of us." When the humanity of the preacher is communicated in this way, many listeners find it easier to absorb what the sermon is trying to communicate. Our warning is to be aware that the relationship (the personal stories and "I'm like you" attitude) can become the focal point of the sermon and thus of some people's listening. People can leave worship knowing more about us than about God or their faith. One interviewee even mentions a disappointment when preachers seem more focused on telling about themselves than God. However, a number of the preachers we interviewed explained they tell personal stories or reveal their humanity in sermons primarily for the reason that they want the congregation to see they are real people. Here are three quotes from different pastors: two men and a woman; one of the men is from a more liturgical tradition. "I try to present myself in a very human fashion. They do not think that I'm special, weird, or unique, but I'm one of them." "We're human. We're hurt, too. Our week's been hard." "I would hope my personal stories tell people that I'm just like everybody else, that I'm a regular thinking, feeling, emotional, spiritual person like they are."

Certainly our research shows people respond positively to personal stories. Consider this typical comment: "Our pastor gives a lot of illustrations and personal stories and is just another one of the congregation." Obviously allowing the congregation to see one's humanity is an asset in many listeners' ability to hear a sermon. For those who need a relationship with the minister in order to connect with the sermon, revealing some of one's personal life may be very helpful.

No one from our study indicated that a bond with the preacher made listening more difficult, except one listener over eighty years of age, whose father was a preacher. When the interviewer asked how that relationship made an impact on listening, the response was, "The main impact that it had was that in growing up it was my father up there talking, so if I wasn't careful, I didn't listen." Yet even this respondent clarified that there was now a desire to know what the preachers are saying, so it is easier to listen.

There are two additional reminders we want to pass along. First, although we were not testing for this, our study has shown that the congregation can be successfully educated not to resent the pastor's absence at certain events. Remember the people explaining to the interviewer that the minister's time was appropriately spent in sermon preparation, not making every hospital call and committee meeting? We guess they learned that from their pastors. And you can teach it, too. You can teach your congregants what is appropriate to expect from you, and how your time is best spent.

Second, remember how little it takes for some people to consider what they have with you to be a "personal relationship." Something as brief as a follow-up visit, a little private signal following worship about the quality of the sermon, a *group* of volunteers gathering before worship to pray for you. Such relationships can be seen as wielding quite a bit of power within the congregation. It makes sense that you consider the proper use of that power.

As you think back over the clusters described in this chapter, we invite you to reflect over your own congregation. Can you tell who feels the need to have a connection with you to hear the sermon? Are there ways (through the sermon or elsewhere) you can establish a better relationship with some of the members who may not feel connected? You may want to note for yourself those who seem not to need a relationship with you to hear what you have to say. One final note: How could the bond people have with you be used to strengthen their faith?

# CHAPTER 5

# Controversy and Challenge in the Preaching Moment

There is hardly a more anxiety-provoking task for the preacher than to address controversial or potentially divisive matters of faith from the pulpit. Whether a public crisis suddenly erupts in the world around us, or we hear congregational murmurings about a difficult issue we have long avoided, there are moments when every preacher feels the need to speak a compelling, if not provocative, word related to some challenging aspect of life and faith. The writers of this book have also wrestled with and wondered about their own ministries of preaching as they relate to critical and challenging aspects of life, and have listened with eager ears to the comments of listeners who responded to the question, "Are some issues too controversial or too explosive for the pulpit?"

With conviction and clarity, the listeners interviewed in this study share a strong desire to hear their pastors address a full range of controversial and challenging issues during Sunday morning sermons. The words of one person reflect well the sentiments of many others: "Whether I agree or disagree with what they say, the pulpit is the place for them to express their Christian feeling and beliefs." A great many listeners express deep longing for an authentic word from preachers who are willing to risk and join with others in the difficult task of understanding God's way amid life's challenges and crises. In describing what is most meaningful and stirring in sermons, one listener reports, "I think they should be provocative and sensitive, but provocative. They should make us think a little. They shouldn't just be pat little messages to make us feel good every week." With enthusiasm and conviction, the listeners in our study voiced their eagerness to hear sermons that address the most urgent issues and questions of our time.

### What These Listeners Say about Preaching on Challenging Matters

When speaking about sermons that address controversial or challenging aspects of life, the comments of listeners in our study reflect four areas of interest. First, they offer strong authorization for preachers to address controversial and challenging issues from the pulpit, often qualifying their support with further words of interest or concern. Second, listeners name several **specific topics they believe should be addressed,** as well as **specific topics that should be avoided** during Sunday morning sermons, including sermons related to political issues and comments regarding sermons preached in the immediate aftermath of September 11, 2001. Third, many listeners voice their **awareness of differences within the congregation** on any given topic of concern, as well as their appreciation for the difficulties pastors and preachers must contend with in preaching about controversial matters. Finally, many listeners describe **what the preacher may do to hinder** the congregation's ability to hear a controversial and challenging word from the pulpit, and **what the preacher may do to help** the congregation to hear, offering specific comments and suggestions.

First, the vast majority of listeners in our survey give **strong authorization for preaching related to controversial issues** and reveal a very strong desire for their pastors to preach more often about difficult matters of life and faith. One listener is adamant: "If it happened in life, if it's possible for it to happen, if it did, will, or is happening, the pulpit is the place for it. God is not a hidden agenda God." When controversial topics are not addressed in sermons, the lament of one listener speaks for several others: "I don't think explosive issues are talked about enough. Not here. Nobody touches it. It breaks my heart." Other listeners find it helpful for their pastors to name and address difficult issues from the pulpit in order to facilitate their own understanding of an issue or to aid their faith development. When asked if anything is too explosive to speak about in preaching, one person voices appreciation for sermons that address controversial issues by saying, "I tend to think those sermons are probably more enlightening. Sometimes you really need to hear that controversial thing to come to grips with it and deal with it."

In fact, nearly all of the listeners in our survey who comment on preaching related to controversial matters of life and faith do so in order to encourage their pastors to preach more often about difficult issues or to challenge their congregation to consider more deeply some important issue as it relates to faith. Across ethnic, gender, denominational, and other differences, people express strong agreement as to what they need to hear from their pastors. For example, one person vividly remembers how the local pastor confronted the church when it was important to do so:

> I remember one week where evidently someone here who was a member was inhospitable to a visitor and it had to do with seating, so that someone was told, "You're sitting in my seat." Our pastor came right to the edge of letting us know that he was downright angry at that. The pastor was really embarrassed that had happened here and I'm sure knew full well there were probably numbers of people, not just that couple, who had held that same thought but just hadn't been highlighted that way. It may have been unpopular to come out and say that, and it could have been handled in a softer manner, but it may not have meant as much.

This listener is aware that the pastor is risking something important when offering a challenging message that confronts the congregation when needed, and views the sermon as a vital opportunity to speak a truthful and corrective word at a critical moment.

However, the vast majority of comments that support preaching related to controversial or challenging issues not only include words of appreciation or encouragement, but also words of advice or concern that qualify these statements of support. For example, many listeners not only voice their interest in sermons that are relevant to the most pressing and difficult issues of our time, but they also want to hear *how scripture relates to these concerns.* In fact, several listeners of different denominational affiliations insist that no issue is too explosive to address "if it relates to the content of the Bible." One listener is emphatic: "No, I don't think there's any issue that's too explosive to preach about. If the sermons are based on the Bible, then there should be no sermon that's too biblical to preach. If it's in the Bible, then you can retell it." Another listener not only closely associates scripture with preaching about challenging and controversial issues, but also insists that the Bible itself addresses many controversial matters of faith:

> I think all subjects should be addressed because I read in the scripture myself that God, when God calls you, wants you to tell the truth. If it's in the word, it is from God and God wants you to know the truth. There are people who feel like you shouldn't bring certain things up in the church. I'm sorry. They're wrong. They need to read the word.

For these and many other listeners, there is not only a strong desire to hear how scripture relates to controversial matters, but the belief that preaching related to scripture will necessarily involve the preacher in addressing difficult and challenging aspects of life and faith.

Related to this is another qualification many listeners name when speaking about preaching related to explosive issues. Several listeners in our study not only name scripture as important, but also insist, "It's important to *hear the spiritual slant* to all things." These listeners express a genuine desire to hear a distinctly Christian perspective or to keep God foremost in the sermon when the preacher considers controversial and challenging issues. Although it may be surprising to hear that listeners mention this qualification, some people report hearing sermons that miss this vital element of Christian or spiritual focus. After remembering a former pastor who "just gave the entire sermon as a social issue so that Jesus and God were almost never mentioned," one listener expresses deep appreciation and an abiding need for the pastor to relate current events and crises to scripture and to God's presence in the world: "If you're going to do social issues, and you should do them, you somehow need to incorporate the Bible and the Christian viewpoint on why these are social issues. This is why it's a social issue: because the Bible says it is; giving biblical examples of the poor and needy." Similarly, another listener expresses openness to hearing sermons that address a range of controversial concerns, but insists that God's perspective must always be raised by the preacher:

> I really think everything should be talked about from the pulpit, but I think it should be talked about in the context of

what God says and not what we want, not what we say. When people say, "What do you think about it?" I say, "I'm learning." What I think isn't really all that ultimately important. It's really what God says that's important. What I think about it, if it doesn't line up with what God says about it, then I better start changing the way I think about it.

Another qualification that listeners make when voicing their support for preaching about controversial issues is related to their *awareness of children and youth* who are listening to sermons. Several listeners speak with enthusiasm about young people hearing sermons related to current events as well as controversial issues. According to one listener, "It's particularly important to speak to some of the youth in our church. Some of the things that the church may be reluctant to talk about, certainly the world is not reluctant to talk about and they may be getting a lot of misinformation out in the streets, so to speak. It would be better if that information was coming from the church." However, although many of these listeners want youth and children to hear sermons that address controversial and difficult matters, their comments also include a strong concern for the preacher to be cautious about naming specific sexual behaviors or violence in sermons. In the words of one listener,

> In the times that we're living in, you need to talk about those things, especially even with the children. I think they need to know about that stuff. I mean, you don't have to bring in the explicits of sexuality or explicits of murder and violence, but you can talk about it in a way that it doesn't turn them off. It makes them understand and helps them to understand God is there for them.

Another listener issues an even stronger word of caution:

> I probably don't want to have a lot of graphic examples. You can leave it to the imagination because I know that there will be children in the audience, too. You can talk about sexuality, but you don't have to be graphic with it, because I have a fourteen- and fifteen-year-old. I know they're going to be curious as it is, but I don't want them to be that curious till they're grown and married.

A final qualification that several listeners make when voicing their support for preaching about controversial issues is that preachers carefully *consider the impact on the congregation* when addressing potentially divisive or volatile concerns. Some listeners recognize that although nearly anything may be spoken of from the pulpit, not everything will be heard, so the pastor must exercise careful judgment in knowing what to preach about and what to avoid. According to one listener, "When you ask if there are any topics that should not be preached from the pulpit my answer is no, absolutely not...But there are some messages a congregation will not hear so it's a wasted message." Another listener struggles to identify what may or may not be appropriate for preachers to address. "Do I think there are some issues that are too explosive for the pulpit? No. I don't think so...Yes. No. Hmm." Both of these listeners are concerned that preachers know the congregational context of their sermons. Many other listeners hope that preachers carefully consider the impact of the message on the congregation as they decide what to say and what not to say. One listener's comments are representative of many:

> I have realized that it's possible for a given congregation, for its preacher to hit upon things that are going to have a negative impact on the congregation. My personal thought on that is that if they feel confident about it or they feel it needs to be brought, then bring it. Even if I don't agree with it, I'm not going to object. The only concerns I have about it is that the controversial things be brought in a way that bringing them doesn't become the issue. When the bringing of it or the fact that bringing it becomes a real block in Christian walk for everybody in the congregation, you sort of have to say, how controversial is it? How big of a problem is it going to be? What are the chances that going through a congregational confrontation on this is going to be positive?

This listener, like several others, asks preachers who address potentially divisive or volatile concerns to consider the impact of their words on the congregation.

Overwhelmingly, the listeners in our study voice their support for preaching related to controversial and difficult matters of life and they do so in ways that not only include words of appreciation or encouragement but also words of advice or concern that qualify their support. A passion for preaching that relates current issues to scripture and Christian faith, an awareness of children and youth in worship, and concern for the way in which preaching on controversial matters can impact the congregation as a whole reflect a strong desire for sermons that occasion a deeper encounter with life's complex problems and questions in light of Christian faith.

In addition to giving strong authorization for preachers to address controversial issues from the pulpit, the listeners in our study also list a cluster of several **specific topics they believe should be addressed** as well as a list of **specific topics they believe should be avoided.** Many of the same topics appear in both categories. Listed in order from most frequently to least often named on both lists, the listeners in this study cite issues related to human sexuality (including homosexuality, heterosexual practices, marital fidelity, AIDS, and reproductive issues), politics, race relations, divorce, women in ministry, drug and alcohol abuse, and finances.

The vast majority of listeners who favor preaching on challenging and controversial issues name **several specific topics they hope to hear their pastors address**. Among these are various issues related to human sexuality, race relations, drug and alcohol abuse, and financial matters. In the words of one listener,

> I don't think any subject should be shied away from in a sermon. The sermon should be relevant to today's issues, especially if something is real bothersome. One thing I guess I can think about in particular is homosexual issues. That is a very, very touchy subject for many people. I think that should be addressed from the pulpit.

In naming specific issues, listeners in this cluster invariably express their appreciation and longing for preaching that engages the congregation in some of the most urgent issues of our time: "If you don't bring things out in the open and discuss them, you're never going to be able to solve any problem. I guess probably racial differences and homosexuality today are big problems that I think the pulpit should address, talk about, and try to come to some kind of understanding."

It is interesting to note that the listeners in our study rarely disclose their own opinions or viewpoints regarding any given topic and they rarely express a desire to hear their pastor or preacher represent a particular viewpoint when speaking about controversial and challenging issues. As noted earlier, listeners are more interested in their pastor's understanding of how scripture or a Christian perspective influences their ideas. Indeed, one of the most important observations to be made about listeners' comments regarding preaching on controversial topics is that they want the preacher to assist the congregation in learning how to think through issues rather than merely telling them what to think about specific issues. One listener speaks of homosexuality, abortion, and a recent church building program that was potentially divisive for the congregation, then underscores the pastor's role in leading the way for others to engage in difficult issues:

> When there's a topic like that which has to be dealt with, people expect leadership from the minister. The preacher doesn't have to hit it on the head, but if he or she at least will talk about it somewhat, it helps people to focus on it. Some people, I think, do look to the minister for, "How should I think about this?" Maybe not in this church as much as some others, but they take their lead from the pastor.

Among the topics most frequently named by the listeners in our study, *political issues* are of great interest and concern. Second only to matters of human sexuality, many listeners in our study comment about politics in the pulpit in a way that situates this interest between topics that should be addressed and those that should be avoided. On the one hand, nearly all are concerned that pastors do not use the privilege of preaching simply to promote their own political agendas. On the other hand, many would like for the preacher to offer some general guidance in how to think about political issues from biblical and theological perspectives.

As just noted, many do not want the preacher's political interests to be the driving force of the sermon or to override the needs of the congregation. In the words of one listener,

> If you're too radical about something and you lose the congregation or lose the confidence of the congregation, then you can't continue to present the main message, which is the Christian message. You become mired in social things or political things, which detract from your main message. I think preachers have to be cautious about that.

Although a few people are adamant, "I don't like mixing politics in with the sermon," many others are willing to allow some room for political interests to emerge in preaching: "I think that you can pretty much talk about most things, but maybe without getting too much into politics or something like that. But you can even talk about that in a certain way, not necessarily taking sides all the time, being bipartisan or whatever." In fact, pastors who express political partisanship and voice their support for particular candidates during political campaigns elicit some of the strongest reactions from listeners who insist, "That's not appropriate, not in the sermon." Again, listeners do not object to hearing about issues related to politics (e.g., homelessness, war, the presence of the flag in the sanctuary) but they do not want to hear their pastor use the pulpit to endorse particular candidates: "I don't think anybody should campaign in the pulpit for a political person—president or mayor or whatever. I think we all have responsibility to be active and to influence, but I don't think it belongs in the pulpit."

Some of the most compelling comments related to politics and controversy in preaching are made by listeners in the aftermath of September 11, 2001. Twenty-one of the twenty-eight congregations participating in this study had at least one of their interview weekends take place within weeks following September 11, 2001, and several persons referenced sermons they heard following the critical events of that day.[1] In response to the question, "Can you tell me about a sermon that you found really engaging?" one congregant speaks appreciatively of a sermon preached after September 11 that spoke directly to the needs and questions of the congregation and drew the listener into meaningful conversations with others at that difficult and challenging time:

> The most engaging sermon I can think of in a long time is the sermon our pastor gave the Sunday after September 11. I think everyone was there…Everyone had questions for our pastor…The sermon was excellent. It was biblical. It was thought provoking. It hit all of the issues. I think sometimes you can sit in discussions with one another or when someone speaks they'll hit the things that are politically correct but kind of skirt some things that are more difficult to talk about. I became engaged in conversation and wound up giving copies of the sermon to several people, which is not something that I normally do at all, but I felt that strongly that it was something that not only met my needs but people beyond that.

The vast majority of listeners who reference sermons related to September 11 are glad that their pastors "didn't shy away from difficult issues but faced them and talked about them." However, some people are less than affirming of the *way* in which their minister approached this critical event:

After September 11, our pastor preached a sermon. I think the idea was to ask us to examine ourselves and see if we could determine any higher purpose to this event. But I didn't interpret it that way. I interpreted it as an attack on our society...Our pastor was very upset by this event and struggling to make sense of it. I think in the struggle to make sense of it at that particular time, at a time when the congregation was deeply in need of comfort, what was given to us was blame. The pastor gave us a sense of our personally contributing to the tragedy. I found that very upsetting.

The sense of personal and corporate indictment felt by this listener greatly inhibited an ability to receive the pastor's message. Similarly, another person voices distress over the minister's sermon immediately following September 11, 2001, but then expresses deep respect for the pastor sharing the pulpit on the following Sunday with someone who voiced a different interpretation of events:

The Sunday after the terrorist attacks, I sat there and I didn't agree with one thing the pastor said except that they should ask for forgiveness. I sat and I listened to the sermon and I was thinking, "Pastor, you're way off base..." The following week we had a congregant who gave a sermon, kind of a rebuttal. I don't know many ministers that like to give up the pulpit like that on Sunday morning but ours did to let this person speak from the heart. I felt like we heard both sides.

The pastor's willingness to share the pulpit and to offer opportunities for different interpretations of this difficult event was deeply appreciated by this listener.

Others also agree that it takes more than one Sunday to adequately address such critical and potentially volatile topics:

I have to admit the first week that our pastor spoke, I agreed with what was said and then on each of the following Sundays when the minister put out more thoughtful responses, I think that enabled me to see the real struggle that was there, and that it wasn't just a simple answer. In that way that was very good. I think mostly it's more of a journey, a consistent journey.

For this congregant as well as several others, it is especially important that controversial, complicated, or potentially divisive issues be addressed over a period of time and through thoughtful, ongoing engagement between the pulpit and the pew.

However, for a few listeners interviewed in this study, **some issues are simply too volatile or problematic and should be avoided in preaching**. Some congregants name sexual relationships as something that "the preacher should just leave alone." For these persons, issues related to human sexuality are either personal matters that "should be discussed at home" or have become so divisive that it is all but impossible for preachers to approach them without pulling the congregation apart:

> Personally, I don't think reproductive issues can be discussed. Maybe they should be but it wouldn't be possible and appropriate in this society. They need to be and there needs to be a way they can be but the media has taken some really important issues and polarized people so much that I don't think they can be talked about in reasonable ways. It automatically puts people into camps. Once they're already in camps, to discuss them from the pulpit is probably not a reasonable place for them.

In particular, many listeners recognize that homosexuality is a volatile subject and at least a few listeners interviewed in our study believe that it is simply too problematic to deal with from the pulpit. As one person notes, "gay and lesbian rights would be tough for our church to overcome and make any kind of decision on." Other topics related to human sexuality that are too volatile to address from the pulpit are cited by listeners, who sometimes offer words of caution to their pastors. One person resents the way in which the minister does not seem to appreciate the struggles and circumstances of others when preaching about sexual morality and behavior:

> My pastor talks about sex and when you should do it. I know what the Bible says but you have to think about now and reality and all these peer pressures. I think there are a lot of people who are not going to wait. So he presses that a lot on females. That's one thing I think he shouldn't talk about as much, because he's male. He doesn't understand what goes on with teens nowadays.

For these listeners, there are a few issues they would rather the preacher did not address on Sunday morning.

In addition to naming specific topics that are of concern, many listeners in our study who are supportive of their pastor preaching about controversial topics also voice their **awareness of differences within the congregation on any given topic** of concern as well as their appreciation for the difficulties of pastors who contend with these differences. Those who support their pastor in preaching about challenging issues are generally aware of the risk involved—both for the pastor and the congregation. One listener simply states, "We have a lot of diversity in the congregation. It would be awfully hard to preach [here]." Many listeners agree:

> I think certainly there are a lot of things to be weighing there if you have different ideas and different opinions. People's feelings could be hurt or divisive for the church. That puts a great deal of responsibility on the person leading the sermon to treat that with care and with respect for all involved. But absolutely, we need to address things that are challenging and difficult and potentially divisive. Otherwise, we'll never learn or see other points of view or figure out how we're going to go forward as a church or as a faith.

Although listeners are very interested in hearing preachers address difficult and challenging matters of life and faith, they are also quite aware that the burden of deciding what to preach about and how to speak falls largely on the pastor. When asked if there are some issues that are too explosive to be dealt with in the pulpit, one person responds, "It doesn't bother me if someone preaches something with which I disagree because there's a reason for them believing the way they do and if I think about it, I may later agree with them, so I'm inclined to say no. But if I were a minister, I might think of some."

It may be encouraging for pastors to know that several people in our study focus on the responsibility of the listeners when hearing something with which they disagree. More than a few congregants claim their own part in responding to differences in opinion with the minister, or troublesome comments that the pastor makes:

> If God puts something on the preacher's heart and if that preacher is being used by God, it's going to be said and it should be said. At that time and in that light, there may be something that may be controversial. It may not be accepted, but then it's up to the congregation and me personally. It's up to how I am going to accept it. How I deal with what my pastor has just said. Am I going to look at it in the light of,

"The pastor shouldn't have said that," or am I going to look at it as, "Why was that said?" or am I going to go up to the preacher and ask later on, "Pastor, what was that about?"

Another person sees the possibilities of engaging with others who have different interpretations of scripture as it relates to current events: "We don't all have to feel the same way. Whether we're reading something in the Old Testament or one of the gospels, we can take a different spin on it and feel like there's a different purpose there than the next one thought, and we come back together in a spirit of acceptance."

To be sure, more than one listener acknowledges that it is especially difficult for pastors to address certain issues with their congregations. For example, one person states, "I think stewardship and tithing are hard for preachers to preach about, even though they're also responsible for budgets of our church and responsible for leading people to do what is right between them and God." For this person and many others, care and wisdom need to be exercised by preachers who would serve as both prophets and pastors to their congregations:

> I think a pastor walks a very, very thin line because you've got this responsibility to this congregation for whom you have pastoral care responsibility, and you have people who are in all different places in their faith. You have to care for them, and you have issues that you feel passionately about. You are in this teaching role, and you can't teach somebody by beating them over the head with it, because I think the pastor has a responsibility to his or her congregation. The ultimate responsibility is to God's call, and that has to come first, but you can't just throw out the congregation because of that.

With considerable compassion, a great many listeners in our study not only appreciate the preacher's struggle to address controversial and challenging issues, but they also offer specific suggestions as to **what the preacher can do to hinder or help the congregation's ability to hear** a controversial and challenging sermon. For many listeners, when it comes to hearing about a difficult issue, "It depends on how the pastor goes about it."

Several listeners indicate **what hinders their ability to hear** what the preacher has to say about difficult issues. These listeners are concerned about preaching that *singles people out* or names individuals in an accusatory manner: "I think it's okay for the pastor to preach about controversial things, but I don't feel it's okay for him or her to point fingers." There is also a vague sense in which several listeners are concerned that preachers should not "make people feel bad" by pointing to the personal struggles or failings of their congregants. However, these listeners do not describe how the pastor may address controversial matters that challenge people's individual lives or life choices without sometimes offending particular people. Instead, the listeners in our study tend to focus on the potential for alienating individuals and so urge the pastor not to "preach about or against an individual in a sermon. I think that would be totally inappropriate." A final concern that one listener names is when pastors appear to say something "for a little bit of *shock value*, just to grab everyone's attention." Neither individual attacks nor dramatic gestures to claim the attention of the congregation are appreciated by these listeners.

With clarity and specificity, many other listeners indicate what **helps them to hear sermons** that address challenging issues. The listeners interviewed for this study offer several insights for preachers to help facilitate a meaningful encounter between preacher and listeners in the preaching moment.

In particular, the comments of listeners in our study cluster around four areas that help them follow a sermon on a challenging subject. First, a great many listeners hope their pastors will discuss challenging issues from the pulpit in ways that *offer more than one perspective* so that what is presented is either a "balanced view" or a spirit of openness to alternative views. One listener urges the preacher to present "the pros and cons and try to bring in some scripture, but not make a definitive decision." Another listener agrees that it is better for the preacher to "lay the facts before you and give you the opportunity to finish the story." Many other listeners hope that the sermon will open the way for a deeper consideration of difficult issues. In the words of one congregant:

> Abortion and homosexuality are the two really good examples
> of hot issues. I believe that our pastor has made reference to
> both of them in sermons in recent years, but they haven't
> been the subject of the sermon. But they have come in and
> the minister is able to use scripture to present maybe two
> ways of looking at those particular topics. You have to know

your congregation, of course. I think the pastor is probably hoping that people who are convinced that there is one right way of looking at something may be open to understanding that there's really another way or maybe more than two ways of seeing it, and that there's actually scripture that can be drawn upon to encourage us to look at something a little bit more openly.

This listener not only speaks positively of preaching that allows for different ways of viewing matters, but also suggests a second practice that several people commend: Namely, several listeners in our study mention that it is sometimes more effective for preachers to *touch on issues over the course of several sermons* than to devote an entire sermon to one controversial issue. For these listeners, it is more valuable for their pastor to address matters gradually and to offer a less direct approach: "It may have to be done very indirectly, with something like allegory, parable, and metaphor, those kinds of things." Such listeners appreciate it when the preacher does not spell everything out but leaves room for listeners to ponder the possibilities for themselves over time. One congregant urges the preacher to be patient with listeners: "I think social progressiveness occurs incrementally. It occurs unevenly within a large population of people. I think that it's good for a minister to facilitate that progressiveness and the pastor needs to recognize that progression will be incremental."

A third piece of advice that listeners offer to preachers relates to *pastoral sensitivity to others* and vulnerability in sharing one's own struggles. The listeners in our study express deep appreciation for pastors who voice their respect for others, especially for those with whom they disagree. In this way, preachers can speak "in love, not in a judgmental way." One listener is appreciative of a priest who "makes room for the freedom of a person's passions," and another listener speaks with great respect for pastors who "really take into account where people are, and then talk about their own conflictedness. That's one of the reasons I really appreciate and admire our pastor." One person speaks candidly about the pastor's humble and caring approach:

> I think our pastor's general attitude of, "I'm not pontificating; I'm struggling through this life just like you," frees up people to express their own views. Through experience, you learn that you can say some things that are in direct conflict with

what the pastor says and you and the pastor still care for each other. The pastor cares for us and tells us that from the pulpit.

A caring and respectful relationship between pastor and parishioners, expressed not only in one-to-one encounters but during the preaching moment, is deeply appreciated by listeners.

Finally, a few people mention that *the pulpit may not be the best place to address some controversial issues.* Given the volatility of some topics and the need for people to ask questions, some listeners suggest that it may be better to discuss some issues "in a smaller group setting where it's more interactive, where you can get people to actually talk about what they hear or have heard." Another listener reflects on issues, particularly "personal" topics such as abortion and recommends, "I think it makes a better discussion group topic than a sermon topic."

With candor and compassion, the listeners in our study reflect a strong desire to hear sermons that address controversial and challenging issues. They long to hear how faith and scripture relate to some of the most urgent crises and questions of our time; they name specific topics and voice their awareness of differences within the congregation and difficulties that pastors must contend with when preaching about controversial issues. Finally, in suggesting what preachers can do to hinder or help the congregation's ability to hear a challenging or controversial message, the listeners in our study reflect their deep longing for a relevant and faithful word that pertains to the most urgent issues of our time.

## Reflections and Insights on Controversy and Challenge in the Pulpit

Many listeners in our study are not only eager to hear faithful words about challenging issues, but they also express a resounding need for Christian faith to be relevant to the most pressing concerns of our time. Perhaps the most valuable message communicated by listeners who comment on controversy and challenge in the preaching moment is heard in their insistent request for sermons that relate Christian faith to current events, issues, and crises. Because many preachers may be hesitant or fearful to raise potentially divisive issues from the pulpit, it is encouraging to hear that the vast majority of listeners in our study express deep longing for preachers to join with them in the difficult task of understanding God's way amid life's challenges and crises. Just as our earlier chapter on the role and authority of scripture in preaching reveals a very strong desire among listeners to learn more about the Bible and its relevance to their lives and world, so do listeners speak very pointedly about their longing for pastors to take the lead in addressing controversial matters of life that are relevant for today: "I believe the sermon should lead instead of follow society. That would be one criticism I would have if I would have criticisms. Generally, sermons tend not to be on the cutting edge. I would like for the church to lead instead of follow, and I think it starts in the pulpit." As is true for many of the pastors interviewed for this study, many parishioners also long for the church to lead rather than follow society.

As listeners express the need for preaching that occasions a deeper encounter with life's circumstances and problems in light of Christian faith, at least three observations are worthy of further reflection. First, these listeners are describing something more than an interest in topical sermons, something beyond sermons that merely offer opinions about current events and crises. They urgently desire to hear their pastor speak from a Christian perspective, or, more particularly, they want to consider how scripture may relate to specific issues and concerns over the course of sustained discourse. More than hearing simple answers to complex questions, people long to be meaningfully and faithfully engaged amid life's challenges, and many name scripture as integral to this difficult task. Although few use the word *theology* in speaking about sermons that address life's challenges, the comments of listeners reflect a deep theological yearning to be engaged in the important work of discerning God's presence in the world and God's way among us.[2]

A second observation is that most of the qualifications made by listeners who voice strong support for preaching on challenging issues reflect awareness that the work of addressing controversial matters of life and faith is more complicated or problematic than listeners may at first acknowledge. In other words, the qualifications and follow-up comments that listeners make very often take into account the difficulties that pastors face in the preaching moment.[3] Most people seem to understand what is at stake for congregations and pastors when potentially divisive issues are addressed from the pulpit, and their comments suggest that listeners do not simply expect the "right" or "true" response to life's most pressing issues. Instead, many listeners simply hope that their pastors will offer informed, compassionate guidance in light of Christian faith and that the preacher's comments will reflect an awareness of a variety of approaches and concerns when addressing life's challenges. They acknowledge that preaching, like other theological tasks of the church, involves ambiguity and complexity so that faithfulness bids us to speak to life's difficulties without having to resolve every problem or to know every answer.

A third observation to be made is that among the many suggestions offered by listeners is an underlying assumption that preaching about controversial matters takes place in the larger context of a long term relationship between the pulpit and pew, a relationship that is informed by interactions outside of worship and is sustained, nurtured, and challenged by a relationship formed over the course of many sermons. For example, when listeners describe sermons preached in the aftermath of September 11, they not only allude to the first sermon they heard immediately following the events of that day, but to several successive sermons given by their pastors over an extended period of time. In other words, people are influenced by much more than one message and most listeners value a preaching relationship that extends over the course of many sermons. Similarly, several listeners indicate they find it helpful for the preacher to touch on a controversial issue over an extended period of time, offering brief allusions or insights during several different sermons rather than focusing on a controversial issue in one sermon alone. Preachers who address life's most difficult issues with integrity and care will most certainly develop a relationship with listeners over the course of time and will consistently raise questions and possibilities for people to consider in light of scripture and Christian faith.

## A Word to Preachers

With enthusiasm and conviction, the listeners in our study express a need for sermons that address life's most difficult issues. In their longing to hear about God's way among us and their appreciation for the difficulties and risks involved in preaching about controversial issues, these listeners reveal a strong desire for preaching that occasions a deeper encounter with life's questions and controversies in light of Christian faith.

Just as importantly, their words reveal an abiding confidence in God's word in scripture and they call on preachers to draw on the resources of Christian faith to address the crises of the world around them.[4] Although the listeners in this study did not want to hear their pastors dictate what to believe in response to any one question or controversy, they certainly express a longing to know what their pastors think about a range of challenging issues in light of Christian faith and scripture. With respect and pastoral sensitivity shown toward those who may disagree with them, preachers are called on to communicate the grace and truth of the gospel in an informed and compassionate manner. The listeners we interviewed issue a strong word that commands our attention; a word that resonates with the gospel itself and calls forth the prophetic voice in preaching. If the church is to lead rather than follow others in addressing both the personal and public controversies that confront us, then preachers need to speak about challenging issues in the light of Christian faith and the biblical witness.[5]

In addition to this strong mandate, the listeners in our study also offer many insights and suggestions for preaching about controversial matters. Their comments reveal at least three important considerations. First, it is important to have a sense of which questions, issues, and concerns are most difficult or pressing for your congregation at any particular time. To do this, the most helpful word to offer preachers is to get to know your congregation and listen to those who listen to your sermons. This may take several different forms. For example, pastors may interview persons individually or in small groups, asking them what they would like to hear in sermons that relate to their personal and corporate struggles or to the most pressing social or political issues that confront them. Pastors may also request time at church board or committee meetings to raise these questions, asking someone else to direct the discussion so that they may take notes and overhear the questions and comments of others. It is also vital that pastors get to know the congregation as a whole and to understand the larger community of which they are a part.[6] Through listening and careful inquiry, preachers need to keep their ears attuned to the topics and issues that are most challenging for the members of their congregation.

Second, be attentive to what hinders and what helps your congregation when hearing a controversial or challenging word. Listeners are willing and able to articulate what has been meaningful for them in the course of listening to sermons, and preachers are wise to listen to these suggestions in learning how to address difficult issues. For example, although the listeners in our study want to hear their pastor's perspective on various issues, they also insist that it is important for the preacher to present an informed and balanced view that respects the ideas of others when speaking about controversial topics. Related to this, nearly all listeners ask the preacher to show pastoral sensitivity in the pulpit and to avoid an accusatory tone when addressing the congregation.[7] For a sense of what has been helpful or problematic for listeners, pastors may solicit verbal or written feedback from a few trustworthy and truthful members. Once again, it is essential for preachers to listen to listeners.

Finally, consider what it means to engage listeners in ways that may open and continue conversations related to a range of controversial topics. Many of the listeners interviewed for this study voice their appreciation for hearing about difficult issues over the course of several sermons. Although they want to hear preachers offer the best of their insights and interpretations regarding controversial matters, listeners are very much interested in being active participants in the preaching moment, joining with others in discussing life's crises in light of Christian faith and the biblical witness.[8] More than definitive answers or the right position on various topics of concern, preachers are urged to consider how the preaching moment may initiate and sustain ongoing conversations around difficult issues over the course of time. In these ways, listeners themselves provide the best guidance in discerning how preachers may engage others when preaching about controversial and challenging issues.

The three major considerations just discussed generate three questions that a pastor might profit from asking the congregation. What are the questions, issues, and concerns that are most difficult or pressing for the congregation? What hinders or helps your congregation when you need to speak about a controversial or challenging subject? How can you do so in a way that will keep the conversation open and ongoing?

# CHAPTER 6

# Roles of Feeling in Preaching

Feeling is a powerful aspect of the life of an individual and of a community. Our study sought to identify some of the major roles that feeling plays when a congregation hears a sermon. Not surprisingly, we discovered a wide variety of ways that people are affected by emotions that are stirred by a message. Indeed, the immediately preceding chapter noted the powerful effects that feelings can have in connection with sermons on controversial topics. In the process of talking about emotion, interviewees indicated quite a bit about qualities in sermons that stir them, and qualities that leave these listeners cold.[1]

Many people describe their understanding of the functions of emotion in the sermon when the interviewer says, "I'm going to ask you questions about you personally and then similar questions about the congregation. Can you tell me about a sermon that stirred your own emotions?" "What in that sermon stirred you?" The interviewer typically continues, "I would like for you to describe a sermon that seemed to move the congregation as a whole, as a community. What was it about that sermon that seemed to move the congregation? What seems to stir the community's emotions?" Listeners usually respond in ways that illumine how they are moved both as individuals and as communities. Another question brings forward several significant replies–"Would you describe a time when the sermon stirred emotions that made you feel uncomfortable?" Another question probes the life of feeling in the sermon—"When the sermon stirs the emotions of the congregation, what happens after worship?" Some listeners indicate the importance of feeling in the preaching event as they answer the question, "When the pastor stands up to preach, what do you hope will happen to you as a result of listening to that sermon?"

Several interviews were conducted in the months following the destruction of the World Trade Towers in New York City on September 11, 2001. This event powerfully influenced the ways in which many of these respondents spoke. When analyzing the comments in the total body of transcripts, however, we find that remarks made by post-September 11 interviewees differ in degree, but not in kind, from thoughts voiced by other interviewees regarding emotion in preaching.

## What These Listeners Say about the Roles of Feeling in the Sermon

The first five chapters of this book make it obvious that reflecting on how human beings respond to sermons is not a science. We do not have exact categories or standards of measurement to describe what happens in the listener's heart, mind, and will in the same way that we measure blood pressure, bone density, or even IQ. The difficulties of analyzing how people respond to sermons are magnified when we turn to the roles of feeling in the sermon, for listeners sometimes find it difficult to speak precisely in conventional language about the relationship between preaching and feeling. Nevertheless, we notice that things listeners say about preaching and emotion gather into four identifiable (though sometimes overlapping) clusters.

A number of listeners speak appreciatively of messages that create **feelings they associate with awareness of the divine presence.** Awe, for instance, is such a feeling. When asked about being moved by a sermon, a listener recalls such a response:

> I probably couldn't tell you which sermons they are, but I'm thinking of times when there's just this silence. This really heavy silence and know that something has been said that's been sacred, that's taken a sacred moment in sermons. Right now I can't pull out which sermon that was and exactly what was said about that, but I do remember those sacred silences in the midst of worship.

Several people speak of such moments. Others, while not calling attention to such experiences of emotion, still report powerful responses:

> I hope to feel closer to God during the sermon. We're in God's house and hopefully we've prepared ourselves at that point to listen. I want to be drawn as much as possible. Sometimes it's more and sometimes less, and sometimes I think we have something that every person—you just feel like you're getting deeper, and that's what I hope people are preparing themselves for and experiencing.

In a similar mode, a very high percentage of interviewees attribute emotion in the sermon to the presence and work of the Holy Spirit. The Spirit is an agent awakening them to the divine presence in the realm of feeling. The presence of emotion indicates, to them, that the Spirit is at work. Such people seldom believe that the Spirit causes everyone to feel in the same way, but acknowledge that the Spirit can move different people in different ways. A respondent who also teaches a Bible school class reflects both on being personally stirred in the service of worship, and on students in his class being stirred: "I think a lot of that is the Holy Spirit and how the Holy Spirit speaks to us" (i.e., through emotions).

Indeed, as we find in a second cluster, for many listeners **the life of feeling is a realm of knowledge**. For such folk, feeling is seldom just passing emotion but is more a transverbal apprehension of self, world, and God. For example, an interviewee says,

> I think of another sermon in particular that the preacher gave at one point when he was talking about the connection between body and soul and speaking specifically about child abuse and child sexual abuse. He was talking about the body and the soul. You can't touch one without touching the other. That's just huge, just huge. One of those things that are so simple that you think you know, and then you know at a much deeper level.

Another interviewee recalls being moved to tears by a sermon that included liturgical dance:

> *Interviewee*: I think there was a very effective sermon that was done here a couple years ago with liturgical dance—spoken word and liturgical dance, and I felt people were equally impacted throughout the sanctuary that day. I've

found that while the sermon might not have been as effective in word that the Holy Spirit was definitely present and that you could feel the energy, and that people were equally rallied around that sermon and that message and subsequently impacted the people.

*Interviewer:* How would you describe the interaction between the spoken word and the dancing?

*Interviewee:* I would say that the spoken word was supportive of the dance. The spoken word was almost the music, that the dance was taking place in. It was one person doing both. The dancer had a body mike. The repetition of movement and the repetition of the word was happening simultaneously. It was very powerful. The dancer's voice accompanied the body movement. That sort of happened. The two related to one another.

*Interviewer:* I'm thinking of how you were describing the fact that sermons can communicate on different levels.

*Interviewee:* Yes.

The dance stirs the listener in the life of feeling. This experience of feeling is a source of theological insight, albeit one that cannot be fully described by word.

Closely related are those listeners for whom the experience of emotion during a sermon is a test of the reliability of the sermon. When these interviewees experience a significant positive feeling during the sermon, they believe that it is an authentic message. If they are not touched, they tend to think either that the sermon is not a real message from God, or that they did not prepare themselves adequately to hear the message. We see this motif in league with the previous one (the Holy Spirit as agent facilitating emotion) in a comment on the authority of the sermon: "It does have authority in a number of ways. Partly when it touches the emotions, when you get caught by the sermon and I *feel* that the words are inspired and they have reached me." Authority is also contingent on faithfulness to the Bible. "Sometimes being touched is through a story. One of the comments I made was that the senior minister does a really good job of bringing in stories, good illustrations to help make the point meaningful, that make me *feel* the Holy Spirit is speaking through the preacher."

Third, adding to this perception, another listener points out that such sharing experiences in preaching **connect people with one another and even create a corporate sense of community**.[2] This listener is answering the question, "What do you think God is doing during the sermon?"

> I can feel God there. I wish I could think of a Sunday in particular because it doesn't happen all the time, but I know God's with us all the time. I can't think of any, but that happens frequently. There are some times when you can feel the vibration in the people. You can feel it. The experience is palpable and shared. You can feel it.

Another interviewee adds to this perspective when responding to the question of when a sermon has authority: "When it speaks to your heart and you feel that it is something that has moved you. You're filled with the spirit of the message. I can't put words quite on it. I think it's a feeling more than something I can articulate." Although this listener cannot describe adequately what happens when the sermon creates deep emotion, such moments are considered to be at the heart of what happens when listening to a sermon.

A long-time listener occasionally gets an audiotape of the service when it contains a significant moment of emotional insight. The interviewer sums up the preceding part of the conversation by saying, "Oftentimes, when you think back on a sermon that particularly struck you, and you remember that feeling raised by the sermon, you do not necessarily remember the words that were said?" (The congregation has two ministers.)

> Yes. I actually have gotten some of theirs, because they tape every service. I haven't actually like listened to them over and over gain, but I've played bits and pieces of it and I say, "Well, how come I have this tape?" I put it in and, "Oh." It's because the rhythm, the wording, the energy, the dynamics of the whole thing came together to make an awesome moment for the congregation. It may not be specific wording. It's all those parts that create that message and the reaction and the intensity to it.

Playing the tape re-creates the experience of the awesome moment. This listener expands. "I think they're excellent sermons. I really do. From the way they touch me and the way I sometimes have tears in my eyes just because it feels…It may bring up memories that hurt, but they're still important. It's a cleansing type of feeling." Another hearer recalls,

> One time…I can't say that I saw a lot of tears going down people's faces or anything, but I think it was a fairly emotional experience for everyone. Our pastor did a sermon where a letter [was read] from a prisoner who had written to him because [the minister] did prison outreach. It was a letter to our congregation. I don't necessarily remember what the letter even said. It was a letter that caused us to feel or be united with the prisoner in the kingdom kind of way, just realizing that this prisoner was part of us.

This parishioner recollects that from time to time the preacher reads letters from the pulpit from persons in situations of extremity (e.g., people who live in developing nations or people in prison) and that "usually the more emotional experiences around preaching have to do with letters or things like that." When asked why the letters release emotion, this listener continues, "They're honest, and they're that person's soul. They're very open. They show us this life that we're not used to or feeling connected to."

For some listeners, the experience of sharing an emotional experience with other parishioners creates a bond. A respondent says that when the community gives praise to God near the end of a sermon, "You feel connected to other people when you see they have a similar response to the sermon. So I think that's one of the good things you realize when you hear a sermon is that, hey, you're not out there by yourself." This theme is present in many interviews.

A small and final cluster of folk say, as in the comment of this person who claims to most value the intellectual content of the sermon, "**I am not an emotional person**." This congregant, along with several others, claims to have few emotional reactions to sermons. When these people do have a reaction, they do not use it as the basis for determining the importance of making a major life decision. Quite a few people who would not go as far as the person who professes, "I am not an emotional person," still say they do not need to have profound emotional experiences to be stirred to faith or action. They are cognizant of having feelings, but they say they try to make major life decisions on the basis of intellectual considerations.

I'm motivated without it getting to my feelings. That's just me. I don't need somebody to be up there [in the pulpit] in tears in a shaky voice and trembling and that kind of thing. I'm not saying that's wrong if somebody [a preacher] does that occasionally. That's just not something that I need or that particularly makes me feel better or pulls me closer to the Lord.

This listener most wants to learn "hardcore dependence" upon God without being emotionally excited.

Switching now from the major clusters of ways that people say they are affected emotionally by the sermon, we turn to *the kinds of material in the sermon that move these listeners emotionally.* A coterie of listeners indicate that they are *especially open to being moved emotionally when their worlds (individually or socially) are in disequilibrium or when they are facing a significant life decision.* Not surprisingly, many people whose lives are relatively stable are deeply moved by stories in sermons that tell of persons or communities whose lives or worlds are chaotic. A hearer who typically responds to the intellectual elements in sermons comments on responding to preaching after September 11, 2001.

Well, when the preacher stands up to preach, I think I'm looking for God's word to come to me. It can come in a variety of ways. Sometimes it makes you cry. Sometimes, usually because it touches you in some deep way, and especially since September 11, we're emotionally vulnerable. Our senior minister is relevant in the sermons since that event. My emotions aren't easily touched, but after the sermon on the Sunday following September 11, I turned to the person sitting in front of me and said "I could have just wept at how sensitive our pastor was to the events."

The same person "could have sobbed" when a member of the congregation who was a native of the Middle East described that week as "the worst of that person's life" because "so many people treated that person with suspicion and even disdain."

Another common theme is people being touched emotionally by the *preacher telling a personal story from his or her own life*, as one parishioner says.

I think that the things I do remember are when a pastor or someone preaching will personalize the sermon a bit, disclose a little bit of something about himself or herself that shows that person has grappled with the issues. That person is only human after all, as we all are. That person doesn't put himself or herself above the congregation. I think those things—when they're connected to the main theme—for me are really poignant, and often times those are things that I remember long after a lot of the other material.

Another listener reports similarly:

Generally speaking, ministers in our denomination aren't pointing fingers at you. They use themselves as examples, and as soon as you hear that, I'll say the word *condition*, you know if you're behaving like that or not. So you wouldn't necessarily start crying and bawling and hide under the seat, or something, but it does touch you. So you recognize your need to address that.

The emotion stirred by the preacher's personal narrative empowers self-examination.

Many people are also stirred when preachers *tell stories that focus on children,* especially children who are important to them—whether their own children or others whom they know. A woman recalls such a moment that occurred during her first pregnancy. She was experiencing some difficulties in the pregnancy and was on bed rest and was anxious about the child. The reading from the Bible in the service of worship "had something to do with children and God caring for children."

Then I had one of those memorable experiences where we read that scripture and I was sitting right under the picture of Jesus and the children. Then our pastor said something about children having to do with the passage of scripture that we read. For me, that was a very emotional response. It was an emotional time. I felt reassured that my child in the womb would be safe and all those other things.

The woman experienced the emotion at that moment as almost sacramental, that is, as a physical reminder of God's providence.

One of the most common reports of material that affects feelings is being *deeply stirred by the story of the death of Jesus.* One interviewee says, "Every time I hear a sermon about Jesus and his dying and his death and his last day here on earth, that really touches me. It's a spirit moving through me. I'm really touched by his death and dying on the cross at Easter time. That's my most emotional time–being able to thank Jesus face to face some day." Another listener makes a similar report. "I think when you get into the sermon on what Jesus has done for me, that's when I get emotional. Yes. When the preacher talks about that Jesus came and died for me and gave me healing and gave me strength and things of that nature, and when he gets to that high point of the sermon, that's when it touches me. Yes."

Another listener gives a more specific account. "I will say that for myself as an individual, the Maundy Thursday period of the Holy Week is more personal and powerful to me than Easter." One reason is that while in high school this listener heard a deeply moving sermon on Jesus' death.

> What we did Maundy Thursday, we stripped the altar, draped everything in black. We had communion and it was dark. It was silent. I was in high school and was bouncing between cynicism and, "Yeah, rah. I've been saved." It was that time in history. I wasn't sure where I was going or what I was doing. I remember the priest getting up and delivering a fairly short message about the Garden of Gethsemane. The message–I'm sitting here getting goose-bumpy thinking about it. The message was about Jesus basically being very, very human and saying, "I would just as soon pass on this," but, dot, dot, dot. It was told in a setting and in a time that here I am thirty years later thinking about this. I mean there were people in that congregation crying. This was not a Bible thumping sermon. There were no special effects or footnotes. This was just revisiting a very simple message in a quiet, powerful way, a personal human setting. It was very powerful.

As we hear in the interviewee's further reflection, the experience helped this person gain a sense of purpose in life:

> That moving experience caused me to think an awful lot about Jesus making the choice, Jesus walking into the passion. Jesus didn't choose to turn left. Jesus could have turned and left. "I'm going to opt out of this." I'm a good citizen, loyal to my home state and we all have our shrines, and one of these that rings true about one of the battlefields in my home state is that the people could have left. No harm. No foul. Chose not to. I think that, "Here I am again."

Just as Jesus faced the choice, so the deep emotions around the sermon compelled this listener to have the courage to make the hard choices in life.

Sermons that *describe persons and communities suffering injustice* arouse the emotions of several listeners. In the following two remarks, a member of a congregation that takes stands on social issues ties together the purpose of preaching, emotion, and injustice when describing what happens when the preacher stands up to preach.

> I hope that I will be challenged to think about things or see things in a different way. Sometimes I just need to be comforted. Sometimes that's why I come to church, and I'm aware that I can't call ahead to get comfort. So I guess what I hope at my best is to be intellectually challenged. But again I keep coming back to the emotional hook because that's what drives me to change—when something is said in the sermon or if there's some intellectual-emotional connection that I haven't made before.

This listener is able to recall several sermons that stirred emotions in this way:

> A preacher in our congregation gave a sermon one Sunday. I can remember that preacher's own passion for social justice and what was happening with a major retail chain and the information about that really stirred me to look further and deeper into how I was doing my shopping and what small steps I could take to rectify some of the problems.

The preacher's passion ignited the listener's passion, fueling changes in ethical behavior.

A similar response shows how several themes we identify in this chapter interweave—feeling as a realm of knowledge, children, and the suffering of Jesus. A woman recalls a sermon in which the preacher tells about a newspaper article that reports a man who beat his wife and then murdered her while the children were in the house. The preacher describes a newspaper article that says, "The children were not injured even though they were in the house." The preacher goes on, "What is injury? How can the newspaper say these children are not injured?" The listener ruminates,

> The sermon was for me a pivotal force in thinking about Jesus and the presence of Jesus in my faith and giving me

much gentler ways of thinking about my faith and who Jesus was, rather than God being this harsh judge of character and you're always in this box or that box. The sermon talked about Jesus suffering the way the children did in a way. The abused woman had suffered. I think the sermon for me was pivotal in, I guess, maybe deciding to remain Christian and being able to live with Christianity as a faith of love rather than judgment. The preacher told the story of Jesus in such a way as to connect Jesus with the suffering woman. You hear those words over and over and over again, but it just seems to me that at some point a sermon or something else will touch you on a level that you've never been touched before by something else. Something you think you've known all your life, you now say, "Oh! That's right!" You have this profound insight that somebody helps you reach.

When touched, this listener recognizes depths of knowledge that had been previously unconscious.

### Reflections and Insights on Feeling in Preaching

Bernard Meland, a philosopher and theologian, points to one of the central difficulties when attempting to discuss the relationship between preaching and the life of feeling when he says, "We live more deeply than we can think." Consequently, "No formulation of truth out of the language we use can be adequate for expressing what is really real, fully experienced within the mystery of existing."[3] Indeed,

> The grounds for awareness, common awareness, of the realities to which we seek to give recognition through language precede our speaking, our expressiveness through language. Thus there are depths of awareness accompanying the bodily event of living and experiencing that yield conditions of knowing that language may not convey, or perhaps *cannot* convey.[4]

Even people who turn to poetry, figurative and imagistic forms of expression, and other arts, have difficulty bringing the inner life to expression. Philosophers of language, psychologists, and others who study feeling in human life point out that a human being is often not only unable to express aspects of feeling, but people are not always consciously aware of the emotions at work within the depths of a person or community. Even so, emotion often very powerfully affects individuals and communities.

The transverbal dimensions of the life of feeling, as described by Meland and others, call for an attitude of humility on the part of the project team and preachers when thinking and talking about the roles of emotion in connection with the world of the sermon. Much life-shaping experience takes place within individuals and communities in ways that go beyond discursive formulation and description. When attempting to analyze such things we need to recognize that we can achieve only partial understanding of how feeling contributes to the life orientations of listeners. Preachers, likewise, need to recognize that they cannot facilely predict how congregations are going to be affected by certain kinds of material and plan sermons as if they know for certain how the people are going to react. People can be touched at depths and in ways that the preacher can never know or even imagine.

Nevertheless, critical reflection is one of the callings of the preacher, such that preachers need to press as far as possible in naming the feelings that are (or could be) at work in a particular preaching situation and in how feelings function in connection with sermons. Furthermore, listeners venture into uncertain territory when suggesting that the feelings can signal the presence or leading of the Holy Spirit. While some emotions likely come about in response to the Spirit and prompt the community to serve the purposes of the gospel, the doctrine of sin reminds us we live in a broken world. Emotion is ambiguous; just as it can mediate the holy, so it can embody qualities that work against God's aims for the world. Even if a particular emotional experience takes place in response to the Holy Spirit, a congregation can misperceive that experience. Consequently, a community benefits from having criteria by which to gauge the likelihood of whether a specific feeling or experience and the response it calls forth is consistent with the community's deepest convictions about God.[5]

Several listeners object to the use of the sermon as a tool for emotional manipulation. In their own language, they raise the issue of the ethics of preaching itself. According to such listeners (and the writers of this book agree), preachers should always respect the freedom of the listener to affirm or to reject the main proposals of the sermon. On the one hand, a preacher seeks to offer the sermon to the congregation in the most inviting way. To do so, sermons can certainly appeal to the emotions. But, on the other hand, a preacher is ethically bound to try to avoid manipulating listeners. Manipulation occurs when a preacher intentionally or unintentionally creates a listening climate that diminishes the capacity of the hearer to reflect critically on the content of the sermon or that urges the listeners to believe that their options for responding to the sermon are more limited than they really are.

## A Word to Preachers

This chapter reveals that the kinds of sermonic material that evoke feeling are quite diverse. People are moved in as many ways as there are people. A preacher, therefore, needs to become familiar with the kinds of material that stir the emotional lives of persons of the congregation. The preacher can then make theologically appropriate use of the kinds of stories or other sermonic experiences that have a good opportunity to help the congregation connect with the sermon at the level of feeling. A minister might also introduce the congregation to other kinds of material that have a chance to appeal to the congregation's emotional life.

Given the fact that emotions have powerful effects on a fair number of people, one of the most pastoral things a preacher can do is to help members of the congregation name the feelings associated with particular sermons. The interviews reveal that some people have difficulty recognizing feelings and their effects, and trouble giving voice to them, even feelings that are fairly close to the surface. Unresolved anger, for instance, can have pernicious effects for the self and community. More than simply helping people name emotions, sermons can encourage people to respond to them (and deal with them) in ways that are consistent with God's purposes for the world, while discouraging people from responding to emotions in ways that work against the divine purposes for the congregation and the world.

A fair number of people assume that the presence of a certain kind of emotional reaction during the sermon indicates the presence of the Holy Spirit. As we said in the preceding section of this chapter, pastor and parishioners need criteria by which to determine the degree to which it is likely that particular manifestations of emotion are, indeed, coherent with God's purposes.

As noted in interviews reported in *Hearing the Sermon,* a large number of people say that a sermon makes them uncomfortable when it provokes self-assessment and challenges them to live more faithfully.[6] Such self-examination, while important to the practice of

Christian life, can often be threatening. Ministers can help facilitate this important process by naming the discomfort, and by providing support for it through sermons and other aspects of congregational life. In particular, most interviewees say that they feel such support when sermons place God's judgment within the larger frame of divine love. The listeners interviewed for this project, by and large, are ready to be accountable for their own failings and to make efforts to align themselves more fully with God's purposes, but they are turned off by unrelenting references to harsh condemnation.

In chapter 7, we investigate specifically how the sermon functions communally. As a precursor to that material, we note here that several respondents point to a vivid feeling of connection with one another that erupts in the congregation when they are moved by a sermon. Ten minutes of feeling close to one another while gathered in the worship space do not, by themselves, a community make. But a preacher could help the congregation recognize that such moments of mutuality represent, in miniature, the quality of community that should be constitutive of the congregation's life. The sermon could help people build from the limited experiences of relatedness after the sermon toward the comprehensive community envisioned by the gospel.[7]

The preacher can also help the congregation with another important aspect of naming. The transcripts reveal that persons make decisions about what to believe and how to live in many different ways. Some listeners turn to critical analysis of principles and ideas. Some folk accept what authorities say because they trust those authorities. Still other people rely more on experience and feeling. A pastor can help congregants name how they make decisions and reflect critically on the advantages and disadvantages of the different ways that people in the congregation come to conclusions. The preacher can especially help the congregation identify patterns of decision-making that take fuller account of sources of our knowledge of God.

Our focus on feelings in this chapter contributes to a companion discussion in chapter 4, as well as to discussion in the wider preaching community regarding whether preachers should use material from their own lives in the sermon. While some voices in the field of preaching assert that ministerial autobiography has no direct place in the sermon, the general drift of comments in listener remarks related to feeling points in the direction of the preacher using personal material, *provided* it is used carefully to illustrate the content of the message and not simply to call attention to the preacher's own life. Most of the listeners in our survey who address this topic affirm that the use of personal material from the preacher's life not only helps them grasp the main concerns about which the preacher is speaking, it also, as we saw in chapter 4, strengthens the bond between themselves and the preacher and opens them to the preacher's insights because they know that the preacher has experienced much of what they experience. However, the preacher's reference to material from the preacher's own life comes with the significant caution that the minister should bring into the pulpit only material that is suitable for public discussion, and, as quite a few respondents note, in limited amounts.

North American culture is moving away from critical reflection as a standard component of decision-making and is increasingly turning to image and feeling to persuade people to commit themselves to everything from buying a certain skin care product to supporting military actions in other countries. This turn of events leads to people being asked why they buy a certain product or adopt certain positions on social issues, and answering nothing more than, "Because it feels good." While preachers want to honor the life of feeling, and to make use of appeals to the emotions in sermons, preachers need to avoid letting sermons mimic the culture in this respect. Critical reasoning is not the only factor to take into account when developing a perspective for life, but such reasoning can often be an important corrective to undisciplined feeling. Preachers perform a valuable service for church and culture by helping congregations develop habits of discernment of the divine purposes that bring reason and feeling into conversation.

Persons who are touched by feeling indicate that the presence of emotion when they hear a sermon can empower them to deeper theological apprehensions and to more faithful life and witness. The sermon speaks to them in depths of self and community that cannot always be satisfactorily explained in informational speech. As one of our interviewees indicates, many listeners are moved by materials that have the character of poetry, image, and even body movement and dance. The preacher should recognize that using such material is not merely fancy window dressing, but is speaking to the congregation at a significant, albeit transverbal level. Preachers, indeed, should regularly include such material in sermons.

Although this chapter focuses on the role of feeling in the listeners' responses to the sermon, several of the theological reflections and implications for preaching discussed in the preceding pages imply a correlate for the preacher. Just as a preacher needs to help members of the congregation name the network of feelings that gather around a sermon, so the preacher needs to name his or her own feelings as they take life in the preparation of the sermon, the preaching, and the follow-through.[8] A preacher's emotions, especially when unexamined, can intrude inappropriately into the conception and embodiment of the sermon. When named, however, a minister's emotions can often become valuable conversation partners on the way to, and in the midst of, the sermon.

When thinking about the themes of this chapter in relationship to a preacher's own congregation, a preacher might ask, "How can I tell what are the signs at the time of the sermon and afterwards that my congregation responds emotionally to the sermon?" A minister can then press ahead: "What are the emotional reactions in the congregation to sermons?" The preacher can question further, "What kinds of material in the sermon stir feelings among my listeners?" "With which of these kinds of material am I most comfortable (e.g., stories from situations of injustice, stories from the preacher's own life)?" In order to help sermons touch the congregation emotionally, or touch some listeners at greater depths than at present, a minister may want to review the kinds of material the minister uses in sermons and ask, "Do I need to incorporate additional kinds of emotionally moving material into sermons?"

# CHAPTER 7

# How Preaching Shapes the Faith Community

When we think about preaching, most of us assume the sermon is supposed to be doing something in the lives of the individuals listening in the pews. We probably also believe something is happening corporately. That is, we believe something is going on in the life of the congregation as a whole because of the sermon. In the first chapter we looked at what people report they understand as the purposes of preaching. In this chapter, we investigate what people report actually goes on in preaching that helps the persons in the pew and the congregation as a whole to become who they are in the faith.

We entered into the analysis of the data expecting that most people would have a personal sense of the sermon's helping them understand the faith. Perhaps they might also see that the sermon helps shape who they are individually in the faith. We thought they might also have a sense that the sermon helps shape who they are as a congregation. After all, preaching is different from a one-on-one conversation. It is a communal event. The sermon is spoken to a gathered body of believers; it receives a shared hearing in the context of community worship. We expected people might be able to speak most easily and well about the sermon's addressing them as individuals (how the faith applies to their specific life, behaviors, and needs). However, we were also eager to uncover how people would speak about the effect of preaching on their faith community. The questions asked to bring these ideas to the surface included: "What does preaching do in the congregation?" "Can you talk about how preaching helps shape who the congregation is, or how preaching helps form the congregation's identity?" We also asked for examples of sermons that changed the way they thought, felt, or acted (indicating we wanted to know about them individually); then we also asked about changes in the congregation as a whole. It should be noted that there were a few occasions when persons were not asked the question about how preaching shapes the communal identity.

### What These Listeners Say about the Sermon Shaping the Community

As we began to analyze material for this chapter, we were surprised to discover how many different ideas persons had about how the sermon is shaping their faith. Frequently in response to the general question of what preaching does in the congregation, although phrased in the corporate, people answered with a personal expectation about preaching, or a personal story of how a sermon affected their faith, or their individual understanding of how a sermon assists in forming or developing their faith. After hearing about the sermon through their personal faith listening, the interviewers asked more clearly about what the sermon does for the congregation as a community. Although many persons answered this more slowly, quite a few people were able to articulate a distinct understanding about what goes on in the congregation as a result of the sermon.

Respondents offer, in general, three different types of response to questions of faith shaping, which we designate into three separate clusters. The three clusters are composed first of those who are **individual faith listeners**. Second there are those who understand the sermon as addressing the congregation as an **aggregate of individual listeners**. Finally there is a small cluster of persons who hear the sermon as addressing the congregation as a unit. We refer to them as **communal identity listeners**.

First, we present responses from the **individual faith listeners**. Their comments most frequently use the singular. Often they have difficulty answering the question about preaching shaping the congregation into a community, but they easily talk about how they personally appreciate the sermon. Usually the report includes comments about the sermon helping in "my" growth or giving "me" directions about how to live, rather than making references to the congregation or to the listeners in the plural. Hear this person as a typical example of someone whose emphasis is as an individual faith listener:

> When the minister speaks to me, even though speaking to hundreds of people, it's one-on-one to me. I feel like I am being spoken to, even though the face is scanning the crowd, and I realize it's to the entire group. To me it's a one-on-one conversation to me. Sometimes afterwards when we go to lunch or something, which we'll often do after service, a group of us, we will sometimes find out that what I got out of that sermon was not what the person next to me got out of it. In that respect it is one-on-one.

A similar response is given by a person of a different ethnicity from a different denomination. The interviewer asks what would be missing if there were no sermon:

> Christian message is more than just, "I need a family." It's more than, "I need to feel good about myself." It's more than, "This is a connection with my grandmother," which is all good. It's only in the sermon time that it's really premeditated, that if it's a good sermon, then I'm going to touch your heart, your emotions, and your history as an individual in Christ, your history with your family, your future, and your purpose. It's only in the sermon time and the whole corporate worship that you touch everything about an individual in Christ, everything that represents humanity. I'm more than my psyche. I'm more than my sociology. I'm more than my emotions. Only when you have a worship service where all those things come together purposefully do you have something that you won't get any place else.

Interestingly, at first hearing, this person may have seemed to be going beyond the personal in talking of what more the message should be, yet does stay within the realm of the individual.

When asked about a sermon that changed something in one's life, the response given below indicates an individual style of listening. In reviewing the whole interview, the respondent answers question after question with individual experiences from the sermons. In discussing the sermon that caused change,

The pastor said, one night in prayer, God spoke and said, "I have created you." And I was created in the image of God and by God. When God finished, God said, "I'm pleased." And the Reverend said, "I didn't cry anymore, because I knew that I was created in the image of God." He used that story to tell me that I, too, was created by the same God that created everyone else. Some people may not understand my lifestyle or what I'm about. I hope that they understand that God doesn't judge me, and why should they? I think that God used that story indirectly. Reverend never mentioned anything about homosexuality. Reverend did speak of color, but there's the same issue there when maybe a woman is trying to struggle to get into a job that she can't because she's female. It doesn't have to be spoken directly, but the Spirit can tell you.

Sometimes the reply to a question begins with a plural reference, but when we read it, the individual emphasis becomes clear. In the next example, the question is about how the sermon shapes the congregation. The respondent says the sermon instructs "us," but the focus is on "my" life. "It instructs us. It guides us. Like I said for me personally, it helps me with everyday life. It's like my school about life." Another person reveals the individual listening style in responding to the question: "What do you hope to have happen as a result of listening to the sermon?" The response: "That's amazing that one person can get up there and say enough for a whole congregation and maybe fifty to a hundred people and to be able to touch them, each one."

These five answers were given by a Lutheran, an African Methodist Episcopalian, a Presbyterian, a Disciple, and an Episcopalian (not in that order); two were African American and three were Anglos; three were women and two were men.

Part of the study was aimed at finding out what people think is going on in the congregation *because* of the preaching. Although it is interesting to learn what people believe happens individually, the real focus for this chapter is to uncover the communal sense. Curiously enough, there are people who find it difficult to express a sense of what happens communally from the preaching event. Consider this person from a small town church who was asked what preaching does in the congregation: "I don't know. For me it just brings the Bible to life in a way. The sermon just makes me feel good, because I get something out of it." In an effort to move to the more communal sense, the interviewer asks what would be missing if there were no sermon. "It would just be a big social hour." Then the interviewer directly asks how sermons shape the congregation as a whole or who this church is. Although this is leading the respondent quite a bit, the answer is still quite individually focused: "Yes. I guess as a whole I hope everybody is hearing the same thing I am, and then I can relate to them, because we were all in the same place and getting the same message."

Someone in a large city congregation also had trouble thinking of the effect on the congregation as a whole. In telling what important things are happening, the person could easily discuss their outreach to the community: "We seem to be reaching out into the community more. Our pastor seems to be taking part in community relations and community changes and work for the better. That's very important." Yet when the questions turn to the issue of preaching and what happens when a sermon stirs the emotions of the congregation, the person has trouble answering. "For me? What happens for me when the congregation has been stirred up? Is that what you're saying?" When the interviewer affirms the questions, the respondent says, "Ask that again." The interviewer repeats the question, asking what happens when the emotions of the congregation have been stirred up, adding a question about what happens after worship when their emotions get stirred up. Again the response is a question. "For me?" When the interviewer clarifies that the question is about the congregation, the response is quick. "To the congregation? I wouldn't know what happens to the congregation. I don't know."

There are also people who discuss effects within the congregation, yet the focus is still on the individuals within the congregation. Take these examples: "I believe preaching shapes the congregation in that it helps each individual know from the baby on up to the senior citizen how you're supposed to be functioning in that particular age bracket, how God expects us to relate to life, and life in God." The meaning is that the sermon speaks to each individual who happens to be in the particular listening pool. Another example seems to be moving toward a sense that the individual responses to the sermon may eventually make an impact on the congregation as a whole:

> When the sermon or the preaching is well delivered, and connects with the audience, then it enhances the community

of the church. What I mean by that is that the congregation talks about the particular sermon after the fact. It's made an impact on them. Maybe in some cases it's made a change in an individual's thinking or an individual's actions, and that is a good thing when it connects. When it doesn't connect, it's just another Sunday. That's not to say that every sermon is going to connect with every individual or should it be necessary [that] the pastor try from that standpoint. But the more that individual or that message can connect with its audience, then the more impact it will have in bonding that congregation toward a common goal, whatever that message was trying to achieve.

One final excerpt is rather lengthy, but it gives quite a fine description of the individual faith listener, as well as a quick acknowledgement that there are occasions of communal identity listening. The response begins by addressing the question of what happens at the homily:

I think when a sermon is going well, I don't notice what the rest of the congregation is doing, because I'm so fixated. It's like reading a novel. Even though the writer wrote it for a bunch of people, it's a two-person event. It's also a corporate event, but I think primarily it just happens to be a whole bunch of two-person interactions all happening at the same time.

The interviewer then asks how the homily shapes the congregation.

The thing I find interesting is I have talked to people about the sermon afterwards and gotten totally different things out of it from what they did. I think that's good. I think it means that different people are focusing on the aspects that are most important for them to hear. I feel weird using such religious terminology, but I feel like it's the Holy Spirit kind of helping to make it into whatever they need, hopefully if it's working right. It certainly does kind of affect our vision as a congregation.

After talking about the feeling of one-on-one communication, the interviewer asks what happens when the congregation moves from individual listening to listening as a body, or in the respondent's wording, what is happening in the corporate experience of the congregation.

I'm going to sound like I go to a lot of different churches. I went to a Quaker meeting once. The silence was so palatable it felt like another being in the room. I really felt at that point like we were all engaged together, even though no one was speaking at this point. I would like not to have to get mystical about it, but I think it's…My father would say that it's some kind of mass hypnosis or group mentality here. I think it's probably a lot of people who are emotionally in similar states. I think the reason why it worked with the Reverend who preached the Sunday after September 11th is because we were all concerned about the same thing. That's what all of our minds were on, and I think a lot of people were there to really listen. So probably more than most times, nobody was doing their shopping list in their head. So there was probably more attention given to the preacher, and then I think probably everyone's hearts were more open than usual, too. I think everyone was really vulnerable.

But I think when everyone's paying attention, there is kind of like a vibration that happens. Like Thomas Mann talks about: if you put three termites in a room, like in a little box, they just walk around and do nothing. I'm sorry. Yes, it was Louis Thomas in *Lives of the Cell.* But he didn't say what the number was, but at some point you keep adding a termite and adding a termite. There's a critical mass, and they start building one of their termite towers. Yes. I think people are like that. Jesus says when two or three are gathered, but maybe it's more like three percent. That if you've got a certain number of people really focused, then other people can pick up on that, and then everyone focuses. Then I think it does become a corporate entity. I don't know. I think it doesn't happen very often.

This long quote reveals the listener's typical pew experience to be individual, but acknowledges there are occasions when a corporate identity or corporate listening happens. The number of persons who speak of individual results from listening to sermons is significantly less than the number of those who speak in plural terms. We turn now to the two clusters of responses beyond the individual.

This second group of answers comes from those who do have ideas about sermons speaking to the entire congregation. They understand the sermon as addressing the congregation as an **aggregate of individual listeners**. By this we mean the respondents see the congregation as made up of individual people who all share similar ideas (for instance, about how to live the faith) and take help from the sermon for their own individual lives of faith. We might describe them as kernels of "listener" popcorn who are sharing the same congregational worship pot. When the minister applies the "heat" of the sermon, individuals "pop." They respond to different ideas; they "pop" individually, yet they share the same pot.

Here are four brief responses to questions about how preaching shapes the congregation, which reveal this characteristic of understanding the congregation as an aggregate of individuals. "It kind of gives guidelines to live by. It kind of shows us the way we should go." From a member of another congregation:

> I believe it's supposed to get the congregation going in a similar growth pattern toward the Lord, not toward the pastor but toward the Lord. I guess that's why you have so many different personalities in churches, because you have so many different kinds of sermons. Probably just the growth of the community within itself and where it goes from there.

One person gives an informative response when discussing how the people respond to preaching, which actually reveals a belief about congregational shaping: "Well, I think overall they respond very well. They're friendly. They're doing Christ's work as far as helping one another and talking and maybe expressing some of their problems. I think our pastor's sermon opens them up to feel more at ease to do that." A final brief answer to the question of how preaching shapes the congregation: "Shapes them? Yes. Makes them more aware of problems? Yes. And hopefully influences people in their daily thinking and actions." Although these answers are not very developed, they do show a sense of the sermon performing a shaping function in the congregation. They come from a United Methodist, an Independent Christian, an African Methodist Episcopalian, and a Presbyterian. One person is African American and three are Anglos; two are women and two are men. They represent four different decades of life and spread from 42–82 years of age.

Even from these brief answers we can see the difference between this cluster of responses and the first cluster. These responses understand the sermon as addressed to all the people in the congregation and they expect the sermon to be doing something in the lives of different people. Usually the answer is given in the plural.

If we think back to the first cluster, one person remarked that the sermon was a guide for the congregation, and an individual school of life. In the answers in the second cluster, the guidance for the congregation is primary and the individual comment is missing or minor.

Within this second cluster, there are sub-clusters. Various respondents give *analogies* in describing what role the sermon has in shaping the congregation. They remain clearly in the aggregate of individual listeners cluster. An answer above notes the sermon gets the congregation in a "similar growth pattern." A wife and husband who were interviewed together use different images, but have a similar attitude about communal shaping. One remarks: "Our senior pastor's our leader, and through the sermons sets the tone for the congregation and inspires us and directs us. I don't think there's anything else other than the sermon that can do that. There's never a time when there are that many of us all in one place to hear the same thing, to get the same direction." The spouse agrees, "That's where you get the feeling that you're part of the church community as opposed to a subunit that's doing some specific function…During the sermon, that's pretty much where marching orders are laid out…There may be some disagreement at various points, but for the most part people nod their heads and say, 'Yes. That's probably what we need to do.'" Back to the first speaker, "So, together as a congregation, we have that kind of, 'Well, at least we're doing something good, but we have so much more to do. We've got to go out and do that.' That's another example of kind of pulling us together and giving us a directive." The second speaker adds that the unison repeating of the mission statement each week is uniting: "The fact that everybody says it with the minister, that's kind of, 'Okay, we're all on the same team.'"

A person from a significantly smaller congregation provides another image. "How does it shape the congregation? I think that's one of the roles of leadership is to get everybody focused where that we can coordinate our efforts. In other words, so that we're all stroking in the same direction and not flying off in all different directions."

The fact that various people draw analogies to help explain how they understand the sermon to be shaping the congregation may indicate they cannot articulate exactly what is happening, but they are convinced something is going on in the preaching event that helps shape the congregation.

A more senior respondent from a liturgical congregation first talks about what ministers are doing when they stand up to preach:

> I think they're trying to get an assortment of people out there who differ in what they want…I think what they're trying to do is engage listeners in thinking with them about the significance they draw from the scriptures that form the basis for the liturgy of that given day, to try to engage people in some sort of a joint experience, a dialogue. That would be my idea of what they're trying to do.

Then, in describing what would be missing if there were no homily, this same respondent draws a more involved analogy:

> It's kind of like, What would be missing if you didn't have lectures in the university? Students can come there. "Look, read these books, and you're going to learn this subject." So you go to a lecture, and the lecture might cover much of the ground that's covered in the book, but it's a living person giving voice to an important document, and it should drive home the message in a way that the page alone won't do. You've got a human being who's committed to this.

We would be remiss not to mention that some listeners had a sense that preaching is doing something in congregational formation, but they were at a loss to describe what it is. This example is typical of these answers to the question of preaching shaping the congregation: "I don't know that it does. I think our mission does that. I suppose it does influence, because it's influencing our values." Such listeners can feel something going on, but not name it.

Some other people, who find it difficult to describe what is going on in the listeners or how the congregation is being shaped, find it easier to give *concrete examples* of how the congregation has changed as a result of preaching. Within this sub-cluster, for instance, we find this answer:

> Here's how I can answer that with an example. Our church was not as biblically based before our previous reverend came in. The minister shaped and made this church more of a biblically based church…Now where we are, that foundation has been laid and now we need to work on the musical ministry of this church and match it to the spiritual foundation and scriptural foundation of this church. So I always see these things as being built, like pieces of puzzles being put together.

It's always easy to look back once the pieces are in place, but try to figure that out as you go. Yes, I think…I know that preaching helps that.

Another response shows how preaching is at work in a racially mixed congregation: "I think our current pastor recognizes the fact that we have a very diverse congregation, and Pastor's not afraid to bring race into the sermon and talk about race relations. Here's our church. We're able to congregate together and share thoughts together and be friends together."

These examples of preaching that shapes specific aspects of church life show an understanding of the congregation as an aggregate of individual listeners. That is, the listeners understand they are a part of a congregation of persons, each of whom is also being molded by the preaching.

Another important part of how persons understand what the sermon is doing in the congregation has to do with the *content of the faith.* Within this sub-cluster, preaching is heard as helping individuals in the congregation become more mature in their faith, not individualistically but as members of a single group. Such ideas are shown in an answer that points out the individual gifts that exist in the congregation, which the sermon helps people see; but also the sermon is assisting in shaping the congregation by changing individual behaviors.

> I feel like preaching shapes the congregation in terms of bringing people to the realization of the gifts that God has given us in the body—some preachers and some teachers and so forth. The preacher, giving the word and expounding the word and telling these people to become committed to the word, will shape the congregation to follow Christ and to think in Christ-like ways. I think of a time in my current congregation where many members came to church without Bibles, and we were challenged from the preacher to bring your Bible to study. If the pastor is following Christ, which we feel when the message is from the Lord, it will certainly shape the behavior, and it did shape the behavior in our congregation, because you almost never see a member without a Bible.

A congregant from a different denomination explains a similar idea about the importance of the Bible, but instead of showing how the preaching has encouraged people to bring their Bibles, the respondent stresses the importance of the preacher's knowing how to engage the Bible spiritually and intellectually. In both cases, preaching is believed to bind the congregants to one another in matters of faith.

> I think preaching enhances and kind of backs up what you already know. I think that preaching really holds us together. We have to have good preaching. We have to have intellect along with spiritual. We don't want anyone getting up there talking about the Bible and don't know any more than what their grandmother said. We want someone, when they come out of the Bible, they can still function.

In another sub-cluster we find a number of people who seem pleased that the sermon could be changing the shape of the congregation. For instance: "This is a very conservative congregation. The sermons help people understand a different way of looking at things. Maybe we need to be a little more open. We need to be more accepting of different people, different things, and different ideas." From quite a different perspective, the same desire for change is voiced. "What they need here is a lot of teaching. The word of God is where we gather together, and that's where we meet the Lord and we find out about Him."

Two other respondents indicate a belief that sermons bring about change in the faith of people in the congregation. "I think preaching shapes the congregation. The preaching of our priest is one that encourages people to get connected with God, to have a strong personal relationship with God, and also I think it shapes the congregation into believing that God is the source of all of our supply." The other comment is quite brief. "Preaching motivates us, and it also helps bring us together."

These pages of quotations from respondents who emphasize congregational listening as an aggregate of individuals reveal differences within this one cluster. There are folks who come close to thinking of the congregation in terms of individual faith listeners, although they do give attention to the other individuals in the congregation. Their comments occur in the plural. There are also listeners who believe something happens to the congregants as a group through the sermon experience. They are the ones who refer to the congregation's being on the same page or being bound together or "stroking" toward the same goal. There is another group within this cluster that comes even closer to understanding the community of faith as bound together. In this sub-cluster, we have placed those who speak in *familial terms* or *those who understand a shared denominational character* to be binding them into a *singular identity*. Listen for the family ties (biological and emotional) expressed as key elements in these excerpts, which come from small town and rural settings:

> It depends on the sermon really. It can be very motivating to the congregation. It can be very uplifting. It can connect on a spiritual level. I think it should ultimately always keep your congregation pulling together, not entering something that may separate them. That's happened at our church before where we've had some things happen, and we felt our congregation split. It was very hard to take. I feel like very much the sermon needs to unite, unite the congregation. We are very much a family oriented, very close knit, tight knit congregation. We welcome any type of outsider. We get a lot of visitors, tourists, and things like that. We're very open. We're very honest. We're very warm to outsiders. We're a family more than anything. We care about each other a tremendous amount. We are involved in everyone's families. We know what's going on. If there's a problem, you know you can turn around and make a phone call to two or three people, and someone can be praying for you.

The second quote stresses the biological connection. The listener is responding to a question about what important things the church is involved in and what preaching does.

> One of the important things is how well the church as a whole is like a family. What is amazing about this church is that almost everybody in the congregation is somehow related to each other. So that's sort of interesting. What preaching does for me is it opens my eyes to what life should be like, because I'm a teenager and I've done some stupid things in my past. It kinds of helps me relate, to know that somebody out there does care and loves you.

We also were interested in those occasions when the comments about the congregation were wrapped up in a denominational identity or even an identity as a nondenominational fellowship. Here are two:

> In this church, which is a peace church, we have a lot of sermons that are geared toward the Peace Movement, and I think that plays a rather large role in this particular church and maybe in churches in the Anabaptist tradition in general.

I think that helps to shape the essential feelings of this congregation, not everybody, but I think a good part of this congregation.

The other listener reports:

One of the sermons that was brought up was about...Like last Sunday, "What is the United Methodist?" Through that, John Wesley and through all those groups, our minister used that as a sermon topic and brought in where we originated from and how the divisions split and how we become United Methodist Movement. That happens as a family, then that gives us an identification, a basis, how we identify as the United Methodists instead of another Christian denomination.

The third cluster of answers gathered around the understanding of the sermon as not only addressing individuals but also speaking of **communal identity listeners**. An analogy we might use again is popcorn, but this time we might understand the individuals popped in the bowl together, but then as a congregation there is an additional ingredient added from the sermon (perhaps the infusion of the Holy Spirit), and they become something different together, as when we add caramel to the bowl of popcorn and, although the popcorn retains its substance, they gather into something different together. They become a popcorn ball. The individual is not destroyed, but together they have become something more than a gathering of individuals. Again there is diversity within this cluster. Some folks have a limited understanding of the connection, as if they do not think there is much caramel on the popcorn. Other people, to use another food analogy, treat the bonding within the faith community as almost total, as if they were gelatin crystals on which the boiling water of the Spirit is poured during the sermon. In this case, the individual almost disappears, melted into the communal. One of the interviews quoted above contains comments that indicate knowledge of the difference between an aggregate of individuals and a communal identity. The interviewee who talks about the termites hitting a critical mass and beginning to build a termite tower (from Louis Thomas, *Lives of the Cell*) understands that although the termites remain individuals, they also take on a communal behavior.[1] In the preaching experience, we might say people hit a critical moment and begin to understand themselves as a single unit.

Although the individuals never disappear, there is a communal consciousness that predominates.

Here are some examples of how the respondents articulate this sense of communal identity. "If I like to come to Sunday school and learn God's word, but missed the sermon, I think you would miss out on the oneness. Just like when you're in worship service, the scripture says that the Lord says, 'If there are two or three together in my name, I will be in the midst.'" We notice this is not the only person who quotes this scripture. The termite tower example was used to connect to it, although the major part of that person's answer deals with individual listening. Another person gives a colloquial explanation of the congregational identity, centering on the Bible and communion: "Okay. We call ourselves the Church of the Book and Table, because we do have communion every Sunday. Like the pastor says every Sunday, 'if you're looking for a Bible-preaching church.' I think that gives us our identity as a Bible-preaching church." In briefer words, another person says: "I think preaching provides a clear example of what is important and where this church is going." A fourth listener has more to say about the congregation: "For me, it's a sense of belonging to a spiritual community. It's being on a spiritual journey. I feel that others are making that same journey. I consider it an adventure. I actually enjoy the trip. I enjoy the intellectual aspects of it." The respondent goes on to say that if there were no sermon, the respondent would not attend service. The interviewer then asks about the sermon for the congregation.

> I think it's the central part of the service. I think it pulls us together. It's the only opportunity the preacher has to call the church together–to be the voice of the community, to articulate ideas or thoughts or big feelings that people have, to talk to people when they need it. It tends to be directing you along the path of that spiritual search I was talking about.

For each of these respondents there is a personal benefit from the sermon, but the greater sense is that the sermon is doing something in the congregation as a communal entity. Some people were able to discuss not only the congregational shaping, but also the *perceived intention of the pastor:*

> I'll give our priest a lot of credit over the last couple of years in that the messages are very timely for the congregation. I think that's something the church as a whole misses without

a sermon. It's the ability for a minister to address what they consider to be the issues with the church. I think it kind of helps shape and mold the church, because a lot of the sermons help the congregation.

Another respondent finds it easier to give examples:

At a previous church, we rearranged the whole worship space and made it more open and pulled the pulpit down and made it much more accessible to the people. There was a lot of talk across different sermons about what we're trying to accomplish with our physical space, which then is consistent with these kinds of themes that are in our religious teachings. I think that was very useful. It was helpful for people. I think it really helped to kind of bring people together and make them think differently about space.

Another person who mentions examples of sermons shaping and changing the congregation remembers several series of sermons, one of which was preached ten years earlier. Although the members are thought of as individuals, the changes are understood as happening to the congregation:

I think the preaching shapes our congregation because it unifies us on many different topics as far as our belief systems and our steps of faith and also as far as what things are important to us, as far as goals for the Christian life and where our congregation is moving towards. Our pastor preached a series about godly men, and it really caused quite a difference in the men of the church as far as becoming more involved in every area of the church, especially outreach.

In a final representative quote from this cluster, notice the communal atmosphere in the understanding of what is going on *as preaching occurs:*

I think it probably challenges you more than any other element does. I think we also look at preaching to bring us back to the Bible. I think that you can come for the special things, and you can come for the service projects, and you feel good about doing those, but something has to connect it to why you're doing it. I think the sermon is generally the glue that does that. I think it's a cumulative process week after week after week.

The respondent then gives an example of how that "glue" has been activated in the congregational life:

> This is a good example. We did just complete a capital campaign that I was involved in, and part of the design of that for the last four weeks has been that the services and the sermon go to [the idea that] someone built this church for you with the idea that this congregation needed to go on. It exists [today], because somebody did that seventy years ago. Now we need to do that so that the work of this church can go forward from here on out. So yes, there are some definite messages that were woven into the sermon for the last few weeks. We received pledges from the oldest of the congregation, who won't be here much longer to see those things happen, but they really felt strongly that this was the place that had served them well. And we heard it from the kids who could [have] just as easily said, "Don't bother me. Let me play my video games and let me spend my money on fast food."

These examples of communal identity listeners reflect a diversity in how they express their ideas, yet the communal aspect of their listening is striking, especially their recognition of the preachers' intentions and the congregation's reception of those ideas.

### Reflections and Insights on How Preaching Shapes Community

We had some ideas of different ways people might understand the shared hearing of sermons and how they might understand that as affecting the shape of their congregation. Some of our predispositions came from scholars who had written about various ways to view the church. For instance, at twenty-one years of age, Dietrich Bonhoeffer, in *The Communion of Saints: A Dogmatic Inquiry into the Sociology of the Church,*[2] presented a threefold typology that parallels what was discussed above. He taught that we can view the community of the church as a "multiplicity of spirits," where the Holy Spirit approaches persons in their individuality (what Bonhoeffer called "singularity"). The second type is the "community of spirit," the interconnectedness of the individuals in the congregation, who have their being in one another. The individual never disappears, but there is a mutuality, a structure of connection that has its base in love. Third, there is a "spiritual unity of the church–the collective person."[3] It is not too difficult to see that the multiplicity of spirits would be the individual faith listeners. The community of spirit would be the aggregate of individual listeners. And the spiritual unity or collective person is the communal identity listeners.

Our analysis revealed a significant majority of persons answering the question of preaching's shaping the congregation with the sense of listening as an aggregate of individuals (about 60 percent). Almost 30 percent of the respondents, however, spoke in individual terms. Even when asked about what was happening in the congregation, they responded with what preaching was doing in their own lives.

Because we were interested in the relation between the intention of the preacher in shaping the congregation through the sermon, and what actually happens in the sanctuary on Sunday mornings, we spent time looking at how the preachers answered those questions, too. What did preachers think should shape the faith of the listeners? We wondered if the clergy responses would reveal a similar three-cluster breakdown. Most often the preachers' comments were in response to: "What do you hope will happen to the congregation as a result of their listening to the sermon?" But sometimes we also found clues as they discussed how preaching fits into their ministry or some other question. We found they did, in fact, fall into the same three clusters.

Those fitting in the first cluster, the **individual faith listeners**, were the fewest in number. This pastor claims, "If a sermon doesn't challenge the listener to do something as a result of hearing it, then I don't really think that's been a sermon. If the sermon is on helping the least of them, then I think some concrete example should be shared with how we can help the least of them." Later in that same interview, the preacher gave an example of a sermon preached on helping children in our society who need love and direction. The appeal was for individuals to get into a relationship with individual children. Another pastor holds a similar idea, appealing to individual listening, yet expects these individuals to encourage and hold each other accountable:

> I would hope that preaching would provide a good guide for life and for the way that they treat one another, for the way they worship God, a deeper worshiping concept of God; that it would provide a concept of their needing to tithe or to give of their means back to God for the many blessings that God has given; for them to take the religious concepts

they learn in church, and in studying the word, into the workplace and into their own family lives, so that it becomes then a way of life for them.

Certainly these are important aspects of the preaching event. The words of the sermon go into individual ears and they need to be understood as meaning something in individual lives. It is no wonder, however, that some people, listening to preachers who are addressing their sermons most often to individual faith listeners, would tend to hear the sermon individually. Preachers in this cluster span the denominational range from nondenominational to liturgical, both men and women, both African American and Anglo (although comparatively, we found slightly more African American preachers speaking individually).

Another group of ministers seems to focus on an additional function of what the sermon is doing in the congregation: namely, one in which persons listen both for individual direction and for assistance as members of the congregation. The sermon tells them how to live as members of the same congregation (**an aggregate of individuals**). This first example seems to be addressing persons as individuals, but also wants to encourage a congregational model formed in part through the preaching:

> Usually the only education the less active members get is the sermon. We have made a special conscientious effort to challenge people thinking that their obligation is simply to show up and worship as spectators. We are trying to engage in a process of renewal, which hopefully will lead to the transformation of many lives where people are closing the gap between what they say they believe and actually what they act out in their daily lives...Christianity is not rocket science. We try and go back and say, "This is how you can make a difference in this culture." We're trying to get people to be aware that to be a Christian is not to sell out to cultural values.

Another pastor in this cluster sees both the individual and the congregational aspects of the sermon: "I guess my approach to ministry is that we are pilgrims together on this journey, and I like to invite people in the congregation to join me in that journey...I have no doubt that the individual faith is connected or conveyed in the work and ministry of the church...I think just as we have personalities, churches have personalities and growth stages, or don't grow." Another example is from a priest who has a congregational sense of those who listen, yet closes with a desire for people, individuals apparently, to make their own decisions:

> Over the years, I've learned that probably preaching is the most important thing I do, because it impacts the most people with my ministry. From preaching, I hope that you'll end up with an educated people of faith that struggle with the issues of faith and that the process helps to stimulate and challenge and enhance that. I want them to disagree with me. In the end I want them to form their own conclusion about what I've said, about the scripture passage, and about the theme.

This priest speaks of people as a group, but there is still a sense of the change happening individual by individual.

Another minister acknowledges the individuals of the congregation, many of whom may not know each other, yet the direction of the sermon is to point the way, show the shape of the congregation:

> I think the biggest thing is that preaching reminds people of the main thing. What the main thing is…the essential story of the gospel, sent for humanity, that has been reached by a loving God, using the cross and the blood shed on the cross to pay the penalty for sin as the way to be forgiven, saved, and changed. That's the critical role of preaching here, especially with all the different worship services that obviously many people don't know lots of other people. So, what do we have in common? We share the gospel. To a certain extent, too, it not only reminds them, but it paints a vision of where the gospel is leading us as a congregation. So, to that extent, I'm really a cheerleader kind of person. I'm a vision painter again and again and again, pointing, "Here's where the gospel is leading us."

Each of these ministers has the understanding that something is going on in the body of believers when the sermon is preached. They address not only individuals, but a people being shaped into a congregation. This group includes high church, free church, and mainstream congregations; large urban church and small rural fellowship; seminary educated and license schooled; men and women; African American and Anglo. This was the largest of the three clusters of preachers.

The final cluster of ministers is smaller. These identified more clearly an understanding that, in addition to the individual, in addition to the congregation as an aggregate of individuals, the sermon was shaping the congregation into a **communal identity listener.**[4] Some of these persons use the distinguishing key of referring to the congregation in the singular. For instance, this one uses both the singular and plural designations. "I think preaching is a significant part of the worship, which reminds us every week when we gather that we are not individuals with an individual faith, but we are part of a covenant community. We are part of a chosen people, and also that we are the body of Christ."

Another minister reveals the strongest sense of communal identity when giving an example of a sermon preached some time ago. In the preaching, the gathered individuals become a single unit, what Bonhoeffer called the spiritual unity of the church—a collective person. "I hear entertainers talking about how there are certain concerts they give, and then there's a point where you and the audience become one. You're no longer preaching to them or entertaining them or singing to them or speaking to them. You all are now doing whatever you're doing together. That's what happened with this sermon." This spiritual connectedness that happened in that one sermon can be seen as the most vivid example in this cluster. In that moment, the identity of the congregation was as a single unit, no longer a gathering of individuals. We suspect that from such experiences and from sermons preached that address that type of congregational identity, the congregation understands itself across the clusters. That is, the same persons hear the sermon as individual faith listeners at times, as an aggregate of individual listeners at times, as a congregation at times, and on rare occasions as a collective person or spiritual unit. We suspect that preachers who do not preach to the congregation with a sense of community or communal identity will be less likely to experience such moments of connectedness, or if they do experience them they will be less likely to use them to help shape the congregational identity.

Here is one final example of a preacher who addresses the congregation as communal identity listeners:

Initially when I began preaching on a regular basis, I guess I had as one primary goal: just not to bore people, because I had been bored a lot of times myself. Now, for me, the primary goal is for people to be spiritually transformed by

encountering God for themselves...By spiritual transformation,
I mean transformation that is really going to change the way
people live—not just make them more active in the church
or something like that. I want people to live a life that is
ethically transformed, where one's attitude toward life is
changed to one of gratitude and joy. I want wholeness for
people and a wholeness that's going to bring wholeness to
the rest of society. So, it's pretty big. Without the sermon
you do not have a group of people being nurtured in a shared
vision of the Christian experience. It's extremely important
for a congregation to become a congregation, to be connected
to each other, to start sharing some of the same images and
sharing some of the same experiences of truth, because it's
together as a congregation that we can present an alternative
to society, and we can help to transform society. We don't
transform society very well all one on one, but a group, a
community, can help to transform the community in which
it is in. It is through community that we continue to believe.
The Christian faith is always one generation away from
extinction. We need congregations to nurture that faith. The
sermon really plays a crucial role in keeping a congregation
focused, in giving it a focal point, giving it an identity.

These three different clusters display not only different ways
preachers direct their sermons; we believe they reveal that the
preachers expect different results from their preaching. So we want
to add our voices to those who are encouraging a more communal
understanding of the faith. Of course, we come to the faith one by
one, that is, each person must make a commitment to live the
Christian life. However, just as no one learns the faith except from
someone else, so must we recognize the limitations of viewing the
faith in individual terms alone. Over 150 years ago, Alexis de
Tocqueville[5] warned of the hazards of individualism threatening
North American society. Robert Bellah, et al., warned of individualism
exhibited in "Sheila-ism."[6] We believe there are significant limitations
to preaching and listening to sermons from an individual perspective
alone. Perhaps the most significant limitation consists in its divergence
from its source. We believe Christian preaching continues the
preaching of Jesus Christ, whose directives and challenges were most
often addressed in the plural (although the English use of "you" for
both the singular and the plural cloaks this).[7] If our preaching is to

be faithful, it needs to acknowledge not only the individual, but also the communal nature of the church, which is referred to as the body of Christ (not as the *bodies* of Christ).

Although there are correlations between pastors who speak more communally and congregants who fall into the more communal clusters, the correlation seems anecdotal, rather than causative. That is, we are not sure whether the preaching is in fact shaping the congregants directly, or whether they were already more communal listeners and they were attracted to a preacher who spoke communally. What is clear is that congregants often share the pastor's ideas about the community, but again this is not conclusively seen as a direct correlation. Not surprisingly, there are persons representing each cluster in congregations where the pastor spoke more communally. We understand this to be a result of the pastors' inclusion of the individual aspects of the faith in sermons, as well as the communal. However, it is rarer for a congregant to have the more communal understanding when the pastor focuses almost exclusively on the personal aspects of the faith. Again, we are not sure if this is the sermon's formative power or the pastor's style attracting a more limited type of listener.

One of the connections we were eager to investigate was, on those occasions when respondents were aware that something communal could happen in the congregation, how did it happen? That is, did they report a sermon with a pastor's personal story, or was there a sermon describing who we are in the faith, or did they learn the concept elsewhere (as with the person who reads *Lives of the Cell*)? What do the pastor interviews report? Do the preachers give a clue in their conversation about scripture (for instance, are they intentional about clarifying the communal "you-all" instead of the ambiguous English "you")? Sadly, answers to many of these questions are practically impossible to determine. However, we did notice communal experiences around significant shared events. For instance, one congregant shared in depth a congregational experience from the Sunday morning after the shootings in Columbine. Their community had a similar episode during the same time frame, so everyone was focused on that emotional tragedy. However, the pastor did not preach that morning. Sensing the atmosphere in the sanctuary, the minister put down the sermon manuscript and opened the sermon time to personal reflection by congregants. In that moment of shared tragedy and uncertainty, the congregants in effect preached to one another. The minister had a brief closing meditation that reflected the appropriateness of the voice of the congregation being lifted communally before God.

## A Word to Preachers

All four of the writers of this book have served churches. We would agree with many of the pastors we interviewed who claim that preaching is the most important thing they do all week, for in that preaching moment something is happening to who we are as individuals and as a community of faith. So, we want to encourage you to take the time you need to prepare your sermons, and to consider what you want the sermon to do in the congregation. Although we are not able to say exactly what the sermon is doing within the community of faith, we are convinced that week by week, you are helping to shape the people with whom you minister. We encourage you to join with your leadership in determining what shape you believe God is calling your congregation to grow into. Miroslav Volf reminds us that to say, "We are the church," is not merely claiming that we meet as a group to worship occasionally or that we are involved in common mission projects. "Rather, it means basically, 'Each of us in his or her own being is qualified by others.'"[8] In the church, we find our identity intimately interrelated with that of the other members. Preaching helps us know who we are together.

One respondent gives quite an interesting concrete example of what preaching does in shaping the congregation:

> The minister taught to shape us and help us to engage the world in a different way. One example I could think of in particular was when the events happened on September 11. The next Sunday our minister called us to see ourselves as primarily Christian over patriotic things we might be feeling and dealing with at the time and just how to go about that. I saw there was a lot of pulling together and trying to figure out things at this time. How do we respond to this? It went on for three weeks in a row that way, still trying to find a response. Then, in the end, the minister ended up allowing a layperson to also speak about struggling with it. I think that was all the congregation trying to figure out how we sit in the world right now at this time and how we should think about our responses to the events.

Not only were the sermons during that period giving the members information about how to be Christians in a confusing world, but the minister also modeled the importance of taking time to come to terms with social crises and the necessity of allowing other voices to be heard. The modeling was every bit as helpful in shaping the congregation as the content of the sermons those three or four weeks. The congregant's response indicates that teaching had been successful.

In 1988, David Buttrick proposed this catchword: "As the church preaches, so the church believes," claiming: "For obviously preaching shapes our common faith."[9] If in fact preaching is shaping our common faith, it is no wonder ministers have been heard to say that preaching is the most important thing they do. One of the pastors we interviewed commented, "I live to preach." Here is a person who understands the importance of preaching for a vital congregational life of faith. Preaching "forms a community's shared way of knowing," says Susan Bond. "We do, through preaching, structure a communally shared understanding of dynamic faith that is related to the tradition, to the daily life of decision making of believers, and to the ethical projects of the church."[10]

With these thoughts in mind, we invite preachers to ask themselves: What do you think your preaching is doing in shaping who your congregants are becoming as individuals? And what do you think preaching is doing in your congregation communally? We invite you to consider the shape you believe God may be calling your congregation into, and what role preaching may have in manifesting that shape.

# CHAPTER 8

# What about God?

It seems odd to talk about God as just another item in the list of "topics" discussed in the interviews, yet, in some ways, looking at what the interviewees say about how God relates to preaching brings an important focus to the entire project, appropriately left toward the end of our presentation. In analyzing data for this chapter, we consider most carefully the congregants' answers to the direct question, "What do you think God is doing during preaching?" We also note comments made in other places in the interviews, for instance in answer to the question, "What do you most want to hear about God in the sermon?" Answers to these questions often include ingredients of what persons understand God is trying to communicate to them personally. Sometimes answers to these two questions reveal differing, even inconsistent, ideas. In addition, we look at places where congregants discuss other matters, yet make references to God's participation (or lack thereof) in the preaching event.

### What These Listeners Say about How God
### Relates to Preaching

The comments about God's participation in the sermon fall into two clear categories. Some people understand God to be **active** during preaching, while many other people believe God is **passive** during the sermon. There are four general clusters of ideas around the belief that God is active. There are those who believe **God acts**

**in providing the specific message**; there are others who believe **God is active in inspiring the construction of the sermon**; there are those who focus on **God as active in assisting the listeners**; and those who believe **God is active in actually performing tasks in the congregation**.

In the other category, there are two general clusters of ideas around the belief that God is essentially passive during preaching. Of those who see God as passive, there are those who focus on the belief that **God is present in worship** and there are those who believe **God has some private, divine response to the sermon**.

In addition to the clusters of ideas around God's being active or passive, a few persons believe God is either disconnected from worship, or that God is the same in worship as elsewhere. We are not calling these few answers a cluster in themselves. We do, however, list a seventh cluster composed of those who **do not know how to answer the question fully**. These interesting final few respondents express an uncertainty about answering the question about what God is doing, although they usually have some ideas about God that they do express. We are not sure whether they find it difficult to discuss theological claims or whether the consideration of God's participation in the sermon is new ground for them.

We turn now to clusters of answers about the activity of God in the sermonic event. The largest group clusters around the idea that the sermon is from God in a direct way. That is, they believe **God acts in providing the specific message**. The sermon is composed of words that are a direct message from God. Consider this response, which reveals a typical sense that God is speaking in the sermon:

> Well, I guess what I think God's doing is providing a way for each individual in the congregation to hear the message, that they can hear whatever is being presented. The preacher's got a certain, like, one-size-fits-all. So I think God has provided the guidance to that preacher during the week, who then takes that whisper, and tries to have something in that message for what everybody is hearing. If it's a hundred people, and people are going to think different things, maybe twenty of them take one thing away, and five of them take another thing away, and one of them will take something else away.

Those who believe God is speaking through the sermon are not univocal in how they understand that speech. Some, as the person above, believe that God speaks what each person needs to hear. Another respondent seems to believe that God speaks a more general message to the preacher, who then passes it whole to the congregation: "The pastor always says how, while sitting at home, God brings the words. I'm assuming the preacher standing in the pulpit is giving me exactly what was gotten from God. I don't know how pastors do it, because I haven't had to teach it, but if the preacher says it comes from God, to the preacher, to us, and then I have to accept that."

Although this group of persons who believe God speaks through the sermon is the largest cluster, they do not all agree that what they hear is "word of God." Some are brief. "Ideally, what you will hear is a word from God." Another speaks more elaborately, indicating what seems to be more a stirring, a more stimulating, and not so by a word from God but word *of* God:

> Well, I think certainly for a sermon to be effective, God needs to be present in that time. The Spirit of God needs to be present in that room, preparing receptive minds, preparing the minister, making a minister perhaps aware that this is not a show. This is not a theatrical presentation. This is relaying a message from God to the parishioners. I think that's a time of preparation, a time of planting, of strengthening, of opening hearts, opening eyes, opening minds, opening ears to be receptive to God's word.

Another type of answer within this same cluster comes from people who focus more on the minister, who is used by God to pronounce the message. For instance, one response asserts: "As all Christians do, your concern is, 'Is what the pastor saying what God is asking to be said?' instead of taking something on the preacher's own and doing it without God." Another person articulates that God uses the minister, but the actual person of the minister is not important: "When I come in, I know that my God is going to speak to me. Regardless of who is up there [in the pulpit], I think that when the word is delivered, it's not necessarily the messenger; it's the messenger in obedience to being used by God."

The word coming through the willingness of the minister is crucial in many of these answers.

> I think God speaks through the minister in a lot of instances. Most ministers, a lot of times they'll get up, they may change

their sermon. They may sometimes even have a written sermon, and they won't even do that sermon. Something fills them, and it's a word that they feel needs to be spoken at that time. Something comes over them that they need to speak a different word at that time. I think that's what God does, brings the message through a mortal. God's with the preacher bringing the message, and speaks to us through the sermon from the person of the minister.

In the very bluntest terms, one final respondent notes God's total authorship of the sermon. "I think that God has already set the sermon for this person to preach."

Closely related to this first cluster of those who believe God is active in the sermon are those who believe **God is active in inspiring the construction of the sermon**. That is, there are those who believe God is giving assistance, but not giving the full message directly: "I think that God is speaking to us in a number of different ways. I don't think God is necessarily speaking through the minister, or in a way. I think God informs and works through the minister in some ways, but I don't take every word that comes out of the minister's mouth as the word of God, as an oracle." These members often respond with comments indicating an understanding of God's participation, especially in the work of sermon preparation, but not directly providing the specific words. God is active inspiring or prompting the work of the minister, in the study as well as in the pulpit.

Respondents in this cluster regard the communication with God as general inspiration, rather than a word-for-word message. The preacher is esteemed for being filled with the Spirit or being closely connected to God. This relationship allows the preacher to address the congregation with a fitting and spiritual message, which is not thought of as a dictation from on high. The preacher's energy in the pulpit is one key for recognizing that God has been active in inspiring the sermon. One person says as much in affirming that God is involved in the sermon: "I would think so, because God's given the preacher the inspiration. I'm thinking you can pretty much tell from the enthusiasm and the confidence that the preacher has in the subject."

One final quotation shows agreement with those who say God is active in inspiring the sermon, yet believe the preacher does not receive a fixed message: "God doesn't come down and say, 'Now preach this sermon today,' but God'll help the minister see what really needs to be done."

Some persons' responses indicate they believe God is active inspiring the preacher, but these respondents also sense God's presence in the listening. This moves us into the third cluster, composed of those who believe **God is active in assisting listeners**. Note this response, which echoes both the inspiration of God in the preparation and the activating presence of God in the listening:

> Oh, God's ever-present. The Holy Spirit is always there, and I believe as the Spirit goes around, we all hear things. My experience is we hear things differently, and that's why the word is so alive, because what I need to hear and what they need to hear is different, but it comes from the same sermon, which is the Holy Spirit's job. That's what the Spirit does through the whole thing is guiding the minister and guiding and helping us to interpret.

Another person makes a similar claim: "First of all, God has to inspire, teach, illuminate, fire up the preacher. Then the Spirit does the same with us." There are several responses in this cluster that focus just on the listener: "Sometimes God opens my heart to certain things that [relate] to me like what I do outside of church. God makes me pay close attention to certain things in the Bible that warn you about certain things." "I think that the Holy Spirit of God, specifically, is working in people's hearts and minds if they're intently listening to the sermon. That if they're open as fallow ground, as our pastor says, that the Spirit is working up in them, issues or things, bringing things to their remembrance." "I think God's clearing my mind and opening my ears that I would hear the word that it is interpreted by the priest in the sermon. That I take what I've heard and internalize it and try to live it, be responsible." "What do I think God is doing? I think actually opening up my heart and my mind to receive the word." Clearly, quite a few persons believe God is at work not only in the pastor's study and in the pulpit but in the hearts and minds of those sitting in the pews. These persons span quite a range. Four are from Anglo congregations ranging from high liturgical to nondenominational, free church; two are from African American congregations—one mainline, one free church. Three persons are women; three are men. Clearly the belief that God is doing something in the congregation during preaching is present in diverse congregations. Several people draw complex analogies when discussing what God is about during the preaching event. One person likens it to a radio system:

> To me God is…The scripture is just like the radio waves, but you have to have a transmitter and a receiver. God is the transmitter, and God is the receiver. You always have radio waves. The scriptures are always there. It's a static thing until God inspires. God is on both ends. Otherwise, the scripture is just like any other anthology. The word is central, but without God the transmitter and then each individual having the Holy Spirit to be the receiver, it's meaningless. It's just static.

The fourth cluster around God's active participation in the congregation consists of those who believe **God is active in actually performing tasks in the congregation**. We include in this cluster answers that indicate a divine presence, for instance **shaping the response of the congregation** or **changing someone's understanding of the faith**. Again, the diversity of persons indicating God is active within the congregation during the preaching is quite significant. Of special interest is the noticeable theological range evident within these four answers. From an urban congregant: "I think God is drawing. I think God is purging. I think God is directing. I think God is chasing us. I think God is literally saving souls and changing lives." A less specific answer comes from a rural setting: "God's moving and waiting to touch and be with whoever is open to receive the divine presence." A lengthier answer from another urban congregant of a different ethnicity continues the diversity:

> In our church I think God is with us, dwelling in each one of our hearts provided that we have each of us accepted God's presence. It says in the Bible that, "Where two or three are gathered in my name, there am I." I think that God goes before us, walks beside us…I think in some ways, God just moves among us and in that way blesses us. I know that happens when we are in congregation and when we are in church together; I know it happens because I leave feeling a different person. I leave with a different mindset and a different heart set, and I'm a different person.

This final comment from a congregant in a smaller city shows yet another position:

I think God is molding people for what's to come basically. There are going to be some big changes coming. Some people, it's scary to think they might get lost in all the stuff that's going to be going on, because your focus is in the wrong spot, in the wrong place. Just I think in the sermon God's trying to prepare you, talking to you, "Make sure you know me, because [of] the things that are going to be going on."

These differing answers, indicating God is actively performing tasks in the congregation, come from a United Methodist, a Disciple, an African Methodist Episcopalian, and a Mennonite.

A significant number of respondents claim God is active during the giving of the sermon. However, there are persons who understand God's role in the sermon as a passive one. About one third of the persons interviewed use passive descriptions of God's participation in the sermon. As noted above, the passive responses may be clustered into two types: those who stress **God is present in worship** and those who claim **God has some private divine response to the sermon.** These are clusters five and six respectively.

As we turn to those who understand God's role in preaching to be essentially a passive one, we look at the fifth cluster, those who understand that **God is present in worship**. Most often respondents use terms of divine observation rather than participation in this cluster. They speak of God's listening or watching as humanity worships. Several short replies demonstrate the idea. "I think that God is like us in that if the sermon doesn't engage, God's not listening. And if it is an engaging sermon, I think God's listening." "What is God doing? I think God's there. I think God's listening." "I guess I think probably the old cliché of: God's taking care of us, watching over us, and wanting us to understand and do what is right." "I would think God is pretty pleased watching the congregation down there gathering and knowing that they want to hear stories about God and want to hear the word."

One final example of an answer in this fifth cluster shows another developed analogy. When asked what the priest does when preaching, this person responds, "Sweating." Then when asked what God is doing, the analogy is spelled out:

My first impulse was to say I think God is…I think God might be…It's a series of two-person communications. God might be the telephone wire in between. It's like the two cans with the string, because I think there's a piece of God inside one person and a piece of God inside the other. Then God is the connection as well. But I was also thinking, I wonder if God listens, like just as another member of the congregation without doing anything. I think God must.

These final words clarify the understanding that God is passive in the preaching event, one who is listening "just like another member of the congregation without doing anything."

The sixth cluster is small, composed of only a handful of answers showing **God has some private divine response to the sermon**. Most often people report that response as laughing (five responses), although a few limit it to smiling (two responses). These are typical of this cluster: "God might be laughing at us, thinking, 'Boy, they sure are silly down there.' God might think 'They just don't get it.'" Or: "Sometimes I think God really must have a wonderful sense of humor and must really get quite a charge out of some of these sermons." Or, "I think God's smiling." Or, "What is God doing in the sermon? Well, I don't know. Maybe laughing at us and thinking, 'Why aren't you listening? Why is your mind wandering?'" It may not come as a surprise that these answers cross ethnic, age, and denominational lines, although only one male answers that God laughs. Several of the respondents, after positing a divine chuckle, go on to suppose God's presence in additional ways, such as inspiring the preacher or guiding the congregation's listening (thus including their responses in the clusters claiming God is active).

There are more answers that cross boundaries from cluster to cluster, indicating that persons may understand God to be present in one way during the writing of the sermon and present in another way in the congregation during the listening. For instance, this response fits into clusters two and three: "God is working through the pastor and working on us as we listen, taking it in, holding it. Probably most of us come at a time where we're opened and ready to hear."

Another small group of answers clustered around a sense of **not knowing how to answer the question fully**. This seventh cluster has an interesting collection of non-answers. For instance, one person has trouble articulating an answer because of a personal God concept that is too large. "I don't know that God is doing anything. I guess my view of God is greater than God doing something. I feel like if I say, 'Well, God is listening to this sermon and God is listening to me,' then I'm putting God in a little box and making the Divine too

small. I really think that. My view of God is so, so very big. I can't
fathom." Another person has trouble shaping an answer about what
God is doing in the sermon because of a God concept that is limited:
"The concept of omnipotence is, frankly, one I can't relate to. I
realize that the Bible says that God is everywhere all the time, always
has been. There is no beginning; there is no end. Quite frankly,
that's hard for me to grasp or hold up." A third person merely admits
ignorance of God's role in the sermon. It is obvious from the response
that this interview took place two weeks after the September 11,
2001, attacks and the respondent's theology has been significantly
shaken by those events.

> None of us knows where God is during the sermon. This is
> part of my theology. This is where I differ theologically from
> other people who sit in a Christian church on Sunday
> morning. My concept and my idea of God is probably not
> where they are. So to answer that question, I don't know
> where God is. I don't know what God does. I don't know
> what action God plays within the world. I have a lot of
> questions about that. I think the past two weeks have
> reaffirmed those doubts that I have about who God is and
> what God does and how God acts. Not saying that I do not
> believe in God, but I'm talking about God in action; where
> God participates. So to answer your question, I have no idea
> where God is in the sermon, what God's doing.

There are also respondents who merely find it difficult to answer
the question. This person, for instance, stops and starts with various
attempts: "Well, hmm. I would hope that maybe the minister has
talked with God about what to say. I don't know. I'm not sure how
to answer that. Well, what is God trying to do with the sermon?" It
seems to us that some people's answers indicate they have perhaps
not often thought about what God's role is in relation to the sermon.
"Frankly, I have no idea. I would assume God is simply waiting and
listening for the sermon, but I hadn't really thought about it." Or,
"God might be thinking about the water bill during the sermon. I
don't know. I hope God's present during most of them. I hope
listening. Other than that, I don't really know."

A number of answers do not fit neatly into these seven clusters.
Two persons respond that God does during worship what God does
all the time. "Oh, I don't know that God...This is me talking, Heresy
101. I don't know that God is doing anything during the sermon that

God's not doing all the time." This person goes on to clarify the belief that God is always using others to communicate a message, a sermon, throughout the week. The second person's ideas are similar:

> I have a very expansive view of God. I sort of think God is everywhere, in every human being, in my children. So I don't think that it's that different in church. It's just that it's a time to be quiet and engage in your thoughts and feelings and behaviors, at least once a week if you can't do it any other time, and that reminds you as you set about your new week how to be more inclusive and to think more about those issues. For me it's not God is here, and God is nowhere else or that kind of thing. It's much more about taking some time out in a busy life to really think about what matters and to feel more connected to God than you might in a normal day.

There are an additional two persons who seem not to fall into a cluster. One claims God might not do anything during the sermon and the other claims God might not need to be present. "I'm not sure God's doing anything, to be truthful. I'm not so sure God interacts on a daily basis with people. I'm kind of changing my idea of what it is that God is, and I don't think he's an old man sitting up in the sky some place, watching every move we make. I think it's a spirit, a feeling that moves through people." This person goes on to admit that this spirit is present in the congregation, concluding, "I think the Spirit at that point kind of moves through people, at least encourages you to listen and think." The other person's response claims God may be somewhere else on Sunday morning, because the church people are doing what they are supposed to do. "God knows things are under control in that worship service, because God's seen us work, and knows we're not going to mess up. God's probably somewhere in some other place, talking to guys in the subway or something, maybe trying to move them in some certain way." These answers come from persons in mainstream congregations.

From this diverse body of information about what laity believe God is doing in the sermon, it makes sense to take a brief look at how their preachers respond to a similar question. In reviewing the two dozen clergy responses we collected, we were first struck by the narrower span these answers have and the fact that preachers seem to respond easier (and longer) than laity. Almost all the preachers in one way or another say one of three things: It is **God speaking in** the sermon; **God is doing something between the words the preacher speaks and the listener**; and **God brings results from the sermon**. An example or two of each should suffice.

Of those who claim it is **God speaking in the sermon**, there is rarely a mention of the preacher doing anything at all. For instance, these excerpts from longer answers: "I don't know. I actually don't have any control over it. It's completely in God's hands"; and "I think that God is speaking to the people through the sermon. Not only speaking to the people, but also speaks to me." One minister was quite explicit.

> I think that God is speaking in the sermon. Otherwise, I'd shut up and get someone else up there, or we're just not going to do this thing. But I think God is speaking through the message, and this is a credit to God, not to me. Because many times I've stepped down from the pulpit area, and I pray, okay God, you fix that, because that wasn't very good. Then I will have someone say this was the best sermon that you've ever preached. I'm like, really? It must have been a God thing.

Those who explain **God's** participation in the sermon as **doing something between the words the preacher speaks and the listener** voice some variations, but they express the idea that God is taking the words of the preacher and "translating" them into what the listener needs to hear. God is intervening between the speaking and the hearing. One person puts it quite simply: "I pray that God takes the words I say and makes them into words that people need to hear." Another response is more developed:

> In the sermon, God is active. How active? Well, I think God is allowing or refining, if you will, the message to reach the ears and minds of the members who have come to hear it. I can give you an example of that. I said it's odd that we have fifty, sixty, eighty, a hundred people here for worship, and they all hear the same message, but they all walk away with a certain different response to that message. That's what God is doing. God is refining that message.

The final cluster from the pastors is composed of those who claim **God brings results from the sermon**. The responses usually claim the Spirit causes transformation or God is actually doing something in the lives of the congregants. These are typical: "What is God doing in the sermon? I think God is inviting people to live, to be more themselves, to be faithful, to be more genuine, to not apologize about being themselves," and, "Through the sermon, God's working on people's hearts, challenging them in areas that they have maybe not thought about. For some mature Christians, God's encouraging them because they're doing the right things. They're doing what God has said." One pastor goes into detail about how the congregation has changed over the past several years, becoming more lively and participatory in worship. Part of the transformation is credited to the Holy Spirit at work during the sermon and the rest of worship.

Each of these three pastor-clusters have more than a half dozen respondents. In addition to these three areas, some ministers discuss God's significant participation in the preparation process; some mention how God uses the preacher (as opposed to only the preacher's words). Several ministers mention God's role each step of the way—from first reading the scripture, through the study and writing, to the preaching and the results in the congregation. However, only one preacher specifically mentions God's participation in opening up the hearts or minds of the laity before worship.

## Insights and Reflections on God's Relationship to Preaching

Most members from the various congregations display a belief that God has some relationship to the sermon. They also exhibit a strong sense that God's participation is important. Although they may not be in exact agreement or use identical words, they have similar understandings that God is present during worship, that God's Spirit is involved in the preaching and, they hope, the hearing. Their language differs—for example, when some persons refer to the Holy Spirit's moving among the worshipers, while others refer to God's being present—yet we sense a basic agreement (with some few, but significant, exceptions) that God is attentive in worship, although some (as noted above) do not express God's presence as an active force in worship.

When we divided interview materials for analysis according to topics, we discovered that while there were over one hundred fifty pages of comments about the listeners' relationships with pastors, there were fewer than seventy-five pages about God. Some of the discrepancy we can attribute to the questions asked. We asked only two direct questions about God (noted at the beginning of this

chapter); we asked three questions about relationship with the pastor
("Can you tell us about a pastor who was also a good preacher?
What did you like about that person?" [asked as one question], "Can
you tell me about preachers you have had through the years?" and
"Do you think how you feel about the pastor affects your ability to
listen to the sermon?").[1] However, although other questions were
answered with information about how people feel about their
preachers, only rarely would other questions reveal beliefs about
God's activity or how they understood God to be relating to the
congregation (or the world). We were pleasantly surprised throughout
the entire interview process how candidly and easily persons shared
their thoughts and feelings about their pastors; how seriously they
could discuss what they think the role of the Bible in worship is;
what important sermons they had heard; and how preaching might
affect their lives and behavior. Yet far fewer respondents could speak
as fully about God. Some few laypersons used language of mystery
in admitting their limited ability to talk of God. Most people who
were hesitant used more mundane, shoulder-shrug language to
express their limited understanding. In a few cases, the
acknowledgement of not knowing was followed by an expression of
wishing the minister would preach on a specific topic to help them
understand the faith (as when one person expressed a longing for a
sermon on the second coming).

Before we began the analysis, we wondered if there would be an
ethnic distinction in ability to express God's participation in
preaching. Many Anglo respondents were able to articulate beliefs
about God's participation in the preaching event; however, we
detected a larger percentage of African American congregants able
to express ideas about the presence of God in the preaching process,
the movement of the Spirit during the sermon and all of worship,
and the guidance of Jesus in the listening and responding. While
such findings may not be surprising to many, we want to underline
the important theological piece, namely that participants in both
ethnic groups were able to speak of God, yet the percentage of
African Americans was higher. We also note one interesting addition.
Anglo members in predominantly African American congregations
(although a very small sample) also seemed more likely to express
answers easily of trust that God would speak a word to them in the
sermon, of God's Spirit being among them, and of God's presence
making a difference in the speaking, hearing, and responding to the
sermon. It is not clear whether African American preaching had
helped formulate this tendency to speak about God's participation

in preaching easier or whether these Anglos had sought out preaching that reinforced ideas they already held.[2]

Although some respondents–regardless of race, age, denomination, gender, or setting–have a difficult time articulating what God's role in preaching might be, a significant number of persons in all categories do clearly come to worship prepared to hear a direct word from God to them individually or corporately. They do believe God is an active participant in worship, speaking through the preacher to individuals in the congregation. There are some who said exactly or nearly those very words. Others imply as much by explaining that God may have a special message for a particular person in the congregation that is communicated through the sermon. We deduce that if persons believe God may pass a message through the sermon to someone else, then certainly it makes sense that God may pass a message to them. Thus, such persons believe God may have a word for them individually from the sermon.

In addition to the analysis and reflection on the entire field of respondents, we reflected on some of the material about God, congregation by congregation. That is, we looked more closely at what everyone within a particular congregation said about God's participation in preaching.[3] We were particularly interested to see if the congregants agree with each other and if there is a correlation to what the preacher says. Although there is less direct correlation than we first thought there might be, we find some. One of the most interesting areas of correlation we found is in people's comfort or confidence in speaking about God. Often, if preachers speak with some comfort about what God seems to be doing, the level of comfort reappears in congregants' answers, even if the content of the answers is not identical. Conversely, there are several congregations where it is noticeable that people have more trouble discussing what God is doing or trying to do in the sermon. A specific example may clarify. One small town mainstream congregant provides a long explanation of God's activity, which begins with several qualifiers (not wanting to be presumptuous, not knowing exactly), then goes on to describe God's guiding the words of the preacher in the development of the sermon to provide guidance for each person hearing the sermon. This is not an untypical response in the study, believing that God is somehow participating in the writing and delivering of the sermon. But in this answer and in this congregation as a whole, there was more hesitance than in many others. For instance, this person displays insecurity in beginning to answer, then offering several qualifiers and disclaimers before getting started. The other respondents from that same congregation have even more trouble. One remarks, without elaboration, that the Holy Spirit is present in worship; the Holy Spirit is "always trying to get us to feel God's presence." Another, after saying, "Well, I don't know," answers that God may be laughing at the congregants, asking "Why aren't you listening?" After additional prompting from the interviewer, the respondent continues: "God's not taking a nap." Again, the interviewer invites additional thoughts on the topic and finally the person mentions that God might speak to someone through a personal prayer that might go on during the sermon, if that person's mind wanders. The closing comment: "So, maybe God is working." Thus, the person indicates a belief that communication with God is possible through personal prayer, but does not extend that possibility to the pulpit.

Of course, these responses are not exceptional; they sound much like what persons from other congregations say. However, we noticed that, as a whole, these congregants exhibit hesitancy, even insecurity, when expressing what God may be doing in the sermon. Their responses on other topics do not reveal such characteristics. It may not be surprising, then, to hear the minister's answer to the question: "What do you think God is doing during the sermon?"

> Lord only knows. I think God is working in people's hearts. I do hope that people hear God more than they hear me. I'll go ahead and say this. How things go on Sunday mornings, I feel, I feel how well things go depends on how good I am. I guess maybe the typical preacher feels that way. I don't know if this is off the track too, but on Sunday mornings I would much rather think it's not a question of how good I am, but how good God is. They're going to hear me, but I'd like them to also hear God. Does that answer your question?

The minister's answer reveals a similar unsure character, coupled with the inconsistency of depending on the quality of the preacher and depending on God. The preacher believes God is at work, but there is little clue that the preacher knows how personally to be of assistance or a participant in God's communication. The minister would *like* parishioners to hear God, but seems unclear how that might happen.

Because it is so peculiar, we looked at responses from all the participants in the congregation where the person mused that God might be thinking about the water bill. Two laypersons from that congregation noted they believe God is making them receptive (opening their minds); another one hoped God is calling the congregation to faithfulness; the final person talked about God's participation in helping make sense of the day's message for one's own life. Except for the comment about the water bill, there is notable similarity in these answers. They believe God is communicating with them through the sermon, making a connection in their lives. Thus, we were not surprised to read the priest's response, which views God as participating in the preaching, "inviting people to get closer and offering to befriend us and assuring us that there is order in the world and purpose. I think God is inviting people to live, to be more themselves, to be more faithful, to be more genuine." This response is in the minority of clergy answers, in that it deals more with God's interaction with the listeners, rather than with the writing or preaching of the message or using the preacher. In this instance, the congregation seems to echo ideas of the pastor, that God's participation during preaching affects the listeners. We suspect the water bill comment was not the result of this minister's preaching.

In another congregation we looked at as a unit, there was a wide swing in the answers. One person said God doesn't interact with people on a daily basis, another person said God is working on the pastor and working on us; another said God is teaching; another said God is present, "working through the sermon to make it meaningful to the people that are here...but I believe God acts everywhere." Thus, within the same congregation, people understand God not to be specifically interacting through the sermon, specifically working on people through the sermon, directly teaching, and also just acting like God acts everywhere. One key to the diversity may be that this church has co-pastors. In the clergy interviews, one of them bluntly states, "I feel that God is speaking through me"; the other claims, "God is working somewhere between the words that are said and the words that people hear." The congregants seem to echo the diversity.

### A Word to Preachers

At first, it may seem discouraging that our congregants are often not repeating what preachers say about God from the pulpit. But most ministers would probably support the idea of listeners' taking what we say and making it their own. Clearly many have done just that. In addition, although they do not repeat our words, something formative apparently does go on in preaching. Note how all the respondents from certain congregations were able to articulate their faith (even with various differences), whereas persons from other congregations were much more hesitant in saying the smallest thing about God. Although, in discussing these congregational units, we are not able to make a definitive claim that preaching is directly formative, we believe the evidence leans in that direction. We are confident in saying that, in the pulpit, we are modeling theological discourse. From us, people are learning how to think critically about the faith; they are following our lead. We show appropriate techniques for making faith claims and judgments when we preach.[4] A guiding question as we reflect personally on what and how listeners learn from us may be: How do I model thinking about the faith in helpful, theologically adequate ways?

Every time we display theologically adequate thought processes, we teach our congregants how to talk about God, the faith, and our lives. Conversely, when we disregard good models of theological discourse, we leave our congregations wanting. Even though congregants from the same congregation are not repeating whole cloth what their preachers say about God, we believe preachers do have a formative role in how ideas of God are developing within the congregation. A guiding question for further thought may be to ask: How am I assisting my people to talk more freely about the faith? Even more importantly, do we want people to have a consistent faith they can live and cherish? We encourage an intentional plan for more intentional, theologically thoughtful, God talk. It bears repeating that many of the people we interviewed express an eagerness to hear what preachers have to say about God.

Although many of the persons interviewed first claim not to be able to remember specifics of sermons, almost everyone did, at least to some extent. They report Bible stories we told, personal stories from our family life (disagreements we had over furniture, when we received a speeding ticket, our childhood vacations), exhortations and corrections about behavior, our interpretations of national events and life choices, and various other pieces of information. So, we wonder whether those who could not say much about God had either not heard enough about God in the sermons or had not had theological discourse modeled for them very well. A good question for preachers to ask before preaching every sermon may be: "What am I saying about God in this sermon?" And to push ourselves further we could also ask: "How am I modeling how to think about the faith?" The preacher's example should assist congregants in thinking through their own faith, even when they come up with different conclusions.

# CHAPTER 9

# Listeners Respond to Preaching in Diverse Ways

When the authors of this book were serving as pastors of local congregations in different places and at different times, we sometimes wondered (in company with many other clergy) whether our preaching made much difference to the congregations we served. This study reveals that many people take sermons very seriously. Listeners respond to preaching in a variety of ways: from thinking afresh about ideas, through feeling emotions that affect them, to taking actions in the church and beyond.

While interviewees reflect on what sermons mean to them throughout the interviews, we get the most help in understanding how listeners respond to sermons by turning to what they said in response to the following requests: "I'll bet you have heard a sermon that caused you to think or act differently, maybe about some big issue, maybe about a smaller issue. Would you tell me about that sermon?" "What did the pastor say or do that prompted you to change?" Listeners also described how they respond to sermons when recounting their histories as people who listen to sermons, and identifying the high and low points of their histories as listeners.

### What These Listeners Say about How They Respond to Sermons

The responses of the people interviewed in the study can be divided into six broad clusters—**deepening in faith, thoughts, feelings, actions, cumulative responses over time**, and **negative responses**. The interviewee responses often overlap within and among these clusters. Further, within each of these major clusters we also find diverse sub-clusters. For example, thought or a feeling generated by the sermon can prompt an action, while a feeling rising from the sermon can lead to reflection, resulting in action. As in the other chapters, the major clusters are indicated in bold print with the sub-clusters designated by italics.

Perhaps the largest single cluster is those who respond to the sermon with **deepening faith and commitment**. The following remark sounds a dominant note: "I think the sermon helps us focus our attention on topics and issues in our faith. It helps us strengthen our faith. So many of the people who come here to worship don't go to Sunday school and may not participate in other activities in the church. So I think it's the heart and soul of the worship service." Of a particular sermon, one person says, "It made me have more faith that God knows what's going on." Another person hears the preacher reinforcing "our faith by giving us more instruction about the Bible or about the scriptures or about faith-related principles." Still another reports, "We are expecting a message from God that will change lives and restore faith and build unity."

Another response is more detailed but in the same spirit:

> I guess what I hope for is that I'll be drawn closer to Christ and that I'll be drawn closer to my faith and what I believe. I hope that I won't be offended. I hope that I won't be told in a prescriptive fashion how we at this congregation believe things should be done in our day-to-day lives. Again, I really hope to be both intellectually challenged and nourished, which, therefore, tends to me spiritually.

Anticipating the section below on listeners who respond to the sermon by acting, we note that some interviewees believe thoughts (prompted by sermons) can lead to actions. This connection is expressed with particular succinctness here: "I hope there would be a greater understanding of God and helping us in our faith and just trying to live a more effective Christian life."

Another large cluster of interviewees says that sermons prompt them to **think freshly about biblical texts or theological doctrines**. These fresh ideas *often enlarge, reinforce, or reframe the way the listeners think.*

> I think in some cases the sermon makes me change the way I think about something that I'm familiar with, that I've always thought about in one light and now suddenly I'm seeing in a different light. That was the case with the Prodigal Son story. Who's the focus? I think the Good Samaritan one, too. I always thought, "Just be kind to your neighbor." Or the Woman at the Well. These are all things I thought I understood in a particular way, and then because of the sermon, now I see them in a different light. It doesn't tell me how to think about them, but it points out the ambiguity in almost any one of these passages.

For this listener, thinking freshly about texts and doctrines is more than an end in itself. It guards against this listener making an idol of any one line of interpretation or of the Bible itself as sermons lead the listener to recognize "the ambiguity in almost any one of these passages."

Sermons also prompt enlarged thinking about broader theological and ethical matters:

> Well, I think some of the sermons that I've heard here in the Peace Movement have changed my concept of what a conscientious objector is. That wasn't talked about much in the churches previous to the one where we are now. I knew people. One of my best friends in high school is a member of another denomination. That person was a conscientious objector. I don't know. When I was a kid, I didn't think much about it actually. I just accepted that's the way he was and let my friend go with that. I really didn't think that much about religion. I just accepted what I was given. It wasn't until later that I began to have questions about it, tried to delve a little closer into other religions and trying to get some kind of semblance. I still don't have all the information, obviously, that I need, but I'm trying to hear other people's ideas and so forth. But some of the sermons here have changed my ideas about conscientious objectors and the

Peace Movement in general. I don't agree one hundred percent, but then there's a lot of good things that I do agree with.

The interviewer asks whether sermons have helped bring about that change, to which the interviewee replies, "It opened my eyes to somebody else's opinion about things from a different point of view, from a different perspective, and from different philosophies. I try to be open if I can." When pressed still further about the aspects of preaching that have prompted fresh thought, the respondent goes on, "I think their ideas, not necessarily the way they've said it but the meaning behind what they're saying and why they say it, why they believe the way they do." Looking ahead to a theme that is more fully developed later in the chapter, the interviewee indicates that such growth comes about not in response to a single sermon, but, "It's been a progression over a period of time."

Another significant number of interviewees respond to sermons *by interpreting their personal and social worlds from theological perspectives.* The following comments are representative.

Anyone can get up and read the readings and read the gospel lesson, but when someone lends a personal experience to teaching, to me that's what I think the congregation takes away with them. If you think about a time in your life that may have occurred and you start thinking about how you handled it, and you hear about whether you handled it correctly or not, you're going to hear a way you could have handled it differently.

Another interviewee describes in detail a part of a sermon that changed the way in which this person understands Christian life. The preacher…

was talking and told the story about, "You're in a car with your friends." One friend is beside you and some friends are in the back seat. You see Jesus on the side of the road. Jesus has got a thumb up, so, of course, you stop and pick up Jesus. You say, "Hop in, Jesus," and you open the back door where there's room. Jesus just stands there and doesn't say anything. So you think, "Oh, Jesus wants to be in the passenger seat." Okay, we'll give Jesus shotgun. So the person on passenger side leaves and gets in the back seat and you offer Jesus the passenger side. Jesus just stands there. That's when you realize Jesus wants to drive your car. I don't know why that suddenly was this illuminating experience for me, but I just finally understood the difference between trying to be a good person and being a disciple of Christ.

Here, a story that makes reference to an everyday experience, with the twist of Jesus' presence, and it becomes a vivid lens through which this listener's perception of the purpose of Christian life is transformed. As shown by this response, some people can recollect detailed parts of particular sermons for many years.

Another parishioner offers an example of sermons helping this person identify meaning in the workplace:

I can think of a sermon that I heard one time on work, our day-to-day work life. I remember a phrase that was used, or maybe a sentence, which stated something along the lines that our work is the lamp stand upon which our light shines. I don't know that I'd ever thought of that before. I think we have a tendency to think of our workday in terms of the repetition and drudgery and trying to eke out a living by the sweat of our brow and not thinking of it as really a foundation for us to live our Christian lives. It's a lamp stand upon which we set our lamp, which shines for Christ.

Each day that this person goes to work, that sermon continues to be effective in the world.

When asked what preaching does in the congregation, an interviewee indicates that the sermon raises issues that the congregation needs to consider:

I'd say the sermon is probably the main source of–this sounds hokey, but–spiritual enlightenment, if you will, what the Bible says. I think we really look to our pastor for that because the pastor is the one that does the Bible study and has the time for that and knows. What does the Bible say? What should we be thinking about? Even I don't always agree, but what should I be thinking about in terms of what's going on in the world, in terms of what's going on in this city or this congregation?

This congregant believes that the community should respond to the sermon by thinking about issues of personal, congregational, and social concern.

Another congregant offers a similar perspective on how preaching has helped this person *recognize and respond positively to people who are different*:

> One of the things I've learned a lot about in this church, and I don't know if I'm going to have any specific examples, but being challenged to think differently about people who are different than I and what my responsibilities are to be open to people different than I.

This person responds to preaching with a heightened sense of Otherness.

Another interviewee speaks for many when describing what this person hopes to receive from a sermon: "Probably that I will get a new insight, some new way of looking at a passage, simple that I have never seen before." However, fresh insight is not the only thing this person seeks from preaching. This interviewer asks, "Do you hope that it will inspire you to act differently?" The interviewee confirms, "Well, at least to act." This person *wants* the ideas of the sermon to motivate action.

A significant number of people in the study sample say that they **respond to sermons (or parts of sermons) with feeling**.[2] Sometimes these emotions are significant moments in and of themselves, and sometimes they are additionally valued as they lead to personal reflection and even to action. As we noted in chapter 6, "Roles of Feeling in Preaching," the experience of religious awe is one of the most frequent—and most profound—responses of feeling.

People in one of the largest sub-clusters of comments on emotionality notice that when the congregation is emotionally moved by a sermon, the *congregation expresses feeling in the worship space after the sermon*. While the tone of the interactions vary according to whether the sermon is emotionally uplifting or sobering, people often linger, talk, exchange meaningful looks, and hug, as we hear in the following comments. "I've seen times when the folks seemed kind of subdued afterward. There doesn't seem to be as much talking as people leave. This really heavy silence and knowing that something has been said that's been sacred." Another listener says, "I've seen other times when it just really did just buoy the emotions. It lifts the emotions. You can just tell that everyone felt glad they were a part of that." Another participant in the study expands on the latter motif, describing people lingering in the worship space and talking. "They're happy. It's, like, more open, hugging or something. Little things but they're big things, really. You still feel the Spirit so you're acting like it. Yes. Yes. Yes." Another interviewee thinks,

> The hymns are a little louder. Oh, they sing louder. Yes they do. They do. There's a little bit more movement. They're not just standing there still, holding their hymnals, but they might sway just a little. Even the most staunch of people, you see them sway just a tad. A little bit of nodding going on while they're singing. People don't disperse very fast. They converse. There's a lot of people still milling around the sanctuary reflecting on something that impacted them during the service. That's the number one thing I think. There's a different level of energy. It heightens. It's almost palpable. You can almost feel it and almost see it jumping from person to person and emerging throughout the room.

Another person says, "I've been in situations and sermons where people don't leave right away. Kind of like warming yourself by a fire, you're not in a hurry to leave."

Such descriptions were especially common in the interviews after September 11, 2001. For example, one listener says,

> Today I noticed, yes, people seemed to be closer today. I noticed more hugs. I know even when we gave the sign of the peace, we hugged and they hugged—a circle of friends in the congregation. People held hands longer. There was more eye contact, more…but I think that had a lot to do with what happened during the week, but yes, I think it does. It brings us closer together. People do communicate more, start talking about the sermon itself, about the whole service really, the prayers.

Similar reports resounded throughout the interviews conducted after September 11, 2001.

Sermons in the African American traditions regularly end in celebrations that are emotional and even passionate. Even so, several African American congregants report that some sermons are especially moving. One listener reports that after some such sermons, there are "a lot of 'Amens,' praise claps, shouts, just a lot of anticipation. I would really sense the people were on the edge of their seats."

Moving sermons also appear in congregations made up mainly of members of non-Hispanic European origin. For example,

We actually now say, "Amen," after a few statements. We have one very staunch "Amener," so that's pretty cool. I think that person's from another background, but that's okay. We like them, too. I think there's verbal and actually auditory "Yes," or they might not go as far as saying "Amen," but they are very definitely making verbal statements of "Yes," or "Yes, that's right. That's right." And you can hear the mumblings.

While most of the "mumblings" in this congregaton are under-the-breath support for the preacher, there are occasional remarks of disagreement—quiet but audible.

Another large group of interviewees say that *emotionally moving sermons frequently lead them to reflect on their discipleship.*

I think that we had a missionary come speak. What that missionary experience brought that was very unpretentious and not coming asking for a check, if you will, but rather, "Let me share with you what other people go through to live their faith in an environment that is totally alien to your experience." I sat there and that touched me on an emotional level, whereas I sort of went, "Wow. I hadn't realized. I didn't realize. If I were in that setting, do I have the fortitude? If I were in that setting, would I rise to that occasion?" That's a visceral response rather than an intellectual response. I thought that was very provocative.

For this hearer, the sermon becomes a medium through which the listener feels something of what it would be like to be in the world the missionary describes.

Several listeners report a slight variation on feeling leading to reflection on discipleship: *Sermons sometimes become occasions for personal reflection and can even make them feel uncomfortable with their present expressions of discipleship and motivate them to live more faithfully.* Indicating how a sermon can prompt personal reflection, a listener says,

Sometimes you only know you feel good, and sometimes you don't know why you feel good. Or you go, "Oooooh," and you don't know exactly within yourself why the sermon touched that chord to make you all of a sudden go, "Oooooh. Maybe I need to reevaluate."

This listener then confirms, "And I do some reevaluation after messages."

Someone from another congregation provides a more specific example of self-reflection sparked by an emotionally moving message:

> I think a sermon that stirred emotions that made me uncomfortable was along the lines of something I should be doing. Yes. I think it was along the lines of helping other people. Yes. This was one about helping other people that we always can do more to be in relationship with other people. Witnessing, being a witness to other people. Sometimes I wish I had a little stronger witness when I'm out in the community or on my job or things of that nature. So what the sermon kind of stirred me up that way and made me a little uncomfortable that, hey, this is something I've got to do something about.

The congregant has a vision of needing to be a more active witness in the community, but has not acted on that vision. The feeling generated by the sermon ignites the will to act.

One listener testifies concerning sermons that prompt discomfort. "Sometimes that uncomfortableness is because it makes me feel guilty because you want to do the most with the gift that God has given you." Another participant in the study calls such a sermon "a real seat warmer, when you're squirming in your seat" because the sermon makes this parishioner aware of elements in Christian life that need attention. Several times this person refers to such sermons as "squirmers."

When listeners believe that feelings around the sermon are stirred by the Spirit, they can *be moved to leadership in the congregation and the wider community*:

> I guess our denomination has a reputation of being involved, and I've seen what we've done over the years trying to get involved. You have people that do get filled with the Spirit, and they respond. Our church wasn't involved as much [before people began to be filled with the Spirit] because it was like, "Hey, everybody can do that." That's true. Everybody can do it, but people viewed it more as the preacher's responsibility, but you can tell that is changing. That's part of the communication process. I think from the sermons and Bible studies, that's where you're seeing the

involvement, and the preacher has the spiritual leadership to say, "Hey, we have a grand vision."

For this listener, the test of whether the Spirit is the source of the feelings in worship is the degree to which the congregation responds to mission efforts.

Many people not moved to leadership are nevertheless *moved to greater involvement in the congregation* by emotionally moving sermons:

> People seem to volunteer. We had such great success with this capital campaign. They gave more money than we even thought they could. We were afraid we couldn't meet the goal, and here everybody surpassed it. So we know that people were touched. Not only the sermons, though they did make a big difference. I just think the whole process. God does work in the congregation.

Another congregant reports in a similar vein, "Some people will get more involved in the church. Some people get more involved in certain organizations. Sometimes you can see some tangibles, immediate results. Not always, but sometimes that does occur." Feeling overflows into enhanced commitment.

Not surprisingly, several listeners report that they *become so emotional that they weep in response to sermons.* For instance, one says, "I know when I feel the Spirit move on me, I cry, and that's my thing. I cry, I cry, I cry." The parishioner then responds to the question of what prompts the crying:

> The overwhelming emotions of just the calmness: "I love you no matter what's going on in your life." That it's going to be all right. Just that. Just that I love you for who you are. It just doesn't matter. There's nothing that can take that away from you. It's usually during my "Lord, I'm sorry" for what it is that I've done for that day or that week that I know I shouldn't have done. There's a lot of that going on. I know there's a lot of that with me during this time since our pastor's been here. I wouldn't do that [cry in worship] before. Just with this preacher saying you have to let that take place in order for Jesus to make you into who you need to be. You can't hold that back.

For this interviewee, the tears are almost sacramental: they are a sign that "it's going to be all right." The freedom to shed tears in worship confirms growth in faith.

Some interviewees *joined a congregation in response to a feeling* that came upon them at the end of a sermon. Remembering a sermon that stirred emotions, a parishioner says, "I would imagine the one that prompted me to join the church." Since this interviewee had been raised in the church, feelings had been "accumulating for many years, but on that particular day, something really touched a nerve, touched emotion."

People on occasion *feel distant* from sermons when the preacher is too graphic. For instance, one listener says, "The pastor was preaching about Jonah in the belly of the whale. How Jonah got out and wasn't chewed up. Ugh." The interviewee's visceral response is so strong that the interviewee tunes out of the sermon.

Some people *raise cautions regarding the feelings* that are generated in worship. One listener who grew up in a denomination whose services of worship typically contain quite a bit of emotional expression, but who is now a member of a highly liturgical congregation, says,

> The subject of preaching and feeling is interesting to talk about, because a lot of times I think that the church can become all about emotionalism...I've come to think of it very similarly to the love in a marriage. That at times you might feel like you hate the other person. You might just be so irritated, but you still choose to love. It's the same kind of relationship as the church. There are times when you feel very emotional, but other times you're just pressing on because it's a journey. Just keep going. Emotion can be so fickle at times.

Another person notices, "On the down side, sometimes when you get that large emotional response to a sermon you can lose some of the effectiveness, where you're not hearing what is actually being said because you're so caught up in that emotional high."

Many interviewees report that they respond to preaching by **taking actions in response to sermons**. Quite a few listeners indicate that they *talk about the sermon with family members, friends, and co-workers* in fellowship time after the service and later, during the week:

> We do coffee hour right after church, so sometimes it's immediately following, but probably more than that, you go on. I'm back on Sunday night to work with youth, and we have a devotional group with about five of us, so there are discussions there. I'm in Bible study. When I'm at work,

I don't work with anyone from my congregation, but it just seems to evolve that you begin to talk about in your daily conversations things that are important to you or have impacted you. You'll find yourself talking about what happened and what the sermon was about on Sunday and compare it with what they heard.

Many members of the congregations carry the sermon into the community.

In the same vein, but more specifically, many interviewees say that sermons help them *think and act in ways that help them relate with family members as well as persons outside the home.* Here is one and representative statement: "If you're talking about, 'Did a sermon make me think.' Did it make me think about something differently? Did it maybe make me keep my mouth shut when I might not have?' Yes. I would say, 'Yes.'" Another person says, "Sometimes a sermon helps you with forgiveness or being able to deal with really cantankerous persons. It helps you back off a little and think." Again (from another person): "I specifically stopped drinking alcohol. I specifically stopped attending night club functions, and specifically stopped buying lottery tickets."

In the same spirit, someone recollects how a direct word from a sermon brought about a reconciliatory action:

> Not very long after our present minister got here, the minister did some preaching on forgiveness and the necessity of, even if we were the injured party, that we were obligated to approach the one who had injured us in order to reconcile. I actually acted on that. It was the way the minister made clear that Jesus said this is what we must do. Since I truly want to do what Jesus says I should do, then I felt I needed to act on that. So I was convicted. That would be a good word to use there. That I needed to take that step. So I did.

Referring to acting differently because of something the preacher says, another parishioner affirms, "It has happened. I have known things that I've been doing for years, all my life, and then in a sermon I hear where it was wrong. Not one of the hell-bound wrongs, but wrong in how it relates to me and my family, or me and my neighbor, or something like that." In response to such insights, many interviewees act differently than before the sermon.

In like fashion, a congregant describes how *reflection leads to ongoing changes in behavior*:

> That involves me hearing the sermon and then making a judgment as to whether or not I have been doing what it is that the sermon says that I should be doing. It's pretty clear if I'm doing it or not. If I'm not, then I try to remember that week and hopefully incorporate that into my life so it becomes part of my life and that I continue on each week after that. Sometimes we backslide and have to hear It again. But just trying to practice what I hear.

Preaching leads to changes in this hearer's approach to life.

Another parishioner believes that prompting such reflection is one of the ongoing effects of preaching:

> It's almost like you need to be reminded really on a daily basis, but at least a weekly basis, to always do the right thing. No, not to do it–how to do it. Just encouragement to do it. Like I say, this denomination is big on peace and resolving things in a peaceful manner. So I use that as a tool to help me let go of bad feelings, because it comes out in one way or another through most messages. It just helps me let go of the frustrations of the week or the annoyance or whatever, the people, the acceptance of behaviors or tolerance. Because I know God does that in and through me, and that's what I should be striving for.

This interviewee says of such experiences, "That's why I keep coming back."

Several people who were interviewed in the study affirm *that they volunteered in community service* as a result of hearing a preacher make that suggestion. Several recall hearing sermons in which the preacher described local situations that needed volunteers; these listeners responded by stepping forward. In one small community, for instance, a house burned down. "The preacher brought a message about that. I got involved in helping to organize and purchase a fairly large house, and to tear down the old house afterwards so they [wouldn't] have a dangerous situation there."

Congregants sometimes take *small but practical actions prompted by sermons that are intended to improve their lives*. An ailing parishioner made a note capsulizing the theme of a helpful sermon. "I've made a little scroll on my computer and it says, 'Don't worry about anything, but pray about everything.'" Seeing the phrase helps this person "not feel so depressed or down. That helped me."

Another parishioner recollects hearing a sermon on the inconsistency between gossip and the Christian life and responding immediately.

> It goes back on going to church and being in church, living a Christian life and then turning around and leaving church and going home and talking about everybody or something. I would be lying if I said that I wasn't guilty maybe occasionally. In the last couple of years, somebody did a sermon on that, and it really touched me, and I quit doing it. I just felt really bad. I didn't even realize that I was talking about different people and what so-and-so was doing when I should have been listening. What so-and-so was doing, or what so-and-so did last night, la la la. After the sermon, it really hit home and I was just really touched. I don't do that anymore. That takes the whole meaning out of being a Christian.

Such responses are common in the survey: people stop doing things contrary to Christian identity as a result of hearing sermons.

One of the most frequent ways interviewees say sermons have influenced them is in *giving financially*. One listener says that a sermon "made me think very seriously about supporting the church and its work and about giving." When asked to tell about the sermon, this listener continues,

> Well, the preacher compared the church to other institutions like to your home and to your school. That it has needs that have to be supported. You have a pastor who has to be paid. In fact, we should have a budget. I just never thought of it that way. It's important to support the church. That sermon affected me very much in my life, in my church life, and in my giving.

A bevy of other listeners testify to the fact that in response to sermons they begin to give financially, increase their giving, and even become tithers. The following remark is representative: "I used to hear so much negativism about tithing until I heard a sermon on it years ago. I came to find out that tithing is simply a duty of a Christian. You're just simply being obedient. You don't only tithe just to receive blessings. You tithe because that's what God wants you to do."

Although few listeners think that preachers should endorse particular political candidates, several note that *preaching helps them evaluate candidates and issues*:

> When our pastor preaches, I do not think the pastor tries to favor one side or the other. For example, when elections were going on, the pastor wasn't going to say vote for this person or that person, but I felt like the pastor tried to say what Christians should believe in or how they should feel. So in that way, it changed me to rethink how I should think about a presidential leader. Like, step back, and what different qualities I should look at that maybe I'm not looking at now.

Although the preacher does not endorse specific candidates, listeners sometimes apply theological criteria they receive from the sermon to selecting the candidates for whom they vote.

Another listener comments that *self-reflection prompted by preaching leads to action*. Preaching…

> sort of opened my mind to the fact that you think you're not prejudiced. You think you are open to diversities and all these types of things. Then there are times when you hear something in a sermon, and you realize that you're probably not as open as you should be, as accepting as you should be, and at those times I think it's a matter of enlightenment then. "Okay, I've taken this for granted. There's more that we can do publicly."

The interviewee responds to enlightenment by going to events outside the congregation that seek to eliminate prejudice. Though the interviewee admits that such experiences are sometimes uncomfortable, "I think sometimes when you go outside of your own church, and you're in a different place, you experience things differently. It lets you know, 'We can do better.'"

Several people note that sermons help *empower them toward actions they might otherwise be reluctant to take*:

> You know you hear a lot of sermons over a number of years and they are different styles. Obviously the sermons of Martin Luther King Jr. were extremely motivational. I was in college

at that time. As a child you hear these sermons, and you talk to your family about them and that gives you motivation and the courage to maybe pursue a different type of activity that you might normally have been reluctant to have been involved in. Those were extremely effective sermons. Dr. King had an extremely effective style of oratory. Many of the sermons were very emotionally charged.

While this listener was deeply moved by the preacher King, the listener acknowledges that other kinds of preaching can also motivate. "You know, you hear a lot of sermons over a number of years, and they're different styles. You leave with saying to yourself, 'I'm starting today.'"

Many hearers, while not able to connect their responses to particular sermons, are confident of being **influenced by preaching in a cumulative way over time**. Their faith, thoughts, feelings, and actions are affected by sermons not so much like lightning strikes, but more like water dripping from a faucet into a bowl—starting the evening dripping into an empty bowl, but overflowing by morning.

For instance, one respondent says, "I think many times sermons' effects happen over months and years. Sermons are effective. I don't think it's a dramatic thing necessarily." Another interviewee says, "I can't think of a single sermon that shaped the congregation. I think it's a cumulative process that takes place week after week after week." Still another interviewee speaks similarly after indicating that this interviewee tends to respond to sermons because of the ideas that preachers articulate: "Change has been a progression over a period of time. I can't think of a moment when I say that I was saved or something. Say that at this particular moment at this particular time, I saw a light. I can't say that. My mind has been evolving over a period of time having different perspectives from different people and different cultures."

A more graphic picture comes to expression in the following remarks: "I am like this big [*makes a gesture indicating a large size*]. Seven years ago, I was this shape [*makes another gesture indicating a much smaller size*]. Now I'm this big [*makes original large gesture*]. I know I've got a long way to go." The interviewer summarizes, "That's interesting because I think some preachers think that each sermon works by itself. It either fails or succeeds alone, but what I hear you say is, 'No. They all add up.'" The interviewee agrees: "You've got to build on it."

Another person says, more fully, "Most of the time I think that transformation is pretty slow. I think that's probably a word here, an action there, that takes me, anyway, on the journey towards faithful living." Remembering a particular sermon following September 11, 2001, this listener continues, "On each of the following Sundays, when our pastor put out more thoughtful responses, I think that enabled me to see the real struggle that was there, that it wasn't just a simple answer. In that way, that was very good. I think mostly it's more of just a journey, a consistent journey." This same hearer contrasts the cumulative but effective results of listening to sermons over time with a pattern in a previous denomination:

> In the past I've had plenty of experiences in another church. I know we've had many experiences where we thought, "We're changed! Just in this one moment!" Just exhilarated and all of this, but you kind of eventually crash and burn, not always back to where we were, but thinking in one moment we had been completely transformed and then just making the same mistake or doing the same kinds of things in our lives. How did things become more important than they should once again? Then it's like, "Go back and conquer that thing." Now I think it's just more of a journey. You're slow sometimes, and sometimes it seems like you're moving at a steadier rate or a faster rate.

The interviewer comments, "So very rarely would one sermon completely change your life. It would be a period of time?" "Right, right." However, the listener does recognize, "I think that singular moments of transformation happen pretty rarely, although it can happen definitely. There are mystical experiences that can happen. But I have not experienced many of those times." For this listener the effects of sermons are incremental but steady.

While calling attention to the fact that many people respond to the cumulative effect of preaching, we note that the pluralism of perceptions we have found in previous chapters is present here. Some listeners respond powerfully to particular sermons. Indeed, some folk who say the influence of sermons is incremental cite specific sermons that were life-shaping. While the latter are exceptional, their effects are long-lived.

We turn now to a cluster of people who **respond negatively to certain sermons.** One of the questions asked in the survey was, "Was there ever a time when you almost walked out?" Only a handful of respondents said, "Yes," but many others report times they felt like walking out. Their responses are illuminating.

Many people who walk out on sermons do so because they believe that the preacher misinterprets the gospel or the complexity of the issues, or the character of the preacher renders the preacher untrustworthy. For instance, one listener tells about walking out...

> because there have been things that were said that I thought were rather flagrant against scripture and as well as having known what was going on behind the scenes. It made me so ill that I couldn't stand to listen to this person speak. I couldn't stay. So I left.

Another person goes into more detail about the reasons for walking out and expresses a very different attitude about doing so.

> The particular guest pastor was speaking to the Pax Americana in a global geopolitical environment as an extraordinarily negative thing, about all the terrible things that America had done abroad, and all the terrible things that American businesses are doing, and about the terrible nature of global corporations and global economy, and how bad and wrong all of that was. I felt that, first of all, it was very, very flawed. It was very inappropriate to use the pulpit as a venue for that, but also I wanted to go, "Yes, and what's your message?" It was a rant as opposed to educate or motivate. It was a rant. In fact, I'll be honest with you, I did get up and walk out. That's the only time I've ever done that. I went out in the parking lot. I felt so dang guilty. I sat there like, *Oh, no. What have I done? I've walked out on the sermon. I should go crawling back in and apologize or something.* It was just so over the top. I thought it was very inappropriate. I felt really bad.

Although the listener continues to object to the preacher's content, the parishioner expresses remorse about walking out. To have stayed would have shown more respect.

Some people who do not actually walk out say that although they felt like doing so, they decided to remain in the sanctuary; however, they stopped giving the sermon serious attention and reacted with annoyance. One person recalls...

> a former minister, who was preaching about gays and lesbians, that they should not be allowed to sing in the choir, for

example. Just talking about the boys having boyfriends, and the girls having girlfriends, and we heard that so much of the time it's become like a broken record. Then when you have members of the congregation that may be that way, then I think it's very offending. I think it's uncalled for.

Occasionally, listeners conclude that when they are angry enough to walk out, they need to reflect on their own attitudes, as we hear in this response to the question of whether the hearer had wanted to walk out: "No. Actually not, because if I have gotten angry, I've learned to recognize that is a signal that either I have some serious work to do with myself or maybe it's something that I need to talk to the pastor about. That it's more a signal that there is a problem with me."

For several listeners, not walking out is a sign of maturity: "I don't think I walked out on a sermon. No. I wouldn't do that, because like I said, I have learned to chew up the meat and spit out the bones. I hope I am more mature than that. I wouldn't just walk out on it. I can disagree…I can still disagree without being disagreeable."

Several people who remember being angry at a preacher also report speaking directly with the pastor about their unhappiness. The following case is representative:

There was one Sunday in particular that the pastor was really challenging to the congregation and almost with a little chastisement to the congregation. Some of the people were quite offended by that, because they felt like they had received a spanking, and they didn't know what for. But I understood where the pastor was coming from. It didn't bother me, because I felt like what the pastor said was the truth. I thought we needed some challenging. We did have some feedback following that, because one of the people expressed the very fact of being upset and had the pastor come into their Sunday school class the following Sunday. They felt like they had received a spanking and didn't know what for. So the pastor came in and expounded upon the subject a little bit more. That led to more understanding. The pastor also indicated being very stressed right then and had made a little bit more strenuous point than what the pastor might have done otherwise. You get feedback like that. Then people dialogue or talk about and then they see the pros and the cons. Hopefully, they'll be able to see then where we needed to do more.

Several unhappy parishioners go to see the pastor and have a conversation resulting in better mutual understanding between pastor and parishioners.

A fascinating response to a sermon involves a parishioner who was deeply disturbed by the preacher's sermon after the destruction of the World Trade Towers on September 11, 2001. The preacher asked the congregation to try to imagine why people outside the United States might want to destroy the United States. "But I didn't interpret it that way," says this listener.

> I interpreted it as an attack on our society. As a consequence I had many conversations with our pastor. I think in the pastor's struggle to make sense of that event, at a time when the congregation was deeply in need of comfort, what the pastor gave them was blame. The pastor gave them a sense of contributing personally to the tragedy. I found that very upsetting. I talked to the pastor. The pastor gave me the opportunity to respond. I preached the next week. I think that's a very healthy church actually. The preacher is big enough to do that.

This congregant's willingness to talk directly with the preacher about an issue on which they disagreed leads to a remarkable demonstration of the church as a community of conversation whose goal is to come to a satisfactory interpretation of the divine presence and purposes. Such conversation requires hearing diverse viewpoints.

### Reflections and Insights on How These Listeners Respond to Sermons

An important part of the preacher's vocation is to help the congregation reflect on the degree to which the lives of the members and the life of the congregation as community are consistent with the gospel. From the perspective of the issues discussed in this chapter, the preacher might be called to help the congregation reflect on the degree to which their responses to sermons are sufficiently faithful, just as the responses of congregants may assist the preacher's reflection on the degree to which her or his sermons are sufficiently faithful. If so, the preacher can reinforce and deepen their responses. If not, the preacher needs to suggest ways in which people can respond more adequately to the gospel.[3] Do people need to think, act, or feel differently to more fully reflect the gospel?

Most of the people interviewed for the study speak of responding to the sermon in terms of their individual lives. Most of the examples in the preceding part of the chapter have to do with self-perception or with attitudes and actions in one's immediate interpersonal world—family, divorce, matters related to the workplace, as well as issues and relationships in the congregation. For example, persons testify that in response to sermons they do things such as change their attitudes toward ex-spouses, stop gossiping, or recognize that a Christian perspective on material resources leads them to share money with others.

Relatively few interviewees indicate awareness of the gospel's concern for social issues. One person, in fact, says this very thing when asked to recall a sermon that prompted this person to think or act differently:

> I don't know that I've ever been challenged to feel that, "Look, I simply cannot go along holding that point of view, those prejudices." I don't think I'm likely to hear from the pulpit things that would challenge me that much. Whatever that says about me, I don't know. But I've never come away feeling, "Boy, I hate that message. The preacher is probably right, but I really don't like what the preacher said." I don't think so. In many ways, the sermons are too bland, generally speaking.

While a preacher certainly wants to help the congregation relate the gospel to their personal and congregational worlds, a part of the preacher's task is to lead the congregation in theological reflection on the larger social world and in how to respond. As we learned in "Controversy and Challenge in the Preaching Moment," many people *want* the preacher to help them think about social issues from a theological perspective.

This aspect of our study implies that many preachers need to help their congregations enlarge their fields of concern and to respond to the sermon with actions that are designed to help larger social worlds become systems that mediate the gospel to all involved. We learn, a listener testifies, that preaching caused this person to reconsider both personal and social issues.

> I think differently about how my money needs to be given. What are my responsibilities both [for] me as a person and doing volunteering in the world? Also, where my money

needs to go. What are the repercussions of things that we do? I've learned in this church about our country and what the far-reaching implications are around the world of what our government does and what I can do. I can make decisions for myself about specific areas. I can put my money or my time or my thoughts that will do good for local people and the problems that they have in their specific areas, their areas of needs, and not just throw money up that may or may not help based on their circumstances. I think I've learned a lot and been challenged in social justice arenas.

The preaching in this congregation addresses social issues in thoughtful and thorough ways over time. This listener has responded to such preaching by interpreting the world as a social system and by thinking ethically about how this listener's life can influence that system.

When describing sermons that prompted them to act differently, many of the interviewees tell about sermons that intersected with their particular issues that were going on in their personal lives or in the life of the congregation or the larger world. The sermon spoke directly to those concerns. This phenomenon suggests that listeners are likely to respond positively when a preacher correlates the content of the message with a felt need in the listening community.[4]

At the same time, congregations are not always aware of things they need to do to live and witness faithfully. In such cases, several listeners indicate that sermons themselves can raises issues to the level of consciousness in the congregation and can prompt the members of the congregation to recognize that they need to respond to the issues raised by the sermon. In this case, the sermon itself creates a sense of felt need in the congregation. The work of the sermon may sometimes be to help the congregation recognize that, from the perspective of the congregation's deepest convictions about the purposes of God, what they really need to know, feel, and do transcends their immediately felt needs. For example, a respondent confessed to being unaware of the personal unconscious collusion with racism. A sermon, however, helped the parishioner become aware of the problem and of the importance of taking actions to urge the church and the larger social worlds to work against racism.

The fact that listeners say they respond most strongly to material that relates to their personal lives and to their life as a congregation suggests that pastoral listening is one of the most important aspects of sermon preparation. With such awareness, ministers can often correlate with the felt needs of the congregation, and can help the congregation become cognizant in the hope that the congregation will be responsive to the sermon. As preachers like to say, the preacher needs to know the congregation. At the most obvious level, a preacher needs to know, insofar as possible, the kinds of things that are happening to members in the congregation that need to be interpreted from the perspective of the gospel—births, deaths, health issues, marriage and divorce, changes in economic and employment status, family concerns, and similar matters. At another level, a preacher needs to know the culture of the congregation as community and the relationship of the congregation to larger contexts (local, state, national, international) of the community.

Different people respond to sermons because of different reasons. Some are struck by the ideas, information, and arguments that the sermon puts forth, and others by feelings that the sermon generates. Several listeners indicate that they respond with particular depth to stories that the preacher tells. In a part of the study discussed in chapter 4, "Listener's Relationship with the Preacher," we also learn that many people's responses to the sermon are affected by their perception of the character of the preacher and their sense of relationship with the preacher. When such persons believe that the preacher is a trustworthy person and one with whom they have a supportive relationship, they are much more likely to take the content of the sermon seriously than if they perceive the preacher as nontrustworthy and one with whom they have a distant or even fractious relationship.[5]

This pluralism in qualities of preaching that motivate listeners to make positive responses to sermons suggests that a preacher cannot rely on one type of sermonic content to connect with the congregation, but needs to be able to develop sermons that present clear and persuasive ideas, that stir significant feelings, and that represent the preacher as a trustworthy person. A preacher cannot rely simply on logical arguments, or stories, or images that evoke feelings. Within the same sermon, or in different sermons, the preacher needs to include material that speaks to different listeners at the points at which the particular people in the listening community are most likely to respond.

Whether a preacher needs to help a congregation reinforce its current theological predispositions or critically reevaluate and possibly change them, several themes in the interviews should give the preacher confidence and can even suggest strategies for developing sermons. Many people in our study are willing to take seriously possibilities that stretch them.

Many parishioners say they are engaged by sermons that have a positive tone, especially sermons that help them see how the world can be a better place if they take up the thoughts, behaviors, or feelings recommended in the sermon. A listener remark summarizes a stream of others in this regard: "I think when someone always preaches from the fear and the negative point of view, you're not telling them what to do about it. You're just telling them what's going to happen to them if they don't do it another way." Instead, a preacher could say, "I know if you really try in this area, that we can get closer to what it is that God intended for us." This listener believes that people respond to "preaching from the positive of maybe having the vision or having the hope of how we can live our lives better, instead of putting labels on people and preaching to them in a negative, fearful way. People, I don't think, come back week after week after week so you can tell them how bad they are." Catching the fact that promise and warning often come together in sermons, another congregant indicates that preaching should be "a very joyous thing" but avers, "I think that it may be hip or trendy or whatever to spend a lot of time dwelling on the ills of the world, the injustices of the world." Such listeners seek a balance between acknowledgement of problems in the world and realistic hope that things can be better. A preacher can help people see how their current views play such roles, or how a change in perspective can bring about a better sense of faithfulness and community.

Several of the people who indicated that they felt like walking out also indicated that conversation with the preacher afterward helped them work through their frustrations. Through formal and informal means, a pastor could communicate such a dialogue attitude to the parish. Such an approach might well help frustrated parishioners be better able to listen to subsequent sermons.

## A Word to Preachers

One of the simplest and yet most important things a preacher can do with the insight that people respond to sermons is to take heart for the vocation of preparing and embodying sermons. As we noted at the beginning of the chapter, many ministers (including the authors of this book) have wondered whether preaching has serious effects. Whether listeners respond immediately to a particular

sermon, or whether their responses accumulate through multiple
sermons over a long period of time, virtually all persons interviewed
in this study cite ways that preaching makes a difference to them.
This awareness should prompt a pastor to discover optimum patterns
of sermon preparation and make sure that the preacher has sufficient
time to prepare each week.[6] The service of worship is the largest
regular gathering of the congregation each week. As a chamber in
the heart of the service, the sermon deserves a preacher's best
attention.

Beyond that, ministers can think of how they would like the
congregation to respond to the sermon in terms of thought, feeling,
and action.[7] Per above, the preacher could correlate these foci with
both the immediately felt needs of the congregation and things that
the congregation needs to think, feel, and do to improve their witness
to the gospel. Indeed, as a part of sermon preparation, the preacher
might ask the following key questions: What would I like for the
congregation to think in response to this sermon? What feelings
would I like for the congregation to have in response to this sermon?
What actions would I like for the congregation to take in response
to this sermon? How would I like for the sermon to contribute to the
cumulative responses of the congregation to preaching over an
extended time?

This strategy comes with qualifications. Every sermon will not
call for all four responses. Some sermons will focus more on thoughts,
others on actions, others on feeling. While the listeners in the study
confirm that individual messages have results in congregations, the
typical effects of sermons are incremental and cumulative. While a
preacher wants to be clear (and bold) in inviting responses to
particular sermons, a preacher also needs to realize that each sermon
is not an apocalyptic cataclysm that is likely to bring about immediate
and profound change. A preacher might set the goals of the sermon
in proportion to the preacher's pastoral awareness of what may be
possible in the congregation. For example, instead of hoping that a
single sermon can cause the congregation to change its attitude
toward the place of homosexual persons in the Christian community,
a preacher might hope that a sermon might help the congregation
become more comfortable in thinking about homosexuality and
talking about it in the context of worship.

Furthermore, a preacher cannot always predict how a congregation
will react to a specific sermon. People cannot be programmed to
respond to sermons in the same way that one loads software onto a

computer to get a (mostly) predictable program. Characteristics in or experiences of the listeners about which the preacher has no awareness and over which the congregation has no control can cause them to make unpredicted associations. Consequently, preachers should not let their self-images ride on how congregations respond to particular sermons. The real indicator of the effectiveness of preaching (and other aspects of ministerial leadership) is the growth of the congregation over time in faith and witness. Periodically a preacher could be encouraged by reviewing signs in the congregation indicating that the congregation is responding to the gospel with growth in faith and witness.

Preachers might ask themselves, "How do I perceive the congregation responding at the time of embodiment, as well as later in the service and afterward—with thoughts? with feeling? with action?" Does the preacher notice characteristics in congregational life (comments, questions, relationships, actions, policies) that reveal cumulative effects of sermons? With such observations in hand, a preacher can reflect on the degree to which the congregation responds to sermons in ways that enhance the congregation as faith community.

# CHAPTER 10

# Preaching and Pluralism in the Congregation

Our study shows that when a minister begins the sermon, the different kinds of diversity in the listening community are remarkable. As we observe throughout this book, and as many ministers know from personal observation, parishioners have differing expectations regarding the purpose of the sermon. Sitting on the same pew, some members are engaged by embodiment that is effervescent, while some others prefer styles that are quieter, and still others say that the preacher's physical presence is of no consequence; for them, the ideas in the sermon are everything. People respond to sermons in as many ways as there are numbers of people. One preacher–so many different kinds of listeners.

We have already considered some ways that preachers can take account of different modes of diversity in the sections entitled "A Word to Preachers" at the end of each chapter. We do not now simply recapitulate those themes we developed, but instead we explore some macro-perspectives on things ministers might do in preaching to help the sermon have a good opportunity to be engaged in by as many people as possible.[1] We begin with a brief theology of diversity in the listening community, and then underscore the basic observation that preachers need to become aware of the diverse clusters in the congregation. Pastors need, as well, to take account of differences between themselves and the various clusters in the parish. We conclude that the diversity of ways people listen to sermons suggests that over seasons of preaching, ministers typically need to develop sermons in diverse ways. Over time a preacher needs to use a variety of sermonic shapes in view of the clusters in the congregation. In appendix A we offer a chart to help the preacher remember to take the various clusters into account in particular sermons and over a protracted period of preaching.

To underscore an important point, we do not recommend that the preacher simply give people what they want to hear in order to win approval from the congregation. Preachers should never violate their integrity. However, the interviewees in the study indicate that preachers can usually develop sermons in ways that encourage congregations to interact seriously with the content of sermons, while still avoiding approaches that needlessly turn off listeners. For instance, engaging a new cluster of listeners may be as easy as noting the preponderance of male protagonists in our illustrations and intentionally adding stories of women to our sermons. We hope to demonstrate ways of communication that give the congregation the best chance of engaging the sermon, hearing the preacher's viewpoint, making their own critical judgments, and responding faithfully.

We also hope the book makes it clear that we do not recommend that the preacher simply try to find the middle of the road through the various clusters. A *via media* is usually not true to the most important theological convictions of the preacher (or the congregation!). In addition, it is not what most of the people in this study group seek. In fact, a middle-of-the-road approach, you may remember, is not possible, since the clusters do not reflect a spectrum (from "hot" to "cold"), but rather a diversity of ways to engage with the sermon. As we observed (especially in chapter 5, "Controversy and Challenge in the Preaching Moment"), many listeners want to know where the preacher stands, while also knowing that the preacher respects them. When preachers explain their own stances, it allows congregants to claim their own (which may differ significantly from the minister's). Many people, in fact, say they are changed in positive ways by positive encounters with relationships, honest presentations of thoughts, and ideas that are quite different from their usual experiences. Indeed, a significant number of congregants look to the sermon to prompt fresh thought. When the congregation senses that the preacher speaks out of love for God and community, they are often grateful for the discoveries that come when they leave the familiar middle of the road and move toward the edge of the road to enter and claim new terrain.

### A Brief Theology of Diversity in the Listening Community

As this book demonstrates, there are sound sociological, psychological, and cultural reasons for attending to the different kinds of pluralism present in the congregation. Beyond those bases, and even more important, respect for diversity in the congregation (and in other areas of life) is a theological matter.

According to the great poem of creation that begins the Bible, God weaves diversity into the very fabric of the world. The day is divided into periods of light and darkness, while the world itself is apportioned among water, land, and sky. God fills the earth with vegetation whose species are manifestly pluriform; the waters teem with multiple modes of aquatic life, and numerous types of birds traverse the skies. The earth brings forth living creatures abundant in number and variety—cattle, creeping things, and wild animals. The creation story claims that God, evidently, not only delights in diversity, but also considers it essential for an optimum world. God intends for the variegated elements of creation to live together in mutual support and community.

Similar themes are implicit in the creation of humankind. Genesis declares that women and men bear the image of God. Many biblical scholars agree that being made in the image of God means that human beings are to represent God's purposes in our limited spheres in the same way that God actualizes the divine purposes in the cosmic sphere: to help the world live as a community of mutual respect, support, and abundance for all. The image of God thus is inherently relational and communal. Yet, whereas God is infinite, each human being is finite. An individual human being can reflect only part of the divine image; because of the fall (Gen. 3), the possibility for a human being to represent the divine image becomes even more complicated by the extent and power of sin. Each person and each community embodies different—but limited—aspects of the divine image and purposes. Consequently, to recover as full a grasp as possible of the divine purposes, people need to gather in community that encourages difference to come to expression. Attention to diversity in community is a theological mandate.

Our research reveals there is diversity within single congregations and similarities across significant denominational or congregational separations. Yet we human beings have difficulty trying to understand each other. Often we misinterpret other persons and communities as being the same. We want others to be just like us, when, in fact, we are each distinct, *and* alike. From this standpoint, an essential part of the preacher's calling is to assist congregations in recognizing ways the listening community is different and ways we may be alike, without reducing persons too quickly one way or the other.[2]

In the background of these concerns is a tendency in human beings to make idols of our own perceptions and devils of others' Idolaters regard finite and relative perspectives as infinite and absolute; they think of their immediate and contextual experience as universal. Bringing the facts of diversity in the congregation to consciousness can be a powerful antidote to our own tendencies toward idolatry by exposing the relativity of our individual perspectives, and can also bring us into a community whose collective understanding of the divine purposes is much fuller and more adequate than the understanding each human being can achieve alone.

We do not romanticize these notions of people gathering into communities that contain diverse manifestations of the divine image. Diverse elements in any community–including congregations–can relate acrimoniously with one another. Becoming aware of one's finitude, and taking steps to relate meaningfully in community with others, can be awkward and painful. However, as noted in earlier chapters, many people interviewed for this study recognize that growth is sometimes prompted and accompanied by discomfort. One of the preacher's tasks is to help congregations recognize this phenomenon, and to take heart in God's presence as they move through it. Certainly moving to become more aware of others is a sign of spiritual maturity, although we admit we will never fully "arrive." If we are not able to appreciate God's pluriform creation in the church, how are we ever to hope to be able to elsewhere?

Furthermore, the Bible repeatedly presents God, the leaders of Israel, Jesus, and the leaders of the church speaking to their respective communities in language that the communities can understand. God and the religious leaders respect the otherness of particular people and particular moments of history, and accommodate communication to the circumstances of the peoples in their particular cultures. To be faithful, we preachers need to do the same in our later times and places.

## Becoming Aware of Clusters in the Congregation

This book identifies clusters of perspectives on a range of topics that are found in the congregations in which these interviews took place. Readers may assume that some of the clusters we uncovered are present in their congregations. At the same time, preachers' own investigations will uncover new ones. One helpful aspect of the preacher's vocation is to identify these clusters and to become familiar with them. Ministers who name and describe the basic clusters present in the congregation can then shape sermons that deal with the congregation as it actually is.

How can preachers identify the clusters functioning in the congregation? Two ways come quickly to mind: one formal and the other informal. First, the preacher can listen for comments (and other signals that people give) in everyday life that reveal clusters in the congregation, such as when members of the congregation indicate values that are important to them about preaching: in comments at the door at the end of the service, in Bible study and other small groups, in church meetings, in the home or workplace when the pastor makes a call, during counseling sessions, when they are hospitalized or in other situations, and, of course, on the proverbial parking lot. The preacher can also pay attention to the congregation's attitude and practices regarding worship and preaching, to the sources of authority that seem important in major church decisions, and to places, groups, and movements in the congregation and wider community in which people invest time and energy. Hearing a remark in a meeting or other setting that sounds like it might help the preacher understand an attitude toward preaching in the congregation, a preacher could easily and unobtrusively ask a question or two that would give the congregant(s) an opportunity to expand on their remark.[4]

In this informal approach, a preacher would always be asking, "What do I learn–if anything–about what the congregants think about issues important to preaching from what I am hearing in a particular Bible study, small group, committee meeting, counseling session, hospital or home visit?" The preacher can look over the record of remarks and notice how they begin to fall into clusters of ideas. For instance, a preacher might notice how people use the Bible in a business meeting, how the lay speaker appeals to the Bible when giving a talk in worship in support of the church budget, what participants look for–and want to take home–from the Tuesday morning Bible study group, the role that an interpretation of the Bible plays in the thoughts and feelings of a person who comes for counseling regarding the possibility of divorce, and what parishioners seek from the Bible in pastoral calling.

In the formal approach to discovering clusters within the congregation, the preacher would bring the congregation into the process. Leaders could initiate interviews in the listening community that are similar to the ones conducted for the study reported in this book.[5] Since it is seldom possible to interview everyone in a congregation, representative groups and individuals could be selected. When parishioners are interviewed by someone other than the pastor, they may speak more candidly, especially if they are assured that their remarks will be handled anonymously. A record needs to be kept of content of the interviews. While interviewers can make extensive notes, we recommend that interviewers make tape recordings of the sessions and that the interviews be transcribed. This approach provides a precise account of what the congregants say. As the pastor and other leaders read the material, clusters will naturally surface.

### Describing the Clusters in the Congregation

Regardless of whether the data is collected through informal or formal means, the preacher could use categories and issues similar to the ones identified in this study as a kind of filter through which to analyze what people say and do in ministry. For example, a preacher might identify clusters of congregational perspective around the categories discussed in this book:

- Purposes of preaching. Find out the answers to: What does preaching do in the congregation that other things do not do? What are the clusters of opinion around what people hope will happen to them and to the congregation as a result of listening to a sermon?

- Role of the Bible. Find out how congregants see the role of the Bible in preaching. To what degree, and how, is the Bible authoritative for different clusters in the community?

- Embodiment. Ask how parishioners are affected by the preacher's physical presence–voice, eye contact, gestures, energy, movement, sense of being in the pulpit.

- Relationship with the preacher. Ask how the people perceive relationship with the preacher affecting their listening.

- Challenging issues. Ask: Are some issues just too explosive for the preacher to deal with in the pulpit?

- Feelings. Ask how listeners are affected by feelings in and around the sermon. What happens when the congregation is stirred?

- Shaping the congregation as community. Ask: What are ways that sermons help (or could help) shape the congregation as community?

- God in preaching. What do people think God is doing prior to, during, and after the sermon?

- Response to the sermon. What clusters surface as people speak of responding to the sermon?

Preachers may find that an additional category of clusters is important.[7] For example:

- Authority in the sermon. In what clusters do people view authority in the sermon?

Preachers, of course, not only want to name the various clusters in the community, but they want to shape sermons so that they will have a genuine opportunity to engage persons across the various clusters.

## Differences between Preacher and People as Occasions for Discovery

The preacher seeks, at least in part, for the sermon to have the qualities of a conversation involving the Bible, Christian tradition, sources from the various arts and sciences, and other arenas of experience that can illumine the subject of the sermon, the clusters in the congregation, the preacher, and God. The sermon aims to give the various voices in the conversation an opportunity to hear one another, and to consider how the different speakers experience one another and the world. The preacher seeks to help the congregation explore ways that interaction with these other voices and ideas can help the congregation interpret the divine presence and purposes.

Before persons become ministers in the church, they are Christians. As ordained leaders of the church, it makes sense that clergy work on their own maturing in the faith. Critical self-awareness is an important ingredient. From the material in this book, preachers should be able to reflect on their own perspectives on the various topics, not just gain information about others in the congregation. It is important for the preacher to give voice to those ideas. We remember that many parishioners interviewed for this study stress that they want to know what the pastor thinks. Preachers are then able to add to the honest give and take of ideas, admitting that there are legitimate differences. When the preacher is aware of the points of contact and points of difference between the preacher's worldview and the worldviews of the clusters in the congregation (assuming that some parishioners will share some clusters with their pastor), the preacher can work conscientiously and critically to open paths of communication, and can help the congregation reap the benefits of diversity and deal with the problems that sometimes come with diversity.

When preachers model their own willingness to listen to other positions respectfully and to disagree, without rancor, they are not only modeling appropriate Christian faith, but the relational compassion of the Divine. Such behavior matters to parishioners. Quite a few interviewees indicated that they will engage a sermon whose ideas are quite different from their own when they believe that the preacher loves them and respects them. This point is quite important, because some preachers are reluctant to articulate ideas in the pulpit that go against commonly held ideas from the congregation, believing this tactic will shut down people's listening. However, it is the perceived lack of respect, not differences of opinion, that results in lowered attentiveness to the sermon.

This study finds that preachers can often invite varied clusters of folk to consider ideas that are quite different from the ideas that they customarily assume. Indeed, as we noted above, such listeners often find that such dissonance becomes an occasion for growth. Indeed, many listeners value the preacher's being honest, and stating what the preacher truly believes, as long as the preacher does so with sensitivity and in such a way as to acknowledge relativities, and to leave room for conversation and differing interpretations. Even when they do not finally adopt the preacher's way of thinking, such listeners often become more critical of their own viewpoints, and more understanding (and accepting of) why other people think, act, and feel differently. In addition, if the congregational conversation is real, change in theology, ethical commitments, and style of leadership is possible, for clergy and laity alike.

## What Facilitates Hearing in Diverse Clusters?

A preacher, of course, needs not only to describe the clusters in the congregation, but to consider how to shape the sermon so as to create optimum possibilities for the congregation to consider seriously the content of the message. A pastor wants to know, "What facilitates hearing in each cluster?" What in a sermon is likely to help members of particular clusters open their minds and hearts to the message? What will the members of a cluster recognize as a sermon worth the investment of their attention?

For example, people in different clusters connect with the sermon in different ways. Preachers may find it helpful from time to time to name and describe the viewpoints of various clusters in sermons in ways that the members of the clusters can recognize as accurate and fair. Such material signals congregants that the preacher has listened carefully to them and respects them. For instance, when interpreting a controversial topic, a preacher sometimes hopes that members of a particular cluster in the congregation will move from one viewpoint or action to another. A preacher will often find that an accurate and sensitive description of the position(s) currently held helps the listeners recognize that the preacher is not dealing with them in caricature, but respects them as they really are. Recognizing that the preacher knows them, they may be more willing to consider seriously the ideas that the preacher invites them to consider.

Preachers can benefit from making a general commitment to touching the many clusters in the congregation. However, from time to time, preachers may also find it helpful to concentrate on a particular cluster or group, especially when an issue is of particular importance or especially timely. In such cases, a preacher may want to consider one of the following approaches (or some combination thereof).

For one, a pastor could focus one sermon on one cluster in the community, or a group of clusters around a single topic. For instance, a congregation typically contains several clusters differing in what they want to know about God from a sermon. In a sermon on a given text, a pastor might ask how theological interpretation of that text can help (or not help) the different clusters in the congregation discover something of what they want to know about God.

For another approach, a preacher might address a particular cluster in sermons over several weeks, or the preacher might seek interchange with multiple clusters across a season of preaching around a particular issue. For instance, the preacher might want to encourage one or more clusters around the role of the Bible in the sermon to stretch their understandings, and, perhaps to entertain other sources that can be authoritative in Christian community. A preacher might take one particular biblical text as a case study for how the perspectives of the different clusters result in differing interpretations of the text in its ancient contexts or in implications for the contemporary church and world. Each week, the preacher could interpret the text and its implications for today from the perspective of a particular cluster's assumptions about the Bible and its place in Christian life. If dealing with the same text for several weeks seems difficult, the preacher might use a series of texts (say, from a lectionary) and bring the assumptions and methods of a different cluster to bear each week.

Of course, ministers can work on multiple issues in relationship with multiple clusters in the congregation. Whatever approaches a minister might use in connection with a single sermon or a short cycle of messages, a preacher will want to be sure, over the long haul of preaching, to make as much contact as possible with a broad range of congregational clusters. A minister who does not take a self-conscious and intentional approach to such matters may end up unconsciously tuning the sermon to the wavelengths of certain clusters while neglecting other clusters.

## Developing Sermons in Diverse Ways for Diverse Congregations and Clusters

One of the most significant findings of this study is that the typical congregation is a remarkably diverse listening community. While similar insights have come to expression in other books and articles, this project goes further than others in giving the parishioners themselves opportunities to interpret how they listen to sermons.[8] We listened to more than two hundred persons in twenty-eight different congregations talk about preaching. The findings of diversity in the listening community in this study point to the need for preachers to be able to develop sermons in diverse ways for different congregations, different clusters, different occasions, and different purposes. This recommendation is in tension with an assumption found occasionally in preaching circles: that a preacher should follow one particular model of developing sermons. For instance, we know devotees of Fred Craddock's inductive approach, Samuel Proctor's dialectical approach, and Eugene Lowry's five-step loop.[9] Other preachers eschew following a set system of how a sermon should move, and seem eager to find their own preaching voices and methods.

Although finding one's own voice, and becoming comfortable using a particular system, have positive qualities, the exclusive use of any one approach will almost necessarily frustrate some members of the listening community and will create the impression (albeit unwittingly) that the particular patterns of listening that are most friendly to that approach are normative. Congregants whose listening is repeatedly frustrated may lose interest and stop trying to pay attention. Such potential listeners may feel excluded or devalued. They may mentally exit the sermon or even stop coming to worship. The preacher thus loses an optimum opportunity to dialogue with them through the sermon concerning the divine presence and purposes in the world. If one of the goals of the realm of God is to create a community in which people who are different relate with one another in mutuality, acceptance, and support, then approaches to preaching that make full use of those rich differences to increase communication of the relational nature of God, and interpret how humans might live into greater faithfulness, are certainly worth our best effort.

To be sure, preachers have preferences for developing sermons. Over time, a preacher usually evolves a style that seems natural to a preacher's theology and personality. But one size does not fit all, either preachers or listeners. One style of sermon does not fit all listening ears. Ministers need to be able to preach in multiple modes to accommodate the sermon to the different clusters of listeners, as well as to different purposes and occasions. Indeed, from time to time, pastors may need to develop sermons whose movement and material is outside the preacher's familiar and comfortable zones. An inductive preacher may need to develop an occasional sermon that is deductive and that is structured according to points. Clergy who are comfortable with philosophical discourse may need to tell stories. A minister who, by nature, puts the message of the sermon in the face of the congregation may need to be content at times with raising questions and inviting the congregation to recognize points of view that are alternatives to the congregation's usual assumptions. A pastor who is afraid of emotion may need to include material in the sermon that evokes deep and sensitive feelings.[10]

## Going Forth in Joy

The different kinds of diversity present in a congregation invite a preacher's most prayerful, disciplined, and imaginative efforts at understanding the context of the community, interpreting the Bible, reflecting theologically, and applying the message to the congregation and its world. Some of these aspects of a preacher's calling can seem complex, even daunting. Yet, in describing what an interviewee hopes to receive from a sermon, this person also describes something of a quality that can pervade sermon preparation and preaching:

> I just hope that the word will be planted in my heart and keep me growing, growing, growing. I want to grow in grace. I love for the ministers to preach the word so that I have a burning desire down in my heart. As the song says, "I feel in no ways tired." I like to come away feeling like that. Even though I'm weary, I'm in no ways tired, and I just want to run on. You just want to do more, more, more. It just makes me want to go on, and go on with joy. Sometimes you go on because you know that's what you should do. But I want to have that joy. Even when I'm weary, I want to have that joy. A good sermon can do that—put the joy down in my heart.

The authors offer this book in the prayer it will help preacher and congregation, even when weary, go forth in joy.

# Charts to Help Preachers Take Account of Diverse Clusters

On page 210 is a sample chart that seeks to help the preacher identify and remember the Purposes of Preaching clusters within the congregation, and to keep track of points of contact between sermons and each cluster. The preacher could prepare similar charts for each of the topics discussed in this book and mentioned in this appendix. Note that cluster ideas may be identified in the far left column of the chart, where there also is a space for the pastor's perspective. Across the top are sermons. The preacher could make a brief note in the chart to recollect how the sermon interacted with particular clusters. Over time clergy who keep such a record can identify the clusters they are attempting to engage, and how, and can note clusters that may need more attention. A preacher and congregation would need to customize these materials to account for the particularity of a local congregation.

## Major Topics of Clusters

*Purposes of preaching.* In what clusters do people think of the purpose(s) of preaching? ("What do you think your pastor is doing when she or he preaches? What do people hope will happen as a result of listening to a sermon? What does preaching do in this congregation that other things do not do? What would be missing if there were no sermon?")

***Role of the Bible***. In what clusters do people interpret the place and authority of the Bible in the sermon? ("What role does the Bible play in the sermon?")

***Embodiment***. In what clusters can we gather ways that people are affected by the preacher's physical presence–voice, eye contact, gestures, energy, body movement, sense of being in the pulpit? ("Would you please describe for me, a preacher whose physical delivery was really engaging? What are some physical things a preacher does while delivering a sermon that help you want to pay attention? Can you think of a time, when you could not hear or see, the preacher well? How did that affect you? What difference does it make to you when you can see the facial features of the preacher?")

***Perception of relationship with the preacher***. In what clusters can we designate how listeners are impacted by the degree to which they perceive they have (or do not have) a relationship with the preacher? ("Talk a little bit about your relationship with the pastors and preachers you have had. Tell me about a pastor you had who was also a good preacher. What did you like about that person?")

***Challenging issues***. In what clusters do people indicate that they are comfortable with, even eager for, the preacher to address challenging or controversial issues? How can the preacher do so in ways that promote dialogue? ("Are some issues just too explosive for the preacher to deal with in the pulpit? Would you name some and tell me why you think they are dangerous? I'll bet you have heard a sermon that has caused you to think or act differently. Would you tell me about that sermon? What did the pastor say or do that prompted you to act differently? Was there ever a time when you almost walked out?")

***Feeling in listening***. What clusters depict how people are affected by feelings in and around the sermon? What kinds of elements in sermons move people? ("Can you tell me about a sermon that stirred your emotions? What in the sermon stirred you? I would like for you to describe a sermon that seemed to move the congregation as a whole, as a community. What was it about that sermon that seemed to move the community? When the sermon stirs the emotions of the congregation, what happens after worship?")

***Connection between sermon and people.*** In what clusters do listeners speak of things preachers can do to help the sermon connect with the congregation? What do preachers do that cause people to feel disconnected? ("Tell me about a sermon that engaged you. What was it about that sermon that engaged you? Tell me about a sermon that did not interest you. What was it about that sermon that left you cold? Tell me about your history as a person listening to sermons. What are high points? What are some low points? Was there ever a time when you almost walked out? If you had one or two things you could tell preachers that would help them energize you when you are listening to a sermon, what would they be?")

***Sermon shaping congregation.*** In what clusters can we sort congregants' understandings of the relationship of the sermon to them—as individuals, as an aggregate of individuals, as a community? ("Tell me about how preaching shapes your congregation—who you are as a community.")

***God's relationship to preaching.*** In what clusters do people perceive God's relationship with the sermon? ("What do you most want to know about God when you hear a sermon? What do you think God is doing during the sermon itself?")

***Responding to the sermon.*** In what clusters do people respond to the sermon? How do they respond by thinking? by feeling? by acting? ("When the sermon stirs the emotions of the congregation, what happens after worship? Tell me about a sermon that caused you to think or act differently. What did the pastor say or do that prompted you to act differently? Tell me about how preaching shapes your congregation.")

***Authority in sermon.*** In what clusters do people view authority in the sermon? What sources do different clusters regard as authorities for the sermon? ("When does the sermon have authority for you?")

***Additional clusters may be identified by preachers or other leaders.***

**Example of Chart to Help Take Account of Clusters** (see page 207 for more details about using charts.)

**PURPOSES OF PREACHING.** In what clusters do people think of the purpose(s) of preaching? "What do you think your pastor is doing when she or he preaches? What do people hope will happen as a result of listening to a sermon? What does preaching do in this congregation that other things do not do? What would be missing if there were no sermon?")

| Individual clusters for this category | Sermon 1 Title | Sermon 2 Title | Sermon 3 Title | Sermon 4 Title |
|---|---|---|---|---|
| Cluster 1 | | | | |
| Cluster 2 | | | | |
| Cluster 3 | | | | |
| Preacher | | | | |

# Notes

## Preface

[1]For a representative review of recent efforts to consider the listener in the preaching community, see Ronald J. Allen, "The Turn Towards the Listener: A Selective Review of a Recent Trend in Preaching," *Encounter* 64 (2003): 165–94.

[2]The interviews took place in two formats: interviews of individuals that lasted about an hour each (128 persons), and interviews of small groups composed of four to six different people in each congregation (135 people in twenty-eight small groups). The congregations include nine whose memberships are predominately African American, sixteen that are predominately European American (which we will usually refer to as Anglo), and three that are ethnically mixed. The congregations come from the following denominations or movements: African Methodist Episcopal Church, African Methodist Episcopal Zion Church, American Baptist Church, Christian Church (Disciples of Christ), Christian Churches and Churches of Christ, Church of the Brethren, Episcopal Church, Evangelical Lutheran Church in America, Mennonite Church, National Baptist Church, nondenominational churches, Presbyterian Church (U.S.A.), and United Methodist Church.

[3]John S. McClure, Ronald J. Allen, Dale P. Andrews, L. Susan Bond, Dan P. Moseley, G. Lee Ramsey Jr., *Listening to Listeners: Homiletic Case Studies* (St. Louis: Chalice Press, 2004).

[4]Ronald J. Allen, *Hearing the Sermon: Relationship, Content, Feeling* (St. Louis, Chalice Press, 2004).

[5]Mary Alice Mulligan and Ronald J. Allen, *Make the Word Come Alive: Lessons from Laity* (St. Louis: Chalice Press, forthcoming).

## Introduction

[1]The questionnaires were filled out prior to the interviews, and were not designed as formal research instruments but as a way to help the interviewees begin to think about preaching. The questionnaires were "warm up" instruments. From time to time we do refer to material that the respondents wrote on the questionnaires because it helps fill out the meaning of interviewee responses.

[2]For a full explanation of the categorical analysis, see Ronald Allen, *Hearing the Sermon: Relationship, Content, Feeling* (St. Louis: Chalice Press, 2004).

[3]The population of persons interviewed in the study is limited geographically to the Midwest and upper South, and ethnically mostly to African Americans and Anglos. For preaching in other cultures (from the standpoint of the preacher) see *Preaching Justice: Ethnic and Cultural Perspectives,* ed. Christine Marie Smith (Cleveland: United Church Press, 1998); Eunjoo Mary Kim, *Preaching the Presence of God: A Homiletic from an Asian Perspective* (Valley Forge: Judson Press, 1999); Jung Young Lee, *Korean Preaching: An Interpretation* (Nashville: Abingdon Press, 1997); Pablo A. Jiménez, *Principios de Predicacion* (Nashville: Abingdon Press, 2003); *Preaching and Culture in Latino Congregations,* ed. Kenneth G. Davis and Jorge L. Presmanes (Chicago: Liturgical Training Publications, 2000).

[4]Perhaps we should iterate that our sample focused only on Protestant congregations associated with the long-established denominations named in footnote 2. Our Advisory Board did not think we were sufficiently familiar with the cultures of other denominations and movements to undertake responsible research, nor did we have the resources to do so. Thus, our study is missing Roman Catholic, Orthodox, Pentecostal, and congregations of various other sorts, including those with more isolated characteristics. We admit the limitations of our study, although we underline its breadth among Protestants, especially those of the traditional COCU denominations and congregations with an openness to our study. A number of congregations who were invited to participate declined.

## Chapter 1: How Do These Listeners Understand the Purposes of Preaching?

[1]We did not specifically ask interviewees what they mean by the phrase "word of God." In chapter 2 we do identify several references that show that listeners infuse the content of "word of God" with somewhat different meanings.

²Quite a few listeners do not speak of the Bible or the sermon as the word of God. For further exploration of this motif, see chapter 8, "What about God?"

³One respondent even referred to the parts of the service that precede the sermon (singing, prayers, etc.) as "the warm-up."

⁴For overviews of the relationship of preaching and worship, see Richard L. Eslinger, "Church Year and Preaching," in *Concise Encyclopedia of Preaching*, ed. William H. Willimon and Richard H. Lischer (Louisville: Westminster John Knox Press, 1995), 74–78; Gerard Sloyan, "Liturgical Preaching,, in *Concise Encyclopedia of Preaching*,, 311–13; Karen B. Westerfield Tucker, "Lectionary Preaching," in *Concise Encyclopedia of Preaching*, 305–7; and David M. Greenhaw and Ronald J. Allen, eds., *Preaching in the Context of Worship* (St. Louis: Chalice Press, 2001).

⁵In chapter 2, we consider much more fully how the listeners in the study view the role and authority of the Bible.

⁶The relationship of the Bible to the purposes of preaching is tied, of course, to the school of theology to which preacher and people subscribe. For overviews of these matters see Joseph R. Jeter, Jr., and Ronald J. Allen, *One Gospel, Many Ears: Preaching and Different Listeners in the Congregations* (St. Louis: Chalice Press, 2002), 149–73; John S. McClure and Burton Z Cooper, *Claiming Theology for the Pulpit* (Louisville: Westminster John Knox Press, 2003); Ronald J. Allen, *Preaching Is Believing: The Sermon as Theological Reflection* (Louisville: Westminster John Knox Press, 2002), 120–41.

⁷For how listeners perceive feeling as a realm of knowledge, see Ronald J. Allen, *Hearing the Sermon: Relationship, Content, Feeling* (St. Louis: Chalice Press, 2004), chapter 4.

⁸On the interrelationship of various parts of the congregational system as occasions for learning, see Ronald J. Allen, *Preaching and Practical Ministry*, Preaching and Its Partners (St. Louis: Chalice Press, 2001), 29–46.

⁹L. Susan Bond, *Trouble with Jesus: Women, Christology, and Preaching* (St. Louis: Chalice Press, 1999), 16–17, passim.

¹⁰For an example of specific norms in preaching, see Ronald J. Allen, *Interpreting the Gospel: An Introduction to Preaching* (St. Louis: Chalice Press, 1999), 82–91.

¹¹The preacher would need to calibrate these qualities to the aims for each particular sermon.

¹²For approaches to the sermon as an event of teaching and learning, see Katie Geneva Cannon, *Teaching Preaching: Isaac Rufus Clark and Black Sacred Rhetoric* (New York: Continuum, 2003); and Ronald J. Allen, *The Teaching Sermon* (Nashville: Abingdon Press, 1995).

¹³Indeed, the preacher can teach the congregation how to interpret the Bible from the perspectives of contemporary scholarship. Many people already believe that the Bible is important. Many of them would welcome instruction in how to understand the Bible and in how to relate the Bible to other sources of theological insight (e.g., Christian tradition and theology, other disciplines such as the social sciences, the arts, social movements, and personal experience).

¹⁴For a rationale and approach, see Mary Alice Mulligan and Rufus Burrow, Jr., *Daring to Speak in God's Name: Ethical Prophecy in Ministry* (Cleveland: Pilgrim Press, 2002).

¹⁵See further Joseph R. Jeter, Jr., and Ronald J. Allen, *One Gospel, Many Ears*, 49–73.

## Chapter 2: The Role and Authority of Scripture in Preaching

¹Thomas G. Long makes a similar assertion in *The Witness of Preaching* (Louisville: Westminster John Knox Press, 1989), 48.

²This notion of centering the sermon on a biblical text or theme is compatible with Leander Keck's description of the role of scripture in preaching. Keck argues that preaching is biblical when (a) the Bible governs the content of the sermon and (b) the function of the sermon is analogous to that of the text. In this understanding, the number of scripture texts quoted in a sermon does not determine its value or account for the faithfulness of its witness. Rather, "preaching is biblical when it imparts a Bible-shaped word in a Bible-like way." Leander E. Keck, *The Bible in the Pulpit: The Renewal of Biblical Preaching* (Nashville: Abingdon Press, 1978), 106.

³For a helpful review of biblical interpretive methods related to preaching, see David L Bartlett, *Between the Bible and the Church: New Methods for Biblical Preaching* (Nashville: Abingdon Press, 1999).

⁴In his *Proving Doctrine: The Uses of Scripture in Recent Theology* (Harrisburg: Trinity Press International, 1999, o.p. 1975), David Kelsey asserts that the authority of scripture is not

based on some property intrinsic to it, but is established by the manner in which it functions. Tracing the writings of several Protestant theologians in search of the ways scripture is drawn on by each scholar as an authoritative resource, Kelsey notes three different appeals to scripture: (1) those who understand the content of scripture to be authoritative, (2) those for whom the Bible is authoritative on the basis of what it reports about God, and (3) how its images, symbols and myths engage us in revelatory or saving occasions.

[5]For more on the relationship between pastoral care and preaching, see J. Randall Nichols, *The Restoring Word: Preaching as Pastoral Communication* (San Francisco: Harper and Row Publishing Co., 1987).

[6]On the potential dangers and pitfalls of reducing scripture to moral guidelines and moralism in preaching, see James M. Childs Jr., *Preaching Justice: The Ethical Vocation of Word and Sacrament Ministry* (Harrisburg: Trinity Press International, 2000), 17–30; and William Willimon, *Integrative Preaching: The Pulpit at the Center*, Abingdon Preacher's Library, William D. Thompson, ed. (Nashville: Abingdon Press, 1981), 75–84.

[7]For a fuller treatment of the ways pastoral preaching may not only address personal needs but also encourage the well being of communities of faith, see G. Lee Ramsey Jr., *Care full Preaching: From Sermon to Caring Community* (St. Louis: Chalice Press, 2000).

[8]Further comments related to preaching that addresses difficult matters of congregational life are found in chapter 5, "Controversy and Challenge in the Preaching Moment."

[9]For more on the role of preaching as it helps shape communities of faith, see chapter 7, "How Preaching Shapes the Faith Community," as well as Cleophus J. LaRue who, in *The Heart of Black Preaching* (Louisville: Westminster John Knox Press, 2000), describes several "domains of experience" that are integral to black preaching and cites maintenance of the institutional church as one of five key concerns. Although LaRue's comments have particular relevance and meaning for African American congregations, it is worthwhile to note that some of the listeners in our study, both African American and Anglo, value preaching that addresses congregational needs, struggles, and sense of ministry.

[10]In *A Captive Voice: The Liberation of Preaching* (Louisville: Westminster John Knox Press, 1994), David Buttrick strongly advocates biblical preaching that appreciates both scripture's mythic depth and its social message so that sermons may enlarge the listeners' sense of God's liberating word and its relevance for all of humanity.

[11]Similarly, the diverse references to the term "word of God" among our listeners indicate the complex nature of our inquiry, since it sometimes seems to refer to scripture, sometimes to the sermon, and sometimes to a more dynamic presence that moves between scripture and sermon in worship.

[12]See Fred B. Craddock, *As One Without Authority*, rev. ed. (St. Louis: Chalice Press, 2001). Craddock is often credited with having initiated or brought into sharper focus the need to turn to the listener in preaching and to involve others in the process of discovering the meaning of the text through inductive modes of sermon design, just as the preacher discovers the meaning of texts in the process of biblical exegesis when preparing a sermon.

[13]For more on the dangers of moralizing in the pulpit, see Willimon, *Integrative Preaching*, 75–84.

[14]For a practical approach to gathering information about the congregation's questions and perspectives on particular passages, see John S. McClure, *The Roundtable Pulpit: Where Leadership and Preaching Meet* (Nashville: Abingdon Press, 1995).

## Chapter 3: Embodiment of the Sermon

[1]Regarding *embodiment* of the sermon, see the following works: Alla Bozarth-Campbell, *The Word's Body: An Incarnational Aesthetic of Interpretation* (Lanham: Rowman and Littlefield Publishers, 1996); Richard F. Ward, *Speaking from the Heart: Preaching with Passion* (Nashville: Abingdon Press, 1992); idem., *Speaking of the Holy: The Art of Communication in Preaching* (St. Louis: Chalice Press, 2000); Charles L. Bartow, *The Preaching Moment: A Guide to Sermon Delivery*, Abingdon Preacher's Library (Nashville: Abingdon Press, 1980).

[2]For a study of points of connection between preacher and congregation from the standpoint of rhetoric, see Lucy Lind Hogan and Robert Reid, *Connecting with the Congregation: Rhetoric and the Art of Preaching* (Nashville: Abingdon Press, 1999).

[3]Fred Craddock, *Preaching* (Nashville: Abingdon Press, 1985), 24.

[4]A book that benefits both African American and Anglo preachers in this regard is Frank A. Thomas, *They Like to Never Quit Praisin' God: The Role of Celebration in Preaching*

(Cleveland: United Church Press, 1997).

[5]Charles L. Bartow, "Delivery of Sermons" in *Concise Encyclopedia of Preaching,* ed. by William H. Willimon and Richard Lischer (Louisville: Westminster John Knox Press, 1995), 99.

[6]Joseph M. Webb. *Preaching Without Notes* (Nashville: Abingdon Press, 2001), 77–95. Cf. William H. Shepherd, *Without a Net: Preaching in the Paperless Pulpit* (Lima: CSS Publishing Co., 2004).

## Chapter 5: Controversy and Challenge in the Preaching Moment

[1]For an approach to preaching at the time of a crisis, see Joseph R. Jeter Jr., *Crisis Preaching, Personal and Public* (Nashville: Abingdon Press, 1998).

[2]For guidance in identifying the ways scripture informs the prophetic witness of the church, see Walter Brueggemann, *The Prophetic Imagination,* 2d ed. (Minneapolis: Fortress Press, 2001).

[3]For a valuable resource for preachers who hope to shape communities of grace and prophetic witness, see Barbara K. Lundblad, *Transforming the Stone: Preaching Through Resistance to Change* (Nashville: Abingdon Press, 2001).

[4]One very helpful model of how scripture relates to preaching about social conditions and crises is found in James Harris, *Preaching Liberation* (Minneapolis: Fortress Press, 1995); cf. André Resner Jr., ed., *Just Preaching: Prophetic Voices for Economic Justice* (St. Louis: Chalice Press, 2003).

[5]For a fuller exploration of how pastors may take on the role of "ethical prophet" in response to critical social issues, see Mary Alice Mulligan and Rufus Burrow Jr., *Daring to Speak in God's Name: Ethical Prophecy in Ministry* (Cleveland: Pilgrim Press, 2002).

[6]For a helpful resource to aid in the assessment of congregational context and theology, see Nora Tubbs Tisdale, *Preaching as Local Theology and Folk Art* (Minneapolis: Fortress Press, 1997).

[7]For guidance in relating prophetic concerns to pastoral care in preaching, see J. Philip Wogaman, *Speaking the Truth in Love: Prophetic Preaching to a Broken World* (Louisville: Westminster John Knox Press, 1998).

[8]Mary Alice Mulligan and Rufus Burrow, Jr., *Standing in the Margin: How Your Congregation Can Minister with the Poor (and perhaps recover its soul in the process)* (Cleveland: The Pilgrim Press, 2004).

## Chapter 6: Roles of Feeling in Preaching

[1]The concerns of this chapter overlap with a section of chapter 9, "Listeners Respond to Preaching in Diverse Ways," that considers feelings as responses to sermons (174–79). Rather than repeat themes in the two chapters, in chapter 6 we concentrate on general phenomena associated with feeling in preaching, and on the qualities in the sermon that interviewees identify as stirring emotion, while in chapter 9 we concentrate on how people say they respond with emotion to sermons. For discussion of persons who listen to entire sermons through the setting (or lens) of feeling, see Ronald J. Allen, *Hearing the Sermon: Relationship, Content, Feeling* (St. Louis: Chalice Press, 2004), chapter 4. This work also deepens the exploration of several themes in the present book, especially the notion of feeling as a realm of knowledge.

[2]On ways that sermons affect people as individuals, in groups that function as aggregates of individuals, and as communities in which people are aware of being inherently interconnected, see chapter 7, "How Preaching Shapes the Faith Community."

[3]Bernard Meland, *Fallible Forms and Symbols: Discourses of Method in a Theology of Culture* (Philadelphia: Fortress Press, 1976), 24.

[4]Ibid. 29.

[5]For a resource for such criteria, see chapter 1, note 6.

[6]Ronald J. Allen, *Hearing the Sermon: Relationship, Content, Feeling* (St. Louis: Chalice Press, 2004), 80–82.

[7]For guidance in helping congregations develop as communities with prophetic mission focus, see G. Lee Ramsey Jr., *Care-Full Preaching: From Sermon to Caring Community* (St. Louis: Chalice Press, 2000).